PRESERVING
AND MAINTAINING
THE OLDER HOME

PRESERVING AND MAINTAINING THE OLDER HOME

SHIRLEY HANSON   NANCY HUBBY

Illustrations by Betty Anderson

Photographs by Nancy Hubby

McGRAW-HILL BOOK COMPANY
New York   St. Louis   San Francisco   Auckland   Bogotá
Hamburg   Johannesburg   London   Madrid   Mexico
Montreal   New Delhi   Panama   Paris   Tokyo
São Paulo   Sydney   Toronto
Singapore

Library of Congress Cataloging in Publication Data

Hanson, Shirley.
    Preserving and maintaining the older home.
    Bibliography: p.
    Includes index.
    1. Dwellings—Maintenance and repair.
2. Architecture, Domestic—Conservation and restora-
tion.   I. Hubby, Nancy.   II. Title.
TH4817.H325   690'.83'0288   82-15355
ISBN 0-07-026085-0   AACR2
ISBN 0-07-026086-9 (pbk)

1234567890   HAL/HAL   89876543

ISBN 0-07-026085-0
ISBN 0-07-026086-9 PBK.

The editors for this book were Joan Zseleczky and Esther Gelatt,
the production supervisor was Sally Fliess.
It was set in Trump by University Graphics, Inc.
Printed and bound by Halliday Lithograph.

To my husband, Bob, my daughters, Elise and Karen, and my son, Bobby, for their endurance and boundless loyalty during my ventures into historical preservation, especially those that were highly charged and deeply absorbing.

Shirley Hanson

To my family, with my wholehearted gratitude, for their loving support and patient understanding during the many months devoted to creating this book.

Nancy Hubby

To Chestnut Hill, a Philadelphia neighborhood, whose lovely, well-maintained older houses taught us what can happen when:

Residents care for and love the beauty of their homes
and
Builders and architects over the years honor this past and respect the gracious natural setting.

Shirley Hanson
and
Nancy Hubby

CONTENTS

TO THE READER

Our quest for ways to save old buildings and neighborhoods began in 1966. Confronting the crumbling stucco, rotting wood, and partially removed roof of the Veterans of Foreign Wars building in Chestnut Hill, Philadelphia, we organized a successful effort to rebuild this older structure and in the process helped to found a historical society. Over the years our volunteer preservation work in Chestnut Hill has taken two paths. The first continues this initial direction by keeping individual buildings alive in the way each calls for, such as restoration, reconstruction, renovation, and façade easements. Our most dramatic adventure occurred during the three weeks won from the wrecker to rescue a handsome nineteenth-century home. In that time we persuaded the Chestnut Hill Historical Society to "purchase" the building from its institutional owner for one dollar for ten years, located undaunted tenants willing to do the overwhelming amount of work needed to make the house livable, and safeguarded this gem for at least another decade.

The second course is promoting the architectural and historic virtues of Chestnut Hill's buildings and their worth as an irreplaceable resource in this older neighborhood. Conducting a comprehensive architectural survey and publishing its results, arranging lectures by outside experts, training volunteers, presenting slide talks about Chestnut Hill, leading walking tours, writing newsletters, and placing articles in the local newspaper are ways we carried forward this challenge.

Both pathways converged as we worked on *Preserving and Maintaining the Older Home*. It is a celebration of yesterday's houses, those built in this country from the seventeenth century to 1940. In its descriptions and illustrations it applauds the visual excitement of their architectural designs and delightful details. Their careful craftsmanship, prized materials, and imaginative designs make many of these older houses unique. To help keep these treasures, we emphasize ways to maintain, restore, or sympathetically renovate them.

Preserving and Maintaining the Older Home explores the answers to many common questions about older homes. How can we go about understanding an older house and bringing out its best qualities? What is the style of a particular older building? How can we accomplish changes in a sensitive and honest way? What techniques are appropriate for protecting and repairing an older house? Where should we look for trouble spots? How can we find suitable replacements for worn-out materials and missing parts? Which tasks can an amateur do alone? When is professional help needed, especially from an architect or contractor, and how can we find a competent individual or firm to do the job? What can be done to make an older building more energy efficient?

The initial three chapters, Becoming Friends with Older Homes, Architectural Styles, and Preparing for the Work, suggest approaches to an older house. Read them first to gain an appreciation of the inherent values of these buildings and to learn what to consider before beginning repair, renovation, or restoration work. The next eleven chapters focus on the outside of the house, moving part by part from Roofs to Foundations and Basements. Each of these chapters is divided into three sections: Design, Maintenance and Repair, and Replacement. For the thirteen architectural styles selected for the book, the Design sections describe and compare the probable appearance of the architectural characteristics of each featured component — such as chimneys, doors, and dormers. The Maintenance and Repair portions list frequent problems and possible remedies suitable for older homes. Finally, the Replacement sections reveal where to find appropriate parts and materials.

Preserving and Maintaining the Older Home is a practical guide for current owners and renters of older homes, potential buyers of yesterday's houses, individuals investing in older buildings with the intention of renewing them for future rental or sale, persons curious about America's architectural heritage, activists in preservation or in neighborhood rejuvenation, architects, contractors, and students taking courses in architectural history or building restoration. It is for those who wish to become friends with older houses or who already have an abiding passion for preservation.

From our considerable experience we have become trained amateurs, learning the frustrations, fun, and joys of preservation work through on-the-job challenges supplemented by research and study. We do not claim to know about all aspects of the renovation field. In sharing what we have learned, we hope that others will be encouraged to value older homes as we have come to cherish them. To understand yesterday's houses is to love them, and to love them is to care for them tenderly.

Shirley Hanson
and
Nancy Hubby

ACKNOWLEDGMENTS

In writing our book we turned time and again to friends and colleagues for advice and assistance. These lovers of old houses, who share our passion for conserving these matchless resources, offered criticism and wise counsel. Some, drawing on their wide experience in preservation, carefully reviewed the references to history, architectural design, and technical information for accuracy. Others provided excellent editorial suggestions. A few renewed our spirits when the mission seemed overwhelming. To each of the following we give our heartfelt thanks for strengthening our book by generously contributing his or her time, abilities, and knowledge.

We express our warm gratitude especially to Richard A. Yarnall, who diligently applied his considerable talents to all aspects of the manuscript. Almost every chapter bears the imprint of his meticulous reading, his insistence on clear language, his understanding of architecture, construction techniques, and maintenance procedures, and his sensitivity to the special qualities of older houses. Having such a perceptive adviser enriched and deepened this book.

To Jack Hornung, our staunch supporter, comrade in conservation causes, and guide through arduous preservation battles, we are profoundly grateful. His practical renovation experience, sound organizational suggestions, and sharp editorial critiques buttressed this book.

We appreciate the numerous contributions of Jeremy Robinson, our first editor at McGraw-Hill, who wrote the chapter Energy and the Older House.

To the following individuals we pay tribute for their unstinting help: Jack Zankman of the Chestnut Hill Camera Shop for patiently and skillfully assisting us with the photographs; Theodore Nickles for his thorough assessment of the chapter Calling in a Contractor; Hyman Myers and William Cornell for teaching us many on-the-job lessons about restoration work; the employees of Chestnut Hill Stationery for cheering us on as they made copies of seemingly endless drafts and the final manuscript; Robert Tryon for suggesting replacement sources; G. Holmes Perkins for helping us to tap the riches of the University of Pennsylvania's Rare Book Library; the Woodbridge Citizens District Council for the initial inspiration for this book; Mamie Rayford, Mary Bond, and Dr. Victor Rambo for their suggestions and encouragement; the Chestnut Hill Historical Society for use of their library and for their efforts in actively promoting preservation in Chestnut Hill these past fifteen years.

PRESERVING
AND MAINTAINING
THE OLDER HOME

CHAPTER ONE

BECOMING FRIENDS WITH OLDER HOMES

Older homes are treasures to be cherished. Even if they seem worn out and weary, sensitive care can return them to their vigorous former selves. With thoughtful improvements, they can accommodate today's styles of living. Older homes deserve to endure to enrich our lives today and to nurture future generations.

Not everyone agrees. Some individuals consider older homes obsolete relics of the past. In neighborhood after neighborhood evidence of neglect, abandonment, and destruction abounds. Why refresh houses built for previous times? Because they reveal the aspirations and traditions of our forebears. Because the presence of the past shows us where we have come from and helps us to understand ourselves. Because authentic values—beautiful craftsmanship, gracious amenities, and unique personalities—hide beneath their shabby surfaces. Because their artistic workmanship and fine-quality materials are irreplaceable. Because they may be sound financial investments. Because they delight the eyes and nourish the souls of those who encounter them.

Older houses come in all sorts of sizes, shapes, and styles. Some are simple, humble structures; others are flamboyant, imposing edifices. Some are rustic country cottages; others are unpretentious urban row houses, stately townhouses, or ornate mansions. Look for straight-laced, prim residences as well as unpredictable houses which draw you from one unexpected feature to another. Each older home transmits its own personality, whether cheerful or somber, dignified or amusing, restful or playful. Seemingly endless intriguing discoveries await those who learn to see and to appreciate.

The magnetism of an older house may lodge in practical concerns. Often an older home is spacious, offering generous spaces for gatherings and places for privacy. It may be cheaper to buy than a newer house, even accounting for repairs and replacements. Its location may be its attraction, whether a tranquil rural or small-town setting, a vital urban neighborhood, or a convenient place near public transportation.

The appeal of an older home may also arise from its pleasing proportions, its bold or graceful garnishments, or its mellow charm. Its fascination may spring from the careful attention originally given to its details (often missing in newer houses), the surprising personal touches of the initial builder or carpenter, or the traces of former occupants. An older home may be enticing because of the sensuous delights of its glowing waxed floors, stained glass windows, or sumptuously carved newel posts. It is comforting, too, to be surrounded by whisperings of yesterdays.

In contrast, many newer dwellings are stripped-down, look-alike houses in sprawling developments tacked on to the countryside. Gone are the carefully conceived designs, the superb workmanship, the rich diversity of decoration, and the vibrant individual spirit which characterizes older homes, making the survivors from earlier periods take on greater significance and value. With sufficient understanding, ingenuity, and wisdom, those fine older homes which can be made fit for living can continue to survive and to impart joy.

BEGINNING A BEAUTIFUL FRIENDSHIP

Getting to know an older house is an adventure, and in the process the house can grow into a beloved friend. Often its appeal is irresistible—an intuitive love at first sight. The house's endearing qualities and special spirit instantly captivate one's heart. Other times an appreciation of an older home's attractions develops more gradually. The longer you live with an older home of your choice, the richer the experience. When major renovation or restoration work is required, this effort calls for a deep emotional commitment, especially when the owners intend to do most of the work themselves over an

structure of the house. When a home has been brought to a satisfactory condition, inspect it once a year and the vulnerable areas more often to become alert to new problems.

Cultivate a sense of humor. Even after the completion of a painstaking renovation, absurd things can go wrong. Sometimes all you can do is laugh.

WHAT IS THE MOST APPROPRIATE APPROACH TO PRESERVING AN OLDER HOUSE?

Preserving an older house takes many forms. It may mean only small repairs from time to time to keep the house in sound condition. It can occasionally include a precise restoration, taking a home's appearance back to a certain time in its past. Most often the approach called for is renovation: The structure is put into sound repair and its distinguishing features and intriguing details are retained; at the same time, prudent changes may be made for practical reasons. At a minimum, the entire exterior must be made watertight and any hazardous conditions eliminated.

In making these decisions, let the house be your guide. Each has its own problems and possibilities. The choice of what work to do depends on the house's physical condition, its architectural and historical value, and the owner's objectives. Adjustments may also be needed for today's living. A house of exceptional architectural or historical importance may require a careful restoration, and another home may accommodate new dormers or the enclosure of a porch. Other considerations include the style and size of the house and its location. For example, it usually is not advisable to put a contemporary addition on the front of a house or on a highly visible side of a dwelling on a corner lot.

A house evolves over time, experiencing many incarnations, some compatible with the spirit of its style and others insulting its integrity. The present owner must decide, perhaps with competent professional advice, what to retain and what to remove. Alterations which cruelly deform an older home in most cases should not be kept. Sometimes, however, the charm and architectural excitement of later additions, such as porches or decorative bargeboards, make them worthy of being preserved. Often the best approach is to keep the authentic work of several periods rather than to restore the entire house, by new work, to its appearance at one particular time. When in doubt, postpone a decision until you are certain.

Like elderly people, some older homes are remarkably sturdy and in a healthy physical condition. Others show the devastation of time and an absence

extended period. A romance with an older home can become an ardent passion inspiring a dedication overreaching reason. This feeling prompts the owner to persist when setbacks occur.

What is needed for a friendship with an older home to flourish? Start by recognizing and respecting the home's uniqueness. Allow the house to express its own individuality, rather than quarreling with it. Bring sympathy and compassion to an older home's quirks—the outcome of age, perhaps, or the peculiarities of its construction or design. The plumbing may be antiquated and temperamental, the floors may sag, or the windows may stick. Some idiosyncrasies have a remedy; others ask only for tolerance. Be charitable. Friends are not perfect; neither is an older home.

Caring takes repeated effort. This aspect of friendship is less lofty and more mundane but, nevertheless, essential. Once a problem is discovered, always try to locate its source. Do not postpone repairs which will eventually cause costly damage to the

of caring by their former owners. Because of the varying physical states in which older houses can be found, preserving them calls for a range of responses. Perhaps the house is merely a shell, the victim of neglect. In this case, to reproduce the form and details of the earlier structure, a vast amount of new construction is necessary and, except on examples of great architectural or historical value, contemporary building methods and materials are appropriate. Maybe the house is structurally intact, but it is deteriorating. Repainting it, repairing worn-out parts, or rubbing wax into the woodwork may bring the house back to life. Possibly only some parts of the house have been lost or intentionally destroyed. Then the owner may decide to duplicate all of the missing components or to replace only certain of the lost features, adapting others to his or her present needs. Suppose some original features of the house have been camouflaged or insensitively modified. Judicious cleaning or the removal of misguided additions may transform an ugly duckling into a handsome home. Finally, obviously loved and well-tended older houses exist. Any changes they have experienced have been sympathetic. In these instances the response is watchfulness, ongoing maintenance, and thoughtful replacement of aged parts that are no longer useful.

Not all older residences are worthy of preservation simply because they are old. The initial design may be poorly conceived, the house may be shoddily constructed, or its present physical condition may be so dilapidated that attempts to save it are misdirected. Be discriminating and focus on those dwellings worth your efforts.

GUIDELINES FOR CARING FOR AN OLDER HOME

To do justice to an older home, improvements should be sensitive, sympathetic, and honest.

- Discover what is there. Observe the house's shape, the arrangement of its features, and the architectural details and decorations. Study the textures and patterns of the materials and how they are put together. Carefully look at each part inside and outside. Then try to sum up the home's personality. Is it trim and formal? Noble and dignified? Natural and cozy? Playful and unpredictable? Does the house suit your own personality?

- Determine the architectural style of the house and when it was built.

- Allow the house to be itself, and try to bring out its best qualities. Be especially careful with highly visible areas such as the front facade.

- Retain as much of the original house as possible. When in doubt, save what is there.

- Avoid making irrevocable changes. Protect the original parts. Add new work in such a way that it can be undone later, if necessary.

- Do an honest job. Respect the intrinsic worth of an older home. Do not create an impostor pretending to belong to a period or style prior to the date the house was built. Refrain from applying a faddish veneer or taking a cosmetic approach, glossing over severe problems.

- Repair whenever possible to keep the initial ingredients of the house intact.

- Replace only when repair is not feasible, using similar materials, components, dimensions, and finishes. Ruthless remodeling, an unwise substitution of garish modern materials, and obvious imitations of original parts and materials will not only disfigure the historic character of the house but also reduce its financial value.

- Remove any improper alterations such as imitation stone or asbestos siding, preserve appropriate additions, and put back missing original features, if possible.
- Seek the advice of a competent architect or contractor who is familiar with older houses when considering extensive repairs, additions, or replacements.
- Cooperate with your neighbors when making decisions about exterior changes to a twin or row house. These residences are meant to echo each other.
- Check the municipal zoning ordinances and local building codes to be certain any proposed changes conform to zoning and code requirements. Find out if there are applicable local historic district regulations or city redevelopment authority requirements.
- Keep a written and photographic record of any physical changes to the house. Future owners or the local historical society will be grateful for this information.
- Consider the landscaping, gardens, walks, driveways, and fencing on the property and how these can harmonize with the house. Numerous architectural styles had fences designed to enhance the features of the houses, such as the white picket fences accompanying many Eighteenth Century or Georgian Revival homes. Sometimes the architectural features themselves are repeated in the fence designs, particularly evident in the delicate wrought-iron Federal fences. Beware of certain types of contemporary fencing. Chain-link fences, for example, although sturdy, are inappropriate for older homes unless they are concealed in some way, possibly by a covering of ivy.
- Remember that an older house stands in a setting and relates to other homes on the street and in the neighborhood. Think of the house as a permanent guest—a polite and thoughtful one—on its street. The characteristics of each house—such as its materials, the setback from the street, the structure's height and width, the prominence of various components like windows and doors, the roof's shape and pitch, the color scheme, and the decorative details—together with the general condition of every house create the impression received of a neighborhood. How houses affect one another also gives a place its distinctive identity, particularly towns, villages, and urban neighborhoods. The

ideal guest will appreciate its surroundings and never become a disruptive intruder. It will courteously reinforce its setting and help promote a neighborhood atmosphere of livability and loveliness.

A FUTURE FOR THE PAST

Part of the enchantment of older homes is discovering their exciting potentials. They are like rough diamonds waiting to be cut and polished. Witnessing or participating in their metamorphosis is a stirring, triumphant experience. While practicing preservation can be hard, tedious work, it can also be fun and fulfilling for those with frontier spirits who get involved.

By learning what attractions and trouble spots to look for, which remedies to select for maintenance and repair problems, how to avoid costly mistakes, what to ask professionals to do and how to evaluate their work, and where to find replacements for worn-out materials or missing parts, you will be better prepared to conserve and enhance the best of an older home. By approaching improvements with an attitude of enlightened and affectionate care, you can carry out changes in a tender manner and avoid brutal remodeling.

Revitalizing an older house brings many rewards. Among the returns from giving new life to an older home are joy and deep personal satisfaction. The quality of the materials, the beauty of the exquisite workmanship, the charm of the embellishments, and the sense of the past enrich the lives and spirits of the occupants and the persons who encounter the house. An older home refreshed may inspire other individuals in the neighborhood to do similar work. Fine examples of preservation can be contagious. A demonstrated concern for architectural details, sympathetic improvements, intelligent maintenance, or a felicitous choice of exterior paint colors will not go unnoticed but will become a model for neighbors to emulate. Reviving one house can be the beginning of a neighborhood renewed.

Transforming threadbare older houses into gracious, comfortable homes demonstrates more than just an affection for the past. It is a way of promoting intangible, enduring values and of being a responsible caretaker for future generations. It is a way of keeping alive continuity, variety, and beauty in our lives.

CHAPTER TWO

ARCHITECTURAL STYLES

In different eras builders and architects designed houses in varying ways. Each older home is likely to have unique qualities, but a house belongs to an architectural style when several structural and ornamental similarities occur. A repeated combination of specific characteristics creates an architectural style. Shaped by the spirit of their times, architectural styles reflect changing modes of living, social customs, economic conditions, technological improvements, and geographic circumstances. Variations among styles are sometimes glaring, sometimes subtle. To discern differences requires learning to see, educating your eyes to discover a style's distinctive traits.

What should you look for? Houses designed in the same architectural style usually have similar proportions and overall shapes, which may be either symmetrical or irregular. The arrangement of such features as windows, dormers, and chimneys conforms to a recognizable pattern. The components of a house—the type of roof, construction materials, porches and porticoes, embellishments, and details including cornices, corner boards, and moldings around doors and windows—provide further clues indicating a certain style. Naming a house a particular style means its carefully selected parts should work together in a unified composition.

Most older houses belong to one of the many architectural styles; however, few display all the elements of a designated style, and many simpler homes exhibit only a small number of them. The modifications which occur may be because of the initial builder's construction skills and free translation of the style, an architect's interpretation of how the style should appear, the original owner's preferences or budget, a carpenter's personal touches, and adjustments to the climate, available materials, or local customs.

Knowing the architectural style is essential before proceeding with any renovation work on an older house. To avoid careless disfigurations or misguided alterations, identify the style of your house and use this as a guide for preserving its intrinsic components or replacing parts.

HOW ARE THE DATES OF A STYLE DETERMINED?

Assigning specific dates to an architectural style is invariably difficult and arbitrary, for stylistic seasons do not have sharp edges. Only rarely can a precise birth and departure be pinpointed. Usually a style evolves gradually, going through a gestation period before its distinguishing characteristics emerge, flourish, and then leisurely expire. For instance, although some elements of the Greek Revival style originated as early as 1790, this style was not fully mature until around 1820, and by 1840 it had reached its heyday in the East. Elsewhere in the country the Greek Revival style was in vogue up to the Civil War, and it persisted in California throughout the 1870s. For these reasons, the dates accompanying each of the architectural styles described in this chapter are approximations, indicating an era corresponding to the style's American inception and peak of popularity rather than the actual years when the style was built across the country.

The lives of architectural styles frequently followed discernible patterns. Glimmerings of what would eventually become a fashionable new style first shone forth from a few large urban houses located in eastern cities such as Boston, New York, and Philadelphia. Built for affluent pacesetters, these homes established the design standards subsequently copied by others for less ostentatious homes in cities and, later, in the outlying country. Styles generally tended to linger in rural areas long after their novelty had waned in urban centers. In some instances architectural styles advanced westward with the pioneer settlers. By the late nineteenth century and early twentieth century this process occasionally was reversed when architects or builders in the Midwest and West began creating unique styles or notable variations which then traveled eastward.

WHERE DID STYLISTIC IDEAS ORIGINATE?

Each architectural style has its individual roots, yet many styles begin in similar ways. Publications, especially builders' manuals and architectural guidebooks, were important sources for design ideas. In the eighteenth century American builders relied on a few English architectural guidebooks which illustrated the recommended shape and proportions for a house, its plans and decorative details, and the arrangement of components. By following these instructions, a person could, with experience, become a skilled master builder of a specific style. Hired by wealthy clients, these early master builders constructed houses which launched a new style and became prototypes for others to imitate.

Several influential American pattern books and builders' manuals appeared in the early 1800s, and their number multiplied as the century progressed. Simply presented and easy to understand, these pattern books schooled countless carpenters and craftworkers and generated an outburst of new styles. In the latter half of the nineteenth century architectural magazines and millwork catalogs helped to spread additional design ideas.

The contribution made by master builders in the eighteenth century was slowly superseded by architects in the nineteenth century. At first architects, like master builders, were self-taught. Later they received more formal instruction as apprentices to other architects or engineers. Because American architectural schools were not yet established, some apprentices traveled to Europe to study earlier classical buildings or enroll in European architectural programs. Architects receiving a classical training at the École des Beaux Arts in Paris returned to exert a particularly strong influence on American architecture. The American Institute of Architects (AIA) was formed in the late 1860s, pushing the evolving architectural profession a step forward. By the end of the nineteenth century persons practicing architecture were required to be thoroughly trained professionals and to obtain licenses.

Throughout most of the nineteenth century, however, it was a small number of self-trained "architects" who, along with the architectural guidebooks and builders' manuals, set new architectural styles in motion. Most of America's now "older" homes were constructed by carpenters and builders who modeled them after a few pioneering examples.

WHAT WERE THE EFFECTS OF TECHNOLOGICAL CHANGES?

Older homes from successive periods bear witness to advances in technology. Certain late nineteenth century styles, for example, became possible because of changes in building methods and newly invented tools. Knowing when various technological improvements occurred can help in dating a house and in understanding the construction options and restraints shaping a particular style.

Innovations in the production of nails strongly influenced home building. Nail-cutting machines, introduced about 1800, gradually replaced the slow process of making nails by hand. By the 1830s mass manufacturing of nails helped usher in a revolutionary invention: wooden balloon framing. Prior to this time, structural framing consisted of heavy hewn posts and beams, braced and fastened together with wooden pegs and dove-tailed joints. Not only was this earlier method cumbersome, but the rigid frames dictated boxlike houses. Appearing in 1833, the lighter weight balloon frame was easily assembled with nails, hammer, and saw, and it was flexible, permitting a greater variety of house shapes. Composed of vertical studs, floor joists, and rafters, the balloon frame was also efficient, had materials that were simple to ship, and was inexpensive — well adapted to the forthcoming flurry in home building. The advent of the circular saw in 1814 facilitated the production of boards and heavy timbers; but not until the mid-nineteenth century, with the invention of machines for processing wood in stock sizes, were sawmills able to begin supplying the cheap lumber and millwork needed for balloon framing.

Other key inventions in the nineteenth century included prefabricated cast iron around 1850, which became a substitute for the earlier handmade wrought iron used for decoration and fences. The scroll saw for sawing curved outlines emerged early in the century, followed by an avalanche of new and improved tools after the Civil War. Among these were a smaller scroll saw called a coping saw, the motor-driven lathe, the chisel, the gouge, the jigsaw for cutting ornamental patterns and curved or irregular lines in openwork, and the bandsaw, important for creating various shaped wooden shingles in large quantities. These sophisticated tools enabled many mid-to-late nineteenth century homes to burst forth with extravagant embellishments.

Technological improvements in transportation and communication also affected the development of various architectural styles. Canals, built around the turn of the nineteenth century, and railroads, constructed across our country from the 1830s to 1860s, carried building materials and design ideas to remote regions and broke down sharp local differences in architectural styles.

WHAT STYLE IS AN OLDER HOME?

The following sections identify the major architectural styles popular in America from the seventeenth century to the early twentieth century. Along with the descriptions of individual features found in other chapters, these portraits should help to label the style of an older house. Categorizing a particular older home may be perplexing, however, for few houses have survived without changes such as removing or concealing original details. Occasionally, too, when a house was remodeled over time, additions or alterations copied a currently favored style, further complicating a neat classification.

For assistance in solving the puzzle of the style of a specific home:

- Contact the local historical society.
- Search for early photographs showing the original house. Compare these with the house today for indications of design changes.
- Trace the property deed or investigate old maps to find out when the house was built. Knowing the construction date can aid in determining the architectural style.

- Study the house's construction techniques and materials. These may suggest approximate dates and reveal alterations.
- Look around the neighborhood for homes similar to yours which may have more of the original parts still in place.
- Consult an architect or architectural historian who is knowledgeable about older houses in the area.

If you have thought of a particular house as "Victorian," perhaps because it was garnished with gingerbread, you will not find such a "style" in this book. "Victorian" is a general term, relating to the reign of Queen Victoria in England (1837 to 1901) and encompassing a variety of nineteenth century buildings. This chapter and the Design sections of other chapters concentrate on specific features and details of a house, encouraging an observation of the distinguishing differences among older residences. When looking closely at a "Victorian" house, you may find it resembles one of the architectural styles described, such as Queen Anne, Mansard, Gothic Revival, or Italianate.

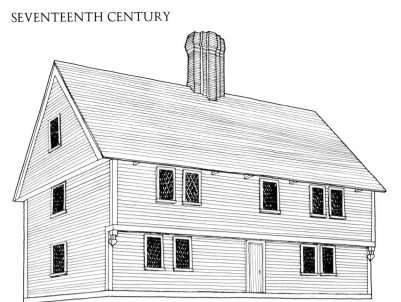

Figure 2-1. New England Seventeenth Century house.

Figure 2-2. Southern Seventeenth Century house.

Seventeenth Century houses are forthright and functional. Lacking the time, financial resources, and probably the skills and tools to construct elaborate edifices, the earliest settlers built plain, serviceable homes without pretense of being other than what they are: staunch, compact shelters. Unfortunately, few Seventeenth Century homes built along the eastern seaboard survive today, and many that do have experienced changes over the years. The Seventeenth Century homes that have endured deserve to be prized.

Early immigrants brought their native building methods with them. Mostly of humble origin, they were accustomed to living in simple homes, and their new dwellings usually were like their former ones. Changes occurred primarily because of differences in climate, locally available materials, and the skills and predilections of the builder. As a result, no two Seventeenth Century homes were exactly alike.

With their steeply pitched roofs, immense chimneys, and small casement windows with leaded panes, the English colonists' homes resemble rural yeomen's houses of the late medieval and Elizabethan period (1558 to 1603). In New England the usual house was a wooden, two-story structure with a massive central chimney and simple plank frames around the windows and doors (Figure 2-1). The placement of the openings was somewhat haphazard and not always strictly balanced. At times the second story on the front or on three sides projected several inches beyond the lower floor. Particularly prevalent in the Connecticut River Valley, houses of this type often had brackets under the overhang on either side of the entrance and in the middle of each end wall. Ornamental pendills, or carved drops hewn from the upper-story corner posts, occasionally acccented the corners. These were almost the only embellishments on Seventeenth Century houses.

The majority of Northern homes were one room deep with later ells or lean-tos providing additional rooms. By the end of the century the lean-to was built when the house was constructed, creating a sweeping, unbroken back roof line. Called a saltbox, this type of house became increasingly common in New England.

Construction techniques were the medieval ones. In New England large boxlike wooden frames were held together by mortise and tenon joints and braced at the corners by additional boards. Chimney girts, or heavy beams, crossed the house, abutting the chimney on both sides. The walls were either planks or lighter vertical boards, called studs, with the spaces between filled with crude bricks (nogging), twigs and clay (wattle and daub), or stones. Narrow clapboard or sometimes shingle siding sheathed the exterior. The rough texture of the siding and other irregularities give these houses a special charm.

Only a few Seventeenth Century wooden houses built in the South remain while more brick homes, typical of the small English house of this period, have endured (Figure 2-2). Most are one-and-one-half-story simple rectangular boxes with two rooms on each floor. The windows and doorway are nearly symmetrical. Like their counterparts in the North, they have steep double-pitched roofs and casement windows. Unlike Northern houses, however, outside chimneys are placed on both end walls, a feature which became a lasting Southern tradition.

Other surviving Seventeenth Century houses also bear the marks of local conditions and of native construction traditions. Stone-ender houses with huge exterior chimneys covering the entire end wall are found in Rhode Island. The Dutch, building in the Hudson River area, favored brick houses boasting tall parapeted gables projecting above the roof line and chimneys on these end walls.

Figure 2-3. Early Georgian house.

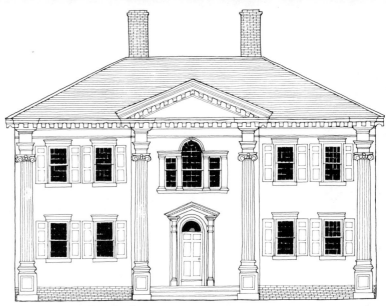

Figure 2-4. Late Georgian house.

Genteel, graceful, and gracious, Georgian houses have a sense of fitness: Their classical parts work together in harmony. Almost all Georgian homes are simple rectangular blocks with their windows, doors, and chimneys carefully balanced. Some are subdued, others are elegant, and still others are fastidiously formal, but all are confidently dignified.

Georgian houses derive from slightly earlier English prototypes which, in turn, were influenced by Andrea Palladio, a sixteenth century Italian architect. Named for the English kings George I through George IV, who reigned from 1714 to 1830, the English examples followed classical rules for proportions and symmetry. The style was introduced to America by English architectural books—such as Palladio's *Four Books of Architecture* and James Gibb's *A Book of Architecture*—and builders' guides including Abraham Swan's *British Architect*, William Salmon's *Palladio Londinensis*, and Joseph Moxon's *Mechanick Exercises*, which illustrated window and doorway details used here on row houses. At the time there were only a few trained architects who designed the larger houses. Carpenter-builders and masons built most Georgian homes, receiving their instruction in classical detailing from the practical manuals. At first, a few Georgian features, such as a paneled door or sash windows, were incorporated into an otherwise Seventeenth Century house. By 1750, when the style had become more academic, designs for entire houses were copied straight from books. These classically correct houses generally were located in urban areas. The less inhibited rural craftworkers often modified the design prescriptions by their own personal touches.

The Georgian style is really two styles: early Georgian from 1700 to around 1750 and late Georgian from 1750 to about 1780. The earliest Georgian homes are trim and functional with only a few modest classical references (Figure 2-3). Two or two-and-a-half stories, a typical early Georgian house has a central entry and hall with two rooms on either side. Five or occasionally seven double-hung sash windows appear across the front on the second story, lining up with the openings below. Central chimneys continued in some New England homes, but paired chimneys placed a few feet from each end of the ridge gradually prevailed. Plain trim surrounds the openings. A rectangular row of small panes appears either in the door or as a transom above it. Pilasters or columns with either a flat horizontal architrave or a low pediment above, framing the door, and a simple cornice with dentils are commonly the only decoration.

Late Georgian houses are more elaborate, imposing, and classically proper (Figure 2-4). The ornate central entrance often has a fanlight above the door, flanking sidelights, and a columned portico. Quoins or pilasters accent the corners, a Palladian window ordinarily appears above the doorway, pediments adorn windows and dormers, and deep carving decorates the lavish cornice. At times, a large late Georgian house has a central projecting pavilion crowned with a triangular pediment. Together, these features give late Georgian houses an opulent appearance.

Local variations occurred in response to differences in climate, available materials, and the builder's own origins. Some of these include pent eaves found on German houses in southeastern Pennsylvania, piazzas and two-story porticoes favored in the South, and houses with broad gambrel roofs with flared eaves built by the Dutch in northern Jersey.

Constructed in cities, towns, and villages along the eastern coast, the Georgian style persisted into the nineteenth century in certain sections such as the South. Popular for modest homes and country mansions, the Georgian style was also employed for row houses in Boston, Philadelphia, Baltimore, and other eastern cities.

Figure 2-5. Federal house.

Refined and reserved, chaste and conservative, the clean lines and graceful decoration of Federal houses point to their classical origins. A quiet graciousness accompanies their dignified and formal bearing. Constructed primarily by carpenter-builders, with a few examples by notable architects, Federal homes are found from Maine to Georgia. Most appear in coastal New England towns, such as Salem, Massachusetts, and in the larger cities of Boston, Providence, New York, Philadelphia, and Charleston. Hardly any were built in the then frontier territory west of the Appalachian Mountains. Look for brick townhouses with wood or stone trim in urban areas, clapboard residences in smaller towns and rural places, and stone homes in Pennsylvania (Figure 2-5).

In some respects the Federal style was America's first national style. Also referred to as the Neoclassic Style and the Adam Style, the name Federal alludes to the new republic. First popular in England as the Adam Style, it was promoted there by the Adam brothers, architects who had studied the archaeological excavations of Herculaneum, Pompeii, and the Palace of Diocletian at Spalato, designed many houses reflecting these ancient buildings, and written *Works in Architecture* describing their architectural concepts. The architect Charles Bulfinch incorporated the Adam brothers' design motifs in his Boston houses during the late 1780s and 1790s, introducing the style to this country. Woodlands, a large Philadelphia house built around 1789, has Federal features. In the early 1800s Asher Benjamin copied and adapted Bulfinch's designs, illustrating these in his widely sold handbook *The American Builder's Companion*.

The Georgian style gradually gave way to the Fed-eral, and features of both styles sometimes appear in a single house. Corner quoins, for instance, persisted until about 1805, and a Palladian window occasionally appeared above the entrance. Differences between the two styles occur primarily in their proportions, scale, and ornamentation. The Federal home usually is a plain, rectangular cube topped with a low-pitched gable roof or a shallow hipped roof encircled by a balustrade. Windows, doors, and two or four tall chimneys are symmetrically arranged. The double-sash windows of six over six panes are narrower than the earlier Georgian ones, and their size is often graduated: Windows on the first and second floors are similar in dimensions, and the third-floor ones are smaller. Embellishments and trim are delicate: thin muntins, slender moldings and door framings, slim portico columns, and fragile, low-relief ornamentation resembling Wedgwood china.

Geometric shapes fascinated Federal builders, forming a counterpoint to the straight lines of the house. A semielliptical fanlight laced with weblike tracery almost always crowns the central entrance door, which is further emphasized by tall rectangular sidelights. Circles, ovals, ellipses, and curving festoons appear as carved or applied ornaments. Samuel McIntire executed exquisite woodcarvings on several Federal houses he designed in Salem. At times, the foundations of Federal homes are raised, and the entrances are reached by curving steps bordered by light iron railings. Occasional octagonal or curved projections may reflect an oval, circular, or octagonal interior room. Now and then, shallow blind wall arches surround recessed windows. Some Federal homes are sophisticated, some are more simple, but all are subtle.

Figure 2-6. Greek Revival house.

Noble and serene, Greek Revival houses have an enduring quality, a tribute to their origins. Turning to ancient Greece, architects and builders discovered in the Greek temple a fitting symbol for the democratic spirit of the young republic. By inference, houses incorporating architectural features from these early temples represented proud expressions of our nation's ideals. Greek Revival homes may be pristine and academically proper or casual and less classically correct, but all are trim and tidily ordered (Figure 2-6).

The first Greek Revival buildings constructed in America were two banks: the Bank of Philadelphia designed by Benjamin Henry Latrobe in 1798 and the Second Bank of the United States, also in Philadelphia, designed by William Strickland in 1818. Architectural guidebooks, such as Asher Benjamin's *The American Builder's Companion* and John Haviland's *The Builders' Assistant* promoted this style by illustrating the Greek orders, which are described in Chapter 9, Porches and Porticoes, and other components of Greek temples, sometimes modifying the original proportions for practical reasons.

By the 1820s the temple form was adapted to houses, eventually becoming a nationwide, authentically American style. First popular in Baltimore and the mid-Atlantic states, the Greek Revival style soon extended to Pennsylvania and western New York, emerging on a large scale in New England by the 1850s. Pioneers moving into the Midwest and West brought this style with them, sometimes shipping parts from New England for their homes. Generally these were not as elaborate as their eastern counterparts. Some of the most imposing Greek Revival houses are found in the South where, as in the West, this style continued long after 1860 when it had subsided elsewhere.

Very adaptable, this style appears in plain farmhouses and homesteads, modest one- or one-and-one-half-story homes, formal mansions, gracious plantations, and stately townhouses. Even the smaller houses have touches of grandeur and, except for homes having an L- or T-shaped plan, are strictly symmetrical. Designs following the pure temple form are carefully balanced, displaying a classical colonnade usually with Doric or Ionic columns supporting an entablature and a low triangular pediment above. The main roof's ridge invariably runs from front to back, and the gable, or pediment, end faces the street. In other instances there may be a projecting portico or a recessed entrance with columns standing on the wall plane. Often, a simplified wooden home is a rectangular block, perhaps with subsidiary wings on either side, and has a wide cornice; corner boards or pilasters marking the corners; broad, flat moldings around the openings; a sill board above the foundation; and tall, evenly spaced windows featuring six over six panes. The entrance doorway, accented by a horizontal transom and flanking sidelights, may be centered or placed on one side. Decoration commonly is restrained, although lacy cast iron graces frieze windows or balconies on some Greek Revival houses in localities such as the French Quarter in New Orleans.

Figure 2-7. Gothic Revival house.

Gothic Revival houses are enchanting creations, fanciful and flamboyant. Their sprightly, sentimental spirits represent a rebellion against the reserve and restrictive formality of earlier classical styles. Born from romantic longings to embrace features from medieval cathedrals, these houses abound with symbolic references to the former Gothic age: pointed arches, window tracery, lancet or casement windows with diamond-shaped panes, cloverleaf-like trefoils and quatrefoils, Gothic crosses, pinnacles, crenelations, and carved foliage reminiscent of the borders on medieval manuscripts (Figure 2-7).

The Gothic Revival style, now and then called the Pointed Style, traces its beginnings to the remodeling of Strawberry Hill, an English estate, in 1747, and to other subsequent English ancestors such as Fonthill Abbey. In 1799 Benjamin Henry Latrobe designed the first American example, Sedgeley, a Philadelphia house. By the 1830s America's most prolific Gothic Revival architect, Alexander Jackson Davis, was designing innumerable cottages and country houses which were illustrated in Andrew Jackson Downing's widely distributed architectural guidebooks. Not as much in vogue after about 1860, Gothic Revival houses continued to be built into the 1880s and 1890s in seashore resorts, such as Cape May, New Jersey, and in the Midwest.

Expect to see an irregular silhouette composed of tall intersecting gables, finials, decorative chimney pots, and, on grander houses, square or octagonal towers or turrets. The plan may be boxlike, recalling the symmetrical arrangement of its classical forebears, or asymmetrical with side wings. Spacious verandas nearly always grace these homes.

Echoing soaring Gothic cathedrals and churches, Gothic Revival houses stress vertical features: pointed arches, slender windows, peaked dormers, steeply pitched roofs, and perpendicular board and batten siding. Fancy woodwork, made possible by the invention of the scroll saw and, in the mid-nineteenth century, by machine-cut millwork, festoons bargeboards along the rake of the roof or outlines gables, window trimmings, and porches. Ingenious ornamentation devised by local craftworkers or put together by builders led to the Carpenter Gothic style, a native offspring of the Gothic Revival.

Except for their interest in churches, Gothic Revival advocates focused their attention on single-family homes ranging from small or medium-sized cottages and country houses to grandiose mansions and a few miniature castles. Popular from Maine to California, most Gothic Revival houses were built in early suburbs (many of which are now urban neighborhoods), towns, villages, or the countryside.

Figure 2-8. Italianate house.

Italianate homes can be quaint or classical, inviting or reserved, but they always have a timelessness and serenity. Highly adaptable, this architectural style is found in a great variety of forms: simple wood cottages or row houses, moderate-sized stucco residences, imposing stone mansions, and stately brownstone townhouses. Prevalent in large cities, such as New York, Philadelphia, and San Francisco, Italianate houses also were built in small towns and in the country (Figure 2-8).

Sometimes called Italian Villa, Tuscan Revival, or Lombard, this style might more appropriately be named the Bracketed Style. These houses are teeming with brackets: projecting from a wide cornice to support the deep overhanging eaves, peaking out from beneath window sills or balconies, and garnishing porches or doorways. The Italianate blocklike forms grouped in an asymmetrical arrangement with protruding ells and windows, irregular floor plans, and projecting towers or cupolas are derived from old northern Italian farmhouses. Windows and

doors usually are evenly spaced. The first English example of this style was built in 1802. Entering America in the late 1830s, the Italianate style reached its height of popularity in the 1850s, largely because of its promotion in architectural guidebooks by Andrew Jackson Downing, Calvert Vaux, and William H. Ranlett.

Earlier Italianate houses tend to be simpler, later ones more ornate. Rectangular or square in shape with a gently sloping hip or gable roof, the plainer home has modest decorations: perhaps shallow pediments or flat architraves above the windows, a bracketed pediment over the entrance doorway, a bay window, and a lantern or cupola crowning the roof. On an elaborate Italianate house, look for tall, round-arched openings on windows, doors, and the loggia; heavy moldings, pronounced pediments, or hoods above the windows; a square corner or central three-story tower; quoins or corner boards marking the corners; balconies; and porticoes or verandas.

Figure 2-9. Stick Style house.

Informal and relaxed, Stick Style homes have a democratic air. Not surprisingly, their roots are American. Traces of the Gothic Revival style and hints of a Swiss chalet are seen in their tall proportions and high roofs with steep intersecting gables, but this unpretentious architectural style is clearly indigenous (Figure 2-9).

Distinctive skeletal stickwork gives this style its name. Superimposed on the wood clapboard siding, the exposed framing suggests on the outside the inner structural balloon framework of the house. Vertical and horizontal thin boards, intersecting at right angles, punctuate the walls (sometimes only on the upper stories), gables, and dormers. You will also find X-shaped crosspieces and diagonal stickwork resembling half-timbering. Essentially nonstructural, the projecting stickwork enhances the house by creating decorative shadows on the surface.

Other adornments on these wood houses tend to

be simple and angular, too, largely confined to the eaves and porches. Pronounced brackets or a series of flat sticks may support the protruding eaves. Otherwise plain porch posts often have diagonal braces or bisected triangles resembling "king-post trusses" on the top. In most examples of this style the window placement is regular, but the jumble of gables, dormers, and chimneys forms an irregular silhouette.

Promoted in architectural guidebooks and builders' manuals, Stick Style houses are found primarily along the northeastern coast and in California. Often having generous porches and verandas, this style was particularly popular in seashore vacation areas. Smaller, simplified homes constructed with balloon framing were well suited to narrow lots, and occasionally building contractors and land developers produced row after row of this style house in their residential tract developments.

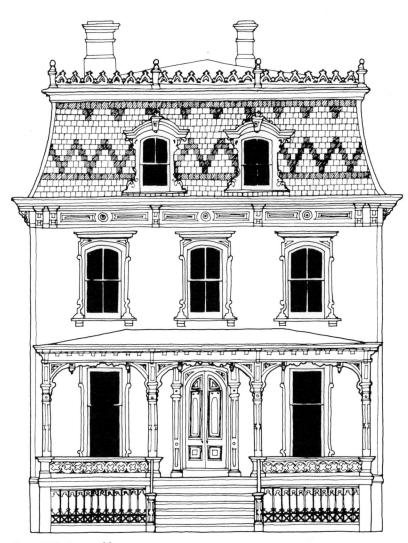

Figure 2-10. Mansard house.

Houses designed in the Mansard style are self-confident, imposing, and stately. Even the smaller homes appear monumental. Opulently ornamented, Mansard houses seem like sumptuous pieces of sculpture with the glitter of sunshine and deep shadows enlivening their surfaces (Figure 2-10).

The imperial bearing of these homes partially comes from their design source: They are modeled after cosmopolitan buildings constructed during the reign of Napoleon III, 1852 to 1870. Sometimes called French Second Empire, the style emerged first in the addition to the Louvre in Paris built between 1852 and 1857. The name Mansard derives from François Mansart, a seventeenth century French architect who created the style's distinctive roof shape. This architectural style is also known as General Grant because the height of its popularity coincided with his presidency.

A high mansard roof with two almost vertical slopes on all four sides is a universal feature of this style. Concave, convex, and S-shaped slopes occur as well as straight ones. Slate roofing with handsome decorative patterns appears often. Curbing edges the top of the roof at its juncture with a second shallow-pitched hipped roof above, and it may also outline the edges of the slopes, adding to the three-dimensional effect. The height of the roof allows space for third-floor rooms. A dazzling assortment of dormers dressed up in ostentatious apparel invariably protrudes from the roof. At times, iron cresting graces the top of the roof or a tower.

Mansard houses are rich in other lively trimmings which often show some classical influence. Ornately carved brackets attached to a molded cornice frequently support the overhanging eaves. Verandas generally have columns with pronounced, flared capitals; columns on porticoes usually resemble the classical Corinthian order. The entrance, nearly always with double doors, has substantial moldings surrounding it. Quoins or corner boards enframing the sides; cornices, hoods, or pediments capping most windows; and decorative detailings embellishing the chimneys give additional vitality to Mansard houses.

Windows in these high-ceilinged homes tend to be tall and narrow. Together with the high foundations, corner boards, and towering roof, they contribute to the vertical appearance of the house. Many homes are wood, but stone and brick versions are also common.

Mansard houses can be both regular and irregular. Towers or pavilions with individual mansard roofs, two-story protruding bays, porticoes, and expansive verandas give some houses an asymmetrical form. As a counterpoint, the window placement is commonly symmetrical, with the first-story windows in line with those above.

Aided by architectural guidebooks and builders' manuals illustrating exterior elevations and interior floor plans, the Mansard style rapidly spread throughout America into most cities along the eastern seaboard and in the Midwest. A few are grand mansions, but many more are moderate-sized residences. Small one-story cottages seemingly overwhelmed by their massive roofs are also found as well as twin houses and townhouses. Sometimes mansard roofs were added to older houses or to new ones of another style, producing third-floor rooms but making these homes seem top-heavy.

Figure 2-11. Romanesque house.

Romanesque houses are robust and resolute, featuring round-arched openings. These solid, straightforward homes at times resemble compact fortresses with their rock-faced masonry walls and deeply recessed windows and doors. Built to last for generations, most Romanesque houses are moderate-sized single-family homes, row houses, or grander residences located in large eastern or midwestern cities such as Chicago (Figure 2-11).

The development of this style was so strongly influenced by the American architect Henry Hobson Richardson (1838–1886) that sometimes it is called Richardsonian Romanesque. Certain characteristics, such as round arches, corbels, and squat columns with foliage capitals, were borrowed from medieval Romanesque architecture. Houses inspired by Richardson's designs also have long bands of windows, belt courses, and wide rounded arches to give them a horizontal emphasis. In many instances the need for light in a particular room determined the window's size and placement, outweighing the desire to treat windows as repetitive units with the same dimensions. Although the windows may align evenly, various components including projecting bays, many-sided turrets, wall dormers, and round or square towers often were arranged in an asymmetrical manner.

Romanesque homes were frequently built with rough stone laid in horizontal rows, but brick, clapboard, or shingles were used on a few exterior walls. Stone of a texture and color different from the masonry walls commonly accents arches, belt courses, lintels, and other trim. Look for additional embellishments such as brick or terra-cotta panels on the gables and belt courses, above the doorways and windows, and along the cornice. In contrast with the rugged stone, the decorative details tend to be restrained, often featuring gentle intertwining floral and foliage designs.

Figure 2-12. Queen Anne house.

Vivacious and uninhibited, Queen Anne houses are entertaining, inviting you to explore how the many complex pieces fit together into a playful puzzle. Surprises abound. Their builders were fascinated by the unexpected: chimneys wrapping around windows or jutting up through dormers, round corners instead of square, or strangely shaped windows appearing where windows do not usually appear. Design limitations dissolved and each home boasts its own idiosyncrasies. But each also has its own special order. Look carefully, you will find it (Figure 2-12).

An English architect, Richard Norman Shaw, launched the Queen Anne style in Leyswood, an 1868 manor house later described in American publications. In 1874 Henry Hobson Richardson designed the first American example of this style, the Watts Sherman House in Newport, Rhode Island, substituting wood shingles and stone for Shaw's tiles and brick. Wide publicity was given to this budding style because of two British buildings constructed for the 1876 Philadelphia Centennial. Highly praised by magazines such as *The American Builder* and *Building News*, as well as by Henry Hudson Holly's articles in *Harpers*, Queen Anne was on its way to becoming one of America's most prolific styles. Soon numerous architectural pattern books, such as Holly's *Modern Dwellings*, promoted the style, and manufacturer's catalogs offered a profusion of suitable parts, among them windows, doors, brackets, and balusters.

The name Queen Anne is misleading. Coined in England, it refers back to a time of fine-quality workmanship and *not* to the architectural features of houses built in the reign of Queen Anne (1702 to 1714). During its popularity, the style had several other names: Neo-Jacobean (alluding to medieval characteristics such as towers and turrets), Free Classic (indicating the incorporation of classic elements such as Palladian windows, columns, and an attic fanlight), Tower Houses, Bric-a-Brac Style, and Modern American Renaissance. The mixture of architectural precedents perhaps combined in one Queen Anne house led to this confusion about what to call it.

Almost all Queen Anne homes have striking silhouettes, often with high, multiple roofs, and are astonishingly asymmetrical: Steep gables, dormers, turrets, wings, balconies, and large porches protrude

in innumerable directions; tall square, round, or octagonal towers with pointed caps, onion domes, or hipped roofs reach high beyond the roof line; and bay and oriel windows bulge outward. The inside layouts, focused on a spacious central living hall and filled with nooks and crannies, determined the outside configurations. Expect contrasts in textures and materials. The first floor may be brick, stone, or clapboard, the second story sheathed in shingles or clapboard, and the attic or gables accented with half-timbers or another kind of shingle. Splendid ornamentation usually is applied above doors and windows and to gables, dormers, porches, brackets, panels, and chimneys. These were borrowed from several sources: ancient Greece and Rome, medieval houses, and the late nineteenth century English Aesthetic Movement which favored the small-scale embellishments, such as sunbursts, flowers, and rosettes, so common on Queen Anne homes. Because these decorations were ready-made and available through catalogs, builders devised endless ingenious combinations of them.

Popular at a time of population growth, national prosperity, and immense construction activity, countless Queen Anne houses, some as late as 1910, sprang up across the country in small towns, the countryside, seashore resorts, suburbs, urban neighborhoods, and cities. Highly adaptable, this style appears as one- or two-story simple cottages, medium-sized homes, grand mansions, and row houses vaunting prominent bay windows capped with cone-shaped or gable roofs. Whether fanciful extravaganzas or subdued shelters, Queen Anne houses reflect the buoyant self-confidence and outgoing spirit of their day.

Figure 2-13. Shingle Style house.

Cozy and comfortable, intimate and informal, Shingle Style houses are homey and inviting. Even the large, rambling houses are relaxed and unpretentious, without any fancy embellishments. Weathered wooden shingles are everywhere: covering the roofs, gables, walls, and porches and giving the style its name. Broad sweeping roofs and a muted silvery gray or rasin brown color make both the smaller houses and the more spacious ones seem generous and gentle. Snuggled close to the earth, Shingle Style homes seem to be a part of their natural surroundings (Figure 2-13).

Authentically American, except for occasional features such as an attic fanlight or Palladian window borrowed from Georgian Revival homes and a round-arched entryway reminiscent of the Romanesque style, the Shingle Style grew out of a renewed interest in the simpler wood shingle homes of our colonial days. The modest late seventeenth century and early eighteenth century shingled homes which dot coastal New England towns and Nantucket were rediscovered by an example displayed at the 1876 Philadelphia Centennial. Soon afterward, in 1879, William Ralph Emerson designed the first Shingle Style house on Mount Desert, Maine. At first, in the 1880s, the style was developed by well-known eastern architects: Henry Hobson Richardson in Boston; Bruce Price in Tuxedo Park, New York; John Calvin Stevens in Portland, Maine; Wilson Eyre in Philadelphia; and McKim, Mead and White, a New York firm which designed several New England Shingle Style houses. Eventually it reached across the country, promoted by the architect J. Lyman Silsbee in Chicago and in 1886 brought by Willis Polk to San Francisco, where the style was sometimes called the First Bay Tradition. In some sections, such as the West Coast, the style flourished into the twentieth century.

Shingle Style houses are strongly horizontal with broad gables, long bands of windows, and low sweeping lines which hug the ground. Wide, recessed porches, balconies, towers, turrets, and slanted bay windows—all sheathed in shingles—create an openness and continuity between the inside and the outside. The textured surface of the roof and walls conceals the structural frame. Most Shingle Style homes are asymmetrical with windows reflecting the interior layouts, gambrel or double-pitched roofs intersecting in unexpected ways, and chimneys jutting up seemingly at random. Now and then rough, coursed stone or natural fieldstone boulders are used on the first story to contrast with the shingles.

At the outset, most Shingle Style houses were summer vacation homes along the northeastern seashores, in mountain resorts, or in the countryside. Later some appeared in city neighborhoods. The key elements of this style, initially devised by architects for wealthy clients, gradually filtered into medium-sized houses and smaller cottages. To keep up with the changing fashions, many owners of Stick Style, Queen Anne, and Colonial Revival homes also covered their houses with shingles to give them a rustic appearance. Identifying a genuine Shingle Style house sometimes is difficult because of this kind of camouflage and because many later owners removed the wood shingles on the roofs and walls, replacing them with asphalt roofing and clapboard siding.

Figure 2-14. Georgian Revival house.

Many Georgian Revival and Federal Revival houses look like overgrown, dressed up cousins of their earlier American ancestors. Invariably larger in size, these homes possess numerous features, such as windows, dormers, and porticoes, having more generous proportions than their forebears. Decorative details and millwork are ordinarily heavier, more pronounced, and quite elaborate. The polished elegance of these formal houses is sometimes opulently ostentatious, sometimes sophisticated, and sometimes just quietly dignified. Always, these proud Revival homes bear witness to their classical antecedents, but in a more ample and often extravagant way (Figure 2-14).

Turning back to earlier styles was a symbolic gesture stimulated by the 1876 Philadelphia Centennial celebration's focus on our country's heritage and by a desire to resurrect the well-ordered, precisely balanced architectural arrangements of former styles amid the free expression and irregularity of several other current styles. Prominent architects and architectural firms took up the Revival banner, searched New England for suitable prototypes, looked into the English origins, and created attractive facsimiles. Handsome Georgian Revival and Federal Revival houses in Newport, Rhode Island, and in Boston, designed around 1885 by the well-known firm of McKim, Mead and White, were among the first examples. Widely copied, they launched what became fashionable architectural styles built throughout the

country. At times both styles were mixed in the same house. In general, Georgian Revival homes were constructed in urban neighborhoods, the suburbs, and outlying areas, while Federal Revival homes were built primarily as townhouses in eastern cities.

Both Revival styles returned to the symmetrically composed boxlike shape embellished with classical details. Georgian Revival homes frequently have pilasters, quoins, or corner boards; wide cornices edged with chunky dentils; substantial chimneys; hipped, gambrel, or double-pitched roofs; and front doors with wide fanlights or transoms above and flanking sidelights. At times an immense central portico or a projecting pavilion crowned with a pediment appears. Some versions have two-tier porches supported by tall two-story columns. Pent eaves were again a popular trait on stone houses in southeastern Pennsylvania. A few characteristics were a marked departure from the earlier Georgian style: Palladian windows may occur on the first floor and not just above the entrance, and spacious open terraces or verandas often project from each side of the house. A Federal Revival home, more elaborate than the original style, retained the shallow hipped roof often with an encircling balustrade; graduated windows; tall, thin chimneys; a formal portico; fanlights above the doorways; and Adam ornaments, such as festoons, although less delicate than the earlier decorations.

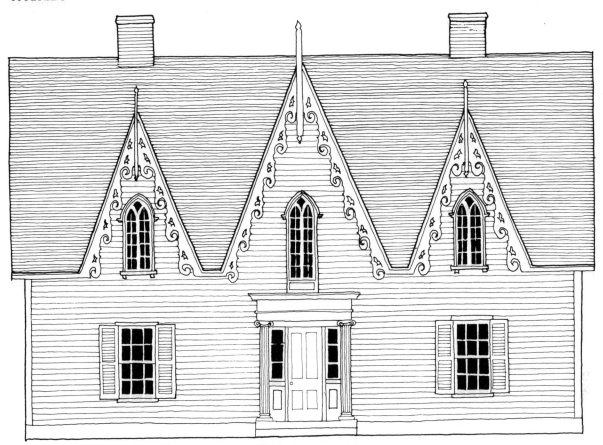

Figure 2-15. Hybrid house.

Some older homes refuse to fit comfortably into one stylistic category. They are mavericks. With zest, they disregard academically correct design prescriptions and combine architectural features from two or more styles. Quite numerous, these houses ordinarily are one of a kind. Whether simple or complex, their distinctiveness is appealing and surprising. Some are conservative, others are spicy or amusing, and still others are eccentric. Always intriguing, hybrid houses simply ask to be accepted as they are (Figure 2-15).

Hybrids come about in various ways, sometimes by intention and other times by accident. Many are transitions between two different styles. These houses mix elements of a former style with components heralding an emerging style. For instance, a home with Federal proportions and windows may boast a Greek Revival doorway. In some cases hybrids represent a consciously selected combination of characteristics from two styles to create a particular effect. A house mingling the Queen Anne and Georgian Revival styles, for example, may be more restrained than a pure Queen Anne but more exuberant and irregular than a typical Georgian Revival. The idiosyncrasies of other mavericks suggest they were fashioned by the whimsy of the original owners or builders.

A house may have been a hybrid initially, or it may have evolved into a composite through graftings by subsequent owners. Perhaps a Greek Revival house was updated with Italianate bow windows, or an Italianate home later was made more fashionable with a mansard roof. When spacious porches became popular, they frequently were added to earlier houses. A Gothic Revival house, for instance, may display a Queen Anne porch with spindles and turned balusters. When all components of a hybrid home are original, the concoction of different architectural styles may have occurred for several reasons: the personal preferences of the first owner or builder, the carpenter's or builder's skills, the materials at hand, the climate, or the budget size.

More hybrids tend to be found in rural areas than in urban centers. Country carpenters, away from the pressures to conform to styles established in the cities, were freer to experiment. Showing the incredible inventiveness of their builders, hybrid houses come in endless combinations. Remember, however, they are derivations, even if tenuous, from the other architectural styles. In identifying hybrids, look for echoes of their prototypes in their features and ornamentation and marvel at the ingenuity of their builders.

CHAPTER THREE

PREPARING FOR THE WORK

Once you and your older home have become friends, you are ready to plan the work. Planning is nothing more than finding thorough answers to several questions. What is to be done? When? Who is to do the work? What is the best technique for accomplishing the job? How much is it likely to cost? The replies involve discovering as much as possible about older houses—a process of investigation and thought no architect or general contractor can perform for you as well as you can.

LEARNING ABOUT AN OLDER HOUSE

You and your house will benefit from an earnest attempt to extend your knowledge about it. This task can stretch out over a long period of time, and each discovery is rewarding. One way to begin is to determine the date the house was built and who designed or constructed it. If the house does not have a date-stone or you are not lucky enough to inherit precise records of your home's past, try to retrace the history of the house through property deeds, building and real estate records, and other public documents. Check with a local historical society. Peruse histories of your neighborhood or street to learn about the date the street was opened, the flourishing of commerce and industry, and the development of railroad or trolley lines which offer additional clues. For guidance, do not overlook neighbors, long-time residents of the locale, families of earlier occupants of the house, and collectors of old photographs. Finding out who designed or built your home can have practical consequences. Studying another house by the same architect or builder may explain mysteries such as the likely appearance of a missing or severely damaged part of your house.

Often an older home has been formed in stages. Limitless curiosity, which may be enthusiastically contributed by any children in the household, aids the search for this information. Evidence of change and additions may be found in the different ways the wood pieces are joined, the various kinds of nails used, or a dissimilarity, however slight, in the stone,

brick, mortar, and other materials of the house. The attic is an especially revealing place to begin. Do not be led astray, however, by the common practice of reusing older materials such as nails. Be a detective, and you may discover transformed room arrangements, tacked-on dormers, hidden fireplaces, or a more up-to-date front door.

Learn as much as possible about the style of the house. The more prominent ones are described in Chapter 2, Architectural Styles. Books and periodicals found in local or college libraries could also enlarge your understanding. Courses and lectures on the appreciation and care of old buildings may answer some questions, as may house tours and visits to house museums. Compare your house with others in the neighborhood and consult with owners of homes similar to yours.

To find out more about older homes, read newspaper articles on home care and magazines about housing and historic preservation. Peruse pertinent books. Browse through catalogs devoted to products and services for older houses and write to the sources listed in these catalogs for more information. Visit lumberyards, hardware stores, and building suppliers to discover what products and materials are available. Organize the findings, whether in files or a notebook, in a useful way. If a professional is hired for subsequent work, share your information with him or her.

Gathering facts about the various materials in your home will become an invaluable aid when confronting decisions about the future of the house. Knowing that good-quality slate is exceptionally durable, for instance, may enable you to question a roofer's opinion that the entire slate roof must be replaced. When changes are contemplated, proceed slowly, for you could easily make a mistake and destroy a valuable legacy or find out too late that the outcome is unsatisfactory. Do research, examine what exists in minute detail, and live with the house as long as possible to allow its nature to unfold. Although planning alone will not produce sweeping changes, it is the only path to a successful renewal where no irrevocable mistakes will be made; no priceless materials and features will be discarded; and your needs will be satisfied, whether the house is for rental, resale, or your own residence.

When an older house is a near ruin, only the crafting of a seeming miracle will make it habitable. Otherwise, it is a good idea to live in a house and let it reveal which components call for repair, rebuilding, updating, and altering. Do not rush into the work. The least expensive, most satisfying way to restore or renovate a home is to live in it while the work goes on. Only then do you discover what really needs to be done. What may at a distance demand to be accomplished first may turn out later to have lower priority, or no priority at all.

CHECKING OUT AN OLDER HOUSE

Inspecting an older house before buying it is always prudent. With this book as a guide, prospective purchasers can carry out the initial examination themselves. Once serious about a certain house, hire an expert to perform the investigation and make an inspection for termites. A professional home inspector will study the dwelling and prepare a written report of the findings enumerating areas requiring minor work and listing major flaws such as a disintegrating foundation, an outmoded electrical system, or rotting joists. Either an architect or general contractor well acquainted with older homes can also inspect the house.

An expert investigation of the "perfect" house may reveal a roof that showers the occupants when it rains, joists weakened by powder-post beetles, and plumbing composed of a hodgepodge of lead, galvanized iron, and copper pipes all leaking somewhere; nevertheless, to the prospective buyer the paragon may remain "perfect." At least, these forewarnings will decrease the number of disagreeable surprises later and can become a bargaining point to reduce the asking price by the amount estimated to correct the problems. The agreement of sale should require the seller to repair any termite damage and to eliminate any termites. When studying the inspection report, be aware that a number of small trouble areas can add up to an astonishing sum. The report, too, becomes the basis for a plan to fix up the house.

Once you have moved into the house, an inspection ought to become an annual event. More frequent checks are essential for items such as wood in or near the ground in a termite-infested area, gutters and downspouts in a wooded location, and fireplace flues when a woodburning stove is in frequent use. A thorough and systematic yearly examination begins with the landscaping, the walks, the driveway, and the slope of the ground to detect where water might be running into instead of away from the

structure. It includes all of the exterior and interior of the building from the murkiest corner of the attic to the dankest spot in the basement. The findings indicate where improvements are necessary to forestall a future calamity. When a defect is uncovered, track down its source and take measures to remedy the cause. The timely patching of wood or caulking of a newly opened gap, for instance, can thwart serious damage to the structure of the house and avert costly repairs.

Be sure the correct procedure is used to solve the difficulty. At best, questionable methods will stave off problems for a brief time only; at worst, they will result in outright harm to the building. When in doubt, seek competent professional advice about how to proceed or expert help in doing the work.

DEVELOPING A WORKING PLAN

You are now ready to develop a working plan which addresses the problems of the house, its characteristics to be preserved, and your requirements. Chapter 2, Architectural Styles, and the Design and Replacement sections of various chapters point out which features inside and outside comprise the riches of an older dwelling and ought not to be removed. Be firm. If a siding expert states that only synthetic siding will solve the problem of disintegrating clapboard and that, to install the siding, the cornices above the windows and their decorative framing must be torn out, seek advice from professionals more sensitive to the assets of an older house and more knowledgeable about the troubles synthetic siding can cause.

If the tasks to be accomplished are few and simple, the working plan may be no more than a list. On the other hand, more extensive work requires more elaborate documents such as floor plans, sketches, and detailed specifications. At this point decide who is to prepare the working plan. You may choose to create the needed drawings and details yourself, to consult a structural engineer for the plans for replacing a foundation or shoring up beams, to get the assistance of a general contractor, or to hire an architect for the entire plan. Chapters 15 and 16, Calling in a Contractor and Considering an Architect, explain the various services contractors or architects provide and how to locate and select these professionals.

An architect can recommend ways to deal with troublesome areas and can visualize design possibilities. Some owners hire an architect only for planning the work, realizing that competent preparation saves money later. You and the architect can agree on just how much is expected of him or her, depending on the nature of the work, your own skills, and the budget.

When devising the working plan yourself, begin with the written list from the house inspection and with the fruits of your research. Divide your ideas into two categories: needs and desires. Arrange to complete the needs first and the desires when, and if, you can afford them. Before proceeding further, check the local building codes to make certain contemplated changes conform to the applicable code. As necessary, produce rough floor plans, measured drawings, sketches of details, and specifications. If drawings of the house as it was built or as it exists are available, proposed changes can be added to these drawings. The only way to prevent misunderstandings later, when workers are on the job, is to supply appropriate details beforehand. The Construction Documents section in Chapter 16, Considering an Architect, explains what should be included.

ESTIMATING COSTS

The working plan provides the information necessary for a contractor to bid on the job. When doing the work yourself, use this plan, whether in the form of lists, rough sketches, or measured drawings, to figure out the amount and cost of supplies. After obtaining the price of materials from suppliers, add about 10 percent for waste and 15 percent for the unexpected. For an idea of the charge for hiring someone else to do the work, talk to a reputable contractor for a rough estimate.

CONSIDERING PRIORITIES

Once a cost estimate has been prepared, the work can be scheduled. The sequence depends on the condition of the house, the nature of the work, the budget, and the objectives. Sometimes certain jobs are done concurrently. Start with the basics. Make certain no fire or other safety hazards exist, the house is watertight and structurally intact, and the heating, plumbing, and electrical systems are operating properly. When the house is safe and sound enough to live in, there is time to mull over the tasks yet to be done. In many cases the work can be carried out gradually. When a contractor is involved, be sure you select one with a good record for completion. By planning ahead, well ahead, you can schedule work for off-season. Furnace work, for example, is always cheaper in the summer, carpentry in the winter. However the work is scheduled, allow time for delays. They almost always happen.

FOUNDATIONS

Whether an intensive renewal or a program of general maintenance and improvements is intended, the work should follow a logical order. Major work on the foundation comes first, encompassing such tasks as straightening a tilted foundation, replacing deteriorated materials, leveling floors, and installing a foundation where none exists. Because this work can crack the walls, open up gaps between the walls and the windows and doors, or cause floors and walls to slant, it tops the list of tasks to be done.

A WATERTIGHT HOUSE

Next, and as soon as possible, make the building watertight. Do whatever is necessary: Repair holes in the roof and flashing, caulk any gaps, regrade the lot so that water no longer flows into the basement, or install new gutters and downspouts where they are missing. Accomplishing this work will avert further damage and safeguard future improvements to the house. Other exterior projects can be done now or, if not urgent, at a later date.

STRUCTURAL WORK

Once the house is watertight, begin the necessary structural work such as strengthening or replacing joists or beams, adding new framing, and installing windows and doors. Tear out parts and materials not to be retained and remove the remains.

UTILITY AND MECHANICAL SYSTEMS

Improving the electrical, plumbing, and heating systems is the next task to consider. Although easiest when the walls are already open, this work can almost always be undertaken in ways that will leave no traces. The more the construction of the house is understood, the less likely the chance of disfiguring or destroying the wooden paneling, plaster ornamentation, and other treasured features. Be inventive. Think about running wires to outlets, fixtures, or switches from the room above or below, through closets, behind baseboards, within unused hot-air ducts, in pipe chases, around door frames behind the casing, or in a protected opening next to the chimney. To prevent hammering nails into the new wiring in the future, make a sketch of where it has been installed. Also, plan the route for new pipes or ducts through existing passages in the house. Explore the possibility of replacing a few sections of wiring, pipes, or ducts instead of installing an entire system. Sometimes, however, completing all major work on the plumbing, heating, or electrical systems at one time can be cheaper in the long run than postponing some projects until later. On these questions seek advice from experts knowledgeable about older homes.

Electrical.   A well-functioning electrical system is pleasurable and convenient. Flaws in the system peril a home and the lives of its occupants. To detect trouble:

- Learn whether the electrical service is adequate. A house will probably require at least 150 amperes, although this amount varies with the size of the house and the number of electrical appliances used.

- Check all wires for cracked or missing insulation.

- Be certain that tree branches do not brush against or hang over incoming service wires.

- Notice whether outdoor wiring, fixtures, and outlets are manufactured specifically for exterior use.

- Find out whether the electrical system is grounded correctly and the grounding connections are secure.

- Look in the attic and basement to learn about the type and condition of interior wiring.

- Be sure the outlets, switches, and fixtures work well and the outlets and switches have cover plates.

- Make a sample investigation of the condition of the wiring inside the walls after turning off the power to the circuit.

- Count the number of outlets in a room. Ideally, every point along the wall should be no more than 8 feet from a receptacle. You will probably settle for fewer outlets in an older home.

Sparking, warmth, or an odor near outlets and receptacles, repeated flickering of the lights, frequently blown fuses or tripped circuit breakers, and a tangle of extension cords in a room signal trouble in the electrical system. Call in an electrician to track down the source of the problem, and make the necessary repairs immediately. Old wiring may call for replacement although knob-and-tube wiring with insulation intact can stay in place. Aluminum wiring is safe only if CO/ALR outlets and switches are installed and transition copper wires are attached to all junctions and other connections. A well-informed electrician or general contractor can advise you about these types of wiring.

Continue with electrical work, except emergency repairs, only after an overall plan for the desired outcome has been devised. Take the time to think about the location of every outlet, fixture, and switch. Seek the answers to questions like the following: Will the addition of a circuit or two be sufficient and possible? Is total rewiring necessary, or will partial rewiring correct the problem? How many separate lines are required for electrical equipment and appliances such as central air conditioning, an electric clothes dryer and range, and an electric furnace? Is it possible to retain and repair the original fixtures (a good idea)? Also, plan on installing smoke and heat detectors.

Before doing any work yourself, find out exactly what tasks are permitted by local building codes, whether an electrical permit is required, and what materials are allowed. If you decide to go ahead with the job, be sure you are familiar with safe work practices and the correct electrical procedures. As a start, always shut off the current by removing a fuse or switching off the circuit breaker.

Plumbing. The plumbing system has two parts: the fresh water supply and its distribution throughout the house to the appropriate fixtures and appliances, and the drain-waste-vent pipes to remove used water and permit harmful gases to escape into the air through a vent stack above the roof. Leaking pipes have caused vast damage in houses, but watchfulness and timely action will diminish the chances of this happening. A careful inspection before buying a house may alert you to the possible staggering cost of replacing deteriorated pipes or a failed septic system; a yearly inspection after moving into the house can avert a disaster. When investigating the plumbing:

- Discover whether the house is connected to a municipal sewer system. Never assume this is true, but obtain verification from the local government. If a private system exists and additional fixtures are contemplated, determine whether governmental authorities will require a new or improved system.

- Learn how often the septic tank, if there is one, has been cleaned. Every 3 to 4 years is usually adequate.

- Be sure that neither puddles nor an objectionable smell occurs over the drainage area of a septic system.

- Be certain the cesspool, if one exists, works properly.

- Notice whether there is a vent stack and whether it projects above the roof. A vent stack opening into the attic is hazardous.

- Check all fixtures for their condition and for good working order.

- Look around the fixtures to be sure they are waterproofed sufficiently to keep water from seeping into nearby wood and causing rot.

- Test the water flow by turning on, at the same time, the hot water at the lavatory and at the tub or shower and also flushing the toilet. Repeat with the cold water. Also, make this test by turning on the hot or cold water at the lavatory on the first floor and the hot or cold water on the highest floor. A sharp drop in the flow indicates a problem, often from a buildup in the pipes carrying the water to those particular fixtures. Pipes in such condition must soon be replaced.

- Examine the pipes to determine their materials. Copper or brass pipes are longer lasting than galvanized iron. Because of the hazard of lead poisoning, replace lead supply pipes with another material. A mixture of incompatible piping materials without any buffering links will cause corrosion of the pipes. Replacing some sections of galvanized iron pipe with copper may accelerate deterioration of the remaining galvanized iron unless plastic transitions are used.

- Investigate the pipes, especially at the joints, for corrosion, leaks, cracks, patches, and mineral deposits. Remove the plumbing access panels, if they exist, to further check the condition of the pipes.

- See whether the pipes are adequately supported by straps or hangers of materials compatible with the pipes.

- Try the main shutoff valve to find out if it is stuck in the open position.

- Be aware of rust on the hot-water heater and of signs of water staining the floor around it.

- Determine whether the drain pipes have an uninterrupted downward slope to the sewer or the septic tank.

Plumbing work is messy; so is a breakdown in the system, but advance planning may help to reduce the chances of a plumbing disaster. An example of foresight is to exchange new copper or plastic (if building codes permit) pipes for aging pipes while the walls are open for other work. When deciding upon the location of new fixtures, keep in mind that having them close together, either back to back or one above the other, is most efficient.

Before attempting plumbing work yourself, know what the local codes allow concerning how much work the amateur can carry out, whether a permit is necessary, and what materials the municipality approves. Although plastic pipe, especially the flexible kind, has a number of advantages, many local governments prohibit or restrict its use. Be familiar with the materials, tools, and techniques the work requires and prepared for the effort that goes into certain jobs.

Heating. Energy conservation and a comfortable house are not incompatible. A properly adjusted, clean heating system is a conspicuous and sound beginning, but the homeowner must do more to reduce heat loss. Warning: A supertight house may be hazardous to your health, sealing in, along with the precious warmth, carbon monoxide, nitrogen dioxide, formaldehyde, tobacco smoke, and radon, a radioactive gas. The owner need not worry in the case of a dwelling with inadequate levels of insulation, cracks and gaps around the windows or doors or in other parts of the house, no storm or insulating windows, and a fireplace with no damper or one that fits loosely. For further information about making a house more energy efficient study Chapter 17, Energy and the Older House. The conscientious few who have already done a superb job of buttoning up the house may be harboring indoor pollution. Airing out the supertight house now and then and proper ventilation will help to lessen the risk.

Where greater heating efficiency is the goal, refrain from painting radiators and consider stripping the paint from those already coated. If radiators must be painted, never apply metallic paint and always paint the visible parts only, using flat black or dark paint. Be aware that drapes, furniture, and radiator covers in front of the radiators can block heat from entering the room.

An important practice is to inspect the heating system once a year for signs of trouble.

- Test the system by moving the thermostat above room temperature. A steam or hot-water system may take as long as 20 minutes to warm up, but heat from a hot-air system will reach the register more promptly.

- Examine the burner for corrosion or mineral deposits. Have the burner cleaned and adjusted by an expert once a year for an oil-fired burner and every two years for a gas-fired one.

- Be aware of corrosion or cracks in the walls of the furnace in a hot-air system. This situation is dangerous because exhaust gases can enter the home.

- Check the boiler in a steam or hot-water system for corrosion, cracks, or leaks.

- Investigate the smoke pipe for corrosion and loose joints.

- Find out if an unlined chimney is used as a heater flue. Heat and summer dampness can cause mortar to decompose and fall to the bottom, often blocking the smoke pipe where it enters the chimney.

- Be certain that ducts or pipes are in good condition and do not leak. If they run through unheated spaces, they should be insulated.

- Notice whether water or water stains appear around the radiators.

- Discover whether radiators slope slightly toward the inlet pipe in a one-pipe system or toward the return outlet in a two-pipe system. If not, water collecting in the radiators prevents them from warming up adequately and also causes loud knocks in a steam system.

- Test the cold-air return grilles in a hot-air system for proper functioning by putting a tissue on the grille. The tissue should remain against the grille.

Examining the heating system before purchasing a house requires two additional steps: Obtain copies of last year's heating bills to verify the cost of heating the house, and check each room for a heat outlet.

OTHER WORK

After the work on the utility and mechanical systems has been completed and before the walls are closed, insulating can be done. Be certain there is a vapor barrier. Once the necessary inspections have been made, the walls and ceilings can be plastered. Next comes repairing and replacing the trim including cornices, moldings, paneling, and hardware. The floors are then put down. At this point the house is ready for the installation of fixtures, for painting and, at last, for finishing the floors.

DECIDING WHO IS TO DO THE WORK

Work gets done in many ways. A few industrious and skilled individuals do it all themselves; others engage workers to take care of everything. Most homeowners, however, seek expert assistance for some tasks, like roofing, extensive wall repairs, wiring, and installing a flue liner in a chimney, and carry out jobs demanding less training themselves. Some shrewd homeowners call on a specialist once for a task, watch the procedure carefully, and ask a few questions. The next time a similar job comes up, the owner is prepared to take it on. Another possibility is to locate a professional who is willing to supervise a crew of amateurs, possibly for a task such as painting. In that way an owner saves money while the work is completed in a reasonably professional way. Intrepid owners may also assemble and oversee their own crew for unskilled labor such as clearing away the dirt, debris, and overgrowth from a house and grounds left vacant for several years and for jobs like painting or cleaning woodwork and floors. Chapter 15, Calling in a Contractor, suggests when a general contractor or subcontractors are necessary.

If you intend to do a large amount of the work yourself, do not wield a hammer, chisel, or pry bar until you have appraised your interests and abilities. Ask the following questions:

- How well prepared are you? Have you had previous experience working on an older building? Remember that seemingly small improvements take more time and effort than anticipated. A good rule is to estimate the longest time it could take to do the job—and then double it. The unforeseen oddities of the house's construction and the falling apart of aged parts under your touch may confront you as you work. Talk with friends and neighbors who have done similar jobs to learn what is involved.

- Do you enjoy accomplishing projects around the house? How patient are you? Coping with worn parts and with peculiar construction methods can be frustrating.

- Do you have the stamina for long hours on the job? Will any physical handicaps prevent you from carrying out the work?

- How much time do you have? Can you devote evenings, weekends, and vacations to the house? Do not forget to add time for organizing the tasks and for purchasing supplies. Even though professionals are hired for much of the work, the energy and taste of the owner can favorably affect the results if the owner will ferret out special items such as mantelpieces, fixtures, hardware, and stained glass windows.

- Have you the skills to do the jobs? Are you adept or awkward working with tools? Be honest with yourself, and do not attempt tasks requiring skills you cannot acquire. Is it possible to learn about the work from books or from experienced acquaintances? Can the project wait until you have taken a course in a particular type of work or a more general course on building restoration?

- Do you have the necessary tools and equipment for the job? Can you borrow or rent them? Items that are expensive to purchase or difficult to locate may cause owners to decide not to undertake certain tasks themselves. Remember to include tool purchases or rental prices in the cost estimate for the job.

- Will the results be satisfactory? Poor-quality work can endanger a life or a home. Fires can start, for instance, in an amateurishly installed chimney flue. Flashing that is not tight can allow water to trickle into a house. Work obviously accomplished by a novice can discourage future prospective buyers or renters of a house; visible shortcomings can offend the occupants. You could be losing money, rather than economizing, because shoddy work will eventually have to be redone by professionals.

The nature of the work determines in part what and how much an owner can do. The owner may elect to scrape paint and haul away debris, but not to rewire or put on a new roof. An owner may be undaunted by repairing a few balky windows, but defeated by replacing numerous badly deteriorated windows. He or she may be willing to fix up the exterior, but not to rebuild a shell. Another consideration is the timing of the tasks. The owner may be able to assume responsibility for more work if it can be spread out over several years. In this case a work plan is essential, for the owner must be certain the initial work will not have to be undone to make a future project possible. In addition, taking on jobs which can be dangerous — roofing, wiring, and working from a tall ladder — is not for everyone.

Homeowners must find out about building codes and zoning restrictions. Additional conversions of single-family homes into apartments, and changes of use may require governmental approval or permits. Also, discover what the filing procedures are and how detailed work plans must be. Certain categories of work, often electrical, plumbing, and gas installations, require a licensed professional to carry out or at least to inspect at completion.

Entering a marathon of fixing up an old house may mean getting hopelessly behind with other commitments. How long will you be able to concentrate on the house? It may be possible to schedule the work in intervals — a few weeks of work alternating with a few weeks of free time. Another disadvantage of doing major work yourself is living with the disarray for long periods while the project progresses slowly in your spare time.

The prime incentive for doing your own work is to save money — often half or more of the cost of hiring a professional — and an added advantage is the ability to spread the expenses over a longer period than when experts are hired. Besides, you probably will obtain better results because of the certainty of having to live with the outcome. Further benefits are the joy of accomplishment and an appreciation for a house which can be acquired in no other way than by mending its defects yourself.

SEARCHING FOR CRAFTWORKERS

From time to time the owner of the older home will require a person skilled in a special craft to pamper a unique old part of the house or to duplicate a valued asset. The right individual can usually be found even though the process may involve seemingly endless telephone calls and discussions with several prospective workers. If you have already located one satisfactory craftworker, begin the search by asking this person for the names of persons with the particular talents you are seeking. When an architect or general contractor has been hired, he or she will often be able to suggest someone. Friends and neighbors, antique shops, businesses specializing in architectural parts, hardware stores, lumber and millwork companies, and local preservation groups may be sources for craftworkers. Another possible place for help is the manufacturer of products for the older home, for such a firm may be able to repair the homeowner's worn items or create a part to the owner's specifications. Also, check advertisements in preservation publications.

Before engaging craftworkers, always look at examples of their work to be certain of its quality. Per-

severe, for only when you have located the right person will you enjoy the results.

REPLACING MATERIALS AND ARCHITECTURAL PARTS

If at all possible, repair a deteriorated part of a house. The situation may not be as hopeless as it first appears. For instance, epoxy resins and consolidants sometimes can strengthen badly degenerated wood. Missing parts of a wooden cornice, a window frame, or another wooden item in a house can be patched with wood cut in the pattern of the original piece. Replace parts only when repair is not possible. In these cases, try to duplicate the dimensions, materials, finish, relationship to other parts of the house, and any other important characteristics of the original. Be resourceful and imaginative.

A surprising array of sources for replacement parts and materials exist. A good place to begin is a wrecking-company yard, which may have countless old doors and windows and used materials as well as a few select mantelpieces, doors, stained glass windows, and decorative pieces. The general-line antique dealer may stock parts from older homes and be willing to hunt for a special item you are seeking. Some auctions feature articles from older buildings. Stores specializing in architectural parts or salvage storehouses managed by historical commissions are worth a visit. Less obvious methods for finding replacements include locating homeowners who live in an area where older houses have been torn down and who have hoarded in their basements whatever they could collect, or negotiating on the spot for that just-right item when a demolition company is razing a building.

An increasing number of firms manufacture reproduction parts for older homes. Catalogs identifying these firms are available, and you can write directly to the manufacturer for detailed information. An expensive, but time-saving, approach is to engage a craftworker or lumber and millwork company to duplicate a cornice, a door, or whatever you require. Standard parts, such as wood moldings, often become excellent replacements, but standard-stock doors or windows may be utterly inappropriate. Be discriminating. A standard item may be a temporary substitute while a lengthy search goes on for the desired material or part.

Patience is essential. Make do with what you have until you uncover a successful alternative. Try a variety of sources. Because stocks change frequently, revisit places already explored or telephone to discover whether what you are seeking is available. The search is fun. You will learn about the past and meet individuals who will be able to offer suggestions for understanding and caring for an older home.

CHAPTER FOUR

ROOFS

Every house must have a sturdy, water-shedding shield against the weather. Beyond being a protective covering, the roof contributes to an older house in other significant ways. Most often a roof is highly visible. Its shape, size, and slope create a unique silhouette, which may be smooth and simple, enlivened with several interlocking roofs, or pierced by a jumble of gables, dormers, and chimneys. The roof's profile may be tall or low, wide or narrow, straight-edged or curved.

Roofing materials can be another noticeable feature. Some are even and uniform; others are somewhat irregular, richly textured, or arranged in creative patterns. A roof may offer extra attractions: iron cresting, finials, bargeboards, brackets, classical moldings, weather vanes, or cupolas.

Roofs are vulnerable, constantly exposed to sun, wind, rain, and snow. A new roof, however, is a major financial investment. Take care of a roof by inspecting it at least twice a year to detect any problems and by making appropriate repairs at once. If a roof has deteriorated to the point where replacement is needed, select a roofing material in keeping with the architectural style of the house and attempt to preserve the original shape of the roof and any ornamentation.

ROOF TYPES

Builders of older houses have used many different roof shapes. Some of the most common types are (Figure 4-1):

GABLE A gable roof, sometimes called a pitched roof, has two sides which slope down from the central ridge. The outline of the sloping sides on each end wall creates a triangle known as a gable.

GAMBREL A gambrel roof has two slopes on two sides meeting at the central ridge. The first slope rises for a distance at a steep angle from the eaves, and the second slope changes abruptly to a more gentle pitch. The juncture where the two pitches meet is called a curb. Each end wall is a wide, four-sided gable.

HIP A hip roof has four sides which slope inward at the same pitch from the eaves toward the central ridge.

MANSARD A mansard roof has steep, almost vertical slopes on all four sides, usually topped with a very low hipped roof.

JERKIN-HEAD A jerkin-head roof is a gable roof with the top of the gable cut off or beveled backward in a small hiplike slope.

RAINBOW A rainbow roof is bowed, as the name implies, in the shape of a rainbow. They are commonly found on one-story houses.

SHED A shed roof has only one pitch.

FLAT A flat roof gives the impression of being without any pitch, but it has a slight slope to shed water.

DESIGN

What considerations influenced the selection of roof designs? Practical questions were decisive. Early steep roofs in New England, for instance, easily shed rain and snow. The desire for additional attic space helped usher in the gambrel and the mansard roofs. Another factor was the availability of roofing materials and their costs. As an example, wooden shingles were much cheaper than slate. Sometimes local traditions shaped decisions—to use a rainbow roof on Cape Cod, pent eaves in Pennsylvania, or a flared gambrel roof in northern New Jersey. Current styles publicized in architectural guidebooks and builders' manuals also affected the choices. In some cases a roof was selected simply because someone liked its shape.

To learn whether the roof on an older house is original or a suitable replacement:

• Ask an architect, contractor, or roofer to examine the roof to determine if it has been raised, lowered, or altered in any other way. A roof on an older home may have been changed from the original because of later additions, the need for usable third-floor space, or a wish to follow roofing fash-

ions. Remodeling with a mansard roof or extending the eaves and adding lavish brackets beneath to give a house an Italianate appearance was not uncommon in the mid-1800s.

- Check to see if there are any roofing materials under the top layer. Reroofing over an older roof is a general practice, and the original roof may be underneath.

- Look carefully at the interior structure supporting the roof, such as the rafters, for clues about construction methods, the wood's age, and any alterations.

- Inspect the junctures where the roof meets the walls for signs of changes.

- Find out if there have been any major additions to the house. If so, compare the added roof with the main roof. Warning: Even though they are different in age and style, both roofs could still be original.

- Search for old photographs showing the initial roof.

- Review the following sections on the types of roofs and roofing materials suitable for different architectural styles.

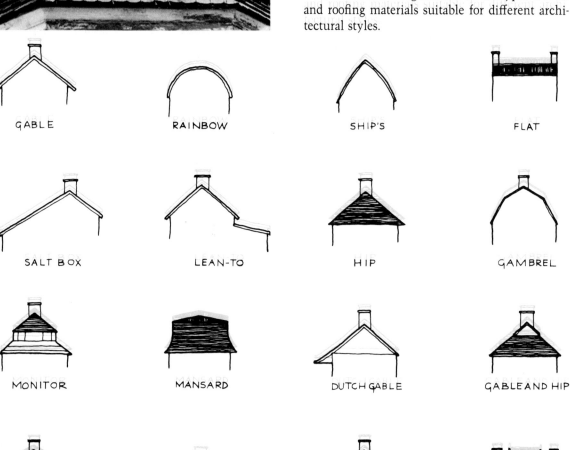

GABLE   RAINBOW   SHIP'S   FLAT

SALT BOX   LEAN-TO   HIP   GAMBREL

MONITOR   MANSARD   DUTCH GABLE   GABLE AND HIP

DOUBLE HIP   DUTCH GAMBREL   GABLE AND MONITOR   CAPTAIN'S WALK

Figure 4-1. Roof shapes.

SEVENTEENTH CENTURY

Seventeenth Century houses have simple, strikingly visible roofs. Throughout the colonies the roofs were almost always gable or double-pitched with slightly projecting eaves. The pitch was extremely steep, rising to a 60-degree angle in the earliest homes and declining to 45 degrees by the end of the century, shedding rain and snow rapidly. Toward the end of the century, vertical faceboards, or fasciae, protected the rafter ends, and soffits boxed in the rafters underneath.

The saltbox and lean-to are variations of the gable roof, found on Seventeenth Century and early Eighteenth Century homes, primarily on Long Island and on Cape Cod and in other areas of New England (*see* Figure 4-1). A lean-to, called a catslide in the South, is a one-story extension at the rear of a house having a separate shed roof which seems to lean against the home. The roof's pitch is somewhat lower than the main roof's pitch. A saltbox also has a single story in the back, but one long roof runs from the main ridge to the first story. Often these rear rooms were later additions.

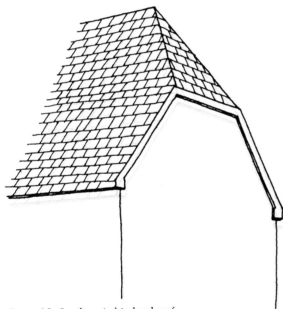

Figure 4-2. Southern jerkin-head roof.

Still another variation of a pitched roof is the Flemish gable found in northern New Jersey and southern New York and on Long Island (*see* Figure 4-1). The Flemish gable projects 2 feet or more beyond the front and back walls. Frequently called a Dutch gable because it was used by many Dutch builders, this type of roof was first employed by the Flemish to protect clay walls from the rain. A few New England and Maryland homes have gambrel roofs and some southern houses have jerkin-head roofs (Figure 4-2).

EIGHTEENTH CENTURY—
GEORGIAN, 1700 TO 1780

Builders of Eighteenth Century homes experimented with many roof forms. Their motives often were practical: to improve construction methods, to lessen building costs, or to increase the upper story's interior space. Other times the designs in builders' handbooks or the builders' own tastes influenced them.

In both northern and southern homes the hipped roof was a particular favorite because the similarity of all four of its sides was considered appropriate for this symmetrical style. The slopes diminished from quite steep in the early 1700s to a lower pitch after 1750. The hipped roof's sides meet at a central ridge except sometimes in a larger house where a flat roof deck tops the roof. A low railing, or balustrade, of turned wooden balusters and taller corner posts capped with knobs, encloses the deck, or captain's walk. After 1750 balustrades were sometimes designed as lattices. A more pretentious home may even have a double hipped roof with the smaller, shallower top hip hidden behind the balustrade.

Also popular throughout the eastern seaboard, especially in New England, were gambrel roofs. The array of gambrel designs, from broad and wide to tall and narrow, frequently reflects local preferences. The Maryland gambrel, for example, has a steeper pitch in the lower section than those in New England. Flemish gambrels, also called Dutch gambrels, have deep overhanging eaves curving gently upward at the ends.

Gable roofs are numerous, too. The roof's pitch is usually lower than earlier gable roofs, possibly a 30-degree angle or less. Local variations did occur: Gable roofs in the South were generally steeper than those in Pennsylvania, which had sharper inclines than those in New England. Lower-pitched roofs created triangular end gables shaped like pediments. As the century progressed, builders applied classical decorations to these gables to make them look more and more like pediments. Wooden moldings and a row of toothlike dentils typically outlined the roof line.

The classical influence also introduced a cornice, or horizontal band, under the eaves at the top of the exterior wall. Early cornices were plain boards, perhaps with a simple molding at the edges. Later cornices, especially on larger houses, contained a series of moldings usually with a narrow strip of dentils and occasionally with blocklike modillions, a wider and heavier version of dentils.

Rainbow roofs with gentle convex curves forming a rainbow-shaped end gable are seen on some New England homes located along the seacoast, such as on Cape Cod. Pent roofs, or pent eaves, common in southeastern Pennsylvania, project like eaves from the wall between the first and second story (Figure 4-3). At times a small triangular pediment juts up from the pent eave above the front entrance. By shedding rain and snow, pent eaves protect the exterior walls on the first floor and provide a slight shelter. Certain brick homes in the South, particularly in Maryland, Virginia, and South Carolina, boast jerkin-head roofs. Both the saltbox and the lean-to continued to be built in rural New England.

Some unusual Eighteenth Century roof designs were attempts to add more light and air to the upper story. Two of these found in New England are a hipped roof beneath a gable roof with a window and a hipped roof with an additional raised roof with windows at its top, called a monitor (*see* Figure 4-1).

Figure 4-3. Pent eaves.

FEDERAL, 1790 TO 1830

The roof lines on Federal houses are simple, serene, and sometimes not even visible. Homes throughout the eastern seaboard have hipped, gambrel, and gable roofs, but the pitch on a hipped or gable roof often slopes so slightly it looks flat. In many instances a wooden balustrade, surrounding the edge of the entire roof or running along only the front and back, hides the roof. These low balustrades sit just above the eaves and have either slender, turned balusters or balusters alternating with wooden panels.

GREEK REVIVAL, 1820 TO 1860

Most Greek Revival houses have low-pitched or moderately pitched gable roofs. The roof's ridge usually extends from the front to the back, particularly when the house resembles a temple. At times low hipped roofs appear on southern plantation homes or on New York houses. Less frequently, the roof is flat, perhaps with a solid parapet, or small wall, at the end. Every once in a while, especially in sections of New York, a square, round, or octagonal structure called a cupola rises above the center of the roof. These cupolas have windows on all their sides, flat or gently sloping roofs, and occasional pilasters. Most often the Greek Revival house has a wide, plain or dentiled cornice beneath the eaves.

GOTHIC REVIVAL, 1820 TO 1860

Gothic Revival houses always have tall roofs. At times the roof lines are simple, but complex silhouettes broken by many gables, dormers, knoblike finials, heavy pinnacles, and pointed spires are more common. Often the roof consists of two intersecting very sharply pitched gable roofs, one ridge running from the front to the back, the other crossing the front. In certain cases the higher peak occurs over the entrance with the lower-sloped roofs elsewhere. One steeply pitched roof may cover the front portion of the house and rest against another which rises at right angles above it over the back section. Elaborate bargeboards, described in Chapter 6, Gables, frequently embellish the roof edges.

ITALIANATE, 1845 TO 1880

Roofs on Italianate homes slope very gently and are hipped, gabled, or combinations of hip and gable. The pitch on hipped roofs may be so slight it seems flat. In almost every house the roof's eaves project dramatically beyond the wall, and imposing wooden brackets attached to a wide cornice support the eaves (Figure 4-4). When these decorations are designed as horizontal scrolls and grouped in twos or threes, they are called modillions.

Italianate roofs are occasionally crowned by a cupola or a lantern in the center (Figure 4-5). Cupolas are smaller structures and may be round, square, or octagonal; lanterns are large, boxlike attachments often having a floor inside. Roofs on cupolas and lanterns resemble the shape of the main roof and have the same deep, overhanging eaves held up by flamboyant brackets. Round-headed windows on all sides are customary in both cupolas and lanterns, and the roof line immediately above the windows may jut up in a triangle or curved arch. Graceful finials may accent their roofs.

STICK STYLE, 1855 TO 1900

Roofs on Stick Style houses are high and steep, often with irregular silhouettes broken by intersecting gables, large dormers, or other minor roofs. In a few instances jerkin-head roofs appear. The eaves sometimes zigzag in a series of peaks over wall dormers below. You will also find boldly projecting eaves supported by brackets.

Now and then the ridge lines and peaks have ornamentation. A low wooden railing in a simple, cut-out design with short end posts may grace the tallest ridge. Minor roofs may have low crenelations, or alternating elevated and lowered squares, along the ridge or, more rarely, cast-iron cresting. Possibly designed as a fleur-de-lis, finials may punctuate a gable's peak.

MANSARD, 1860 TO 1880

Mansard houses have unique roofs, giving the style its name. The roof fits the house like a large hat with a gutter as its brim and has four almost vertical surfaces topped by a low-pitched hipped roof or, less often, by a flat roof. The roof's silhouette looks the same on all sides although once in a while the center of the front roof surges upward like a tidal wave over the entrance.

Ingenious variations distinguish the steep slopes of these roofs. Some are straight, jutting upward sharply; others are convex or concave; and a few are S-shaped. The curves may be sweeping or gentle. A horizontal strip of wood or metal called a coping cornice usually emphasizes the juncture between the two slopes. Although the coping cornice functions to protect the seams between the two roofs, it is often highly decorative, with moldings, fleur-de-lis, dentils, or even brackets upholding a projecting

Figure 4-5. Italianate lantern.

top roof. Pieces of metal or wood known as curbing usually accent the four vertical edges of the mansard roof.

A wide cornice almost always is present, and carved wooden brackets, evenly spaced or grouped in pairs or threes, support the modest eaves. Towers and central projecting pavilions have mansard roofs, too, often with a steeper pitch and generally with the same bracketed cornice.

Delicate cast-iron cresting frequently graces the top of the towers or the lower roof above the coping cornice (Figure 4-6). The cresting's intricate designs encompass upside-down hearts flanked by cupid's arrows, teardrops embellished with foliage, circles enlivened with scrolls, interlocking semicircles, and lacy fleur-de-lis. A series of finials may punctuate the cresting; and taller, more ornate ones, perhaps resembling sunflowers, may accent the corners. Not every mansard roof has cresting. It may never have been there or, possibly, subsequent owners removed it.

Borrowed from the French, the design of the mansard roof proved very practical. Because the roof embraces the entire top floor and the slopes are quite steep, there is enough space and height for extra inside rooms. On almost all mansard roofs, light enters these rooms through large, ornate dormers or, rarely, through a central cupola. When mansard roofs were popular, they were very popular, so much so that some owners of earlier homes tore off their roofs and substituted the more fashionable mansard. Unfortunately, many of these replacements look awkward and ridiculous on houses originally designed for another roof style.

Figure 4-4. Italianate brackets.

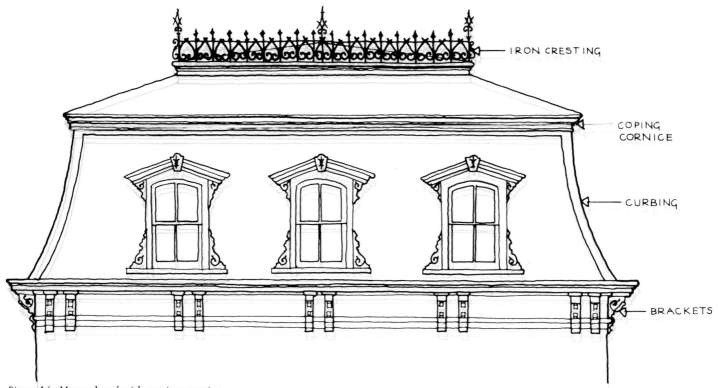

IRON CRESTING

COPING
CORNICE

CURBING

BRACKETS

Figure 4-6. Mansard roof with cast-iron cresting.

ROMANESQUE, 1875 TO 1895

Double-pitched gable roofs are the most common type on Romanesque homes, often interlocking, especially on corner houses. The width of the roof tends to be expansive, emphasizing the overall horizontal lines of the house; the slopes, however, are likely to be quite steep. Among the subtle decorations accenting the roof are delicate finials and terracotta tiles or panels. A cornice may appear, possibly just a wide, dark-colored stone band or at times a more elaborate scroll design. Roofs resembling pyramids typically sit atop square towers, and tall cone-like roofs usually crown bulging, round, or many-sided turrets and projecting bay windows.

QUEEN ANNE, 1876 TO 1900

A quiet, restrained roof line is rare on a Queen Anne house. Most are lively, jagged, and abounding with surprises. Almost all are unique.

A few common characteristics do exist, such as steep gable roofs and intersecting roofs with ridges meeting at right angles. One large gable may embrace another smaller gable at the front, or different roofs varying in size and pitch may interlock in intriguing ways. Hipped roofs also occur. You will notice corner towers with bell-shaped roofs and round or many-sided turrets with tall, pointed cones on top. Often accenting a gable or the dominant roof line are decorative touches including iron cresting or

crenelations on the ridge and slender finials with spires, curves, or fleur-de-lis patterns above the gable's peak (Figure 4-7).

SHINGLE STYLE, 1880 TO 1900

Roofs cover Shingle Style houses like large, flowing capes. Frequently, the roof sweeps down from the ridge to spread over a spacious porch or a portion of the first floor. Because both the walls and the roof are commonly sheathed in shingles, they almost seem to be one.

The roof's shape may be gabled or hipped or a combination of both with intersecting ridges. Gambrel roofs were also popular, occasionally joining gable roofs or interlocking to form double gambrels. Sometimes, broad double gambrels meet so closely that their angles define the shape of the entire house. While you may find steep slopes, the pitch in gable and gambrel roofs tends to be moderate, creating wide gable ends. Some houses are even designed so that the front is one broad gable extending from the ridge to the first story.

REVIVALS OF THE GEORGIAN AND
FEDERAL STYLES, 1885 TO 1940

A Georgian Revival home has a double-pitched, hipped, or gambrel roof, edged by a classical cornice with bold dentil moldings. Hipped roofs are usually shallow, but may have steep pitches on more pretentious homes. Sometimes a flat deck surrounded by a balustrade, referred to as a "widow's walk," tops the hipped roof. The balustrade is most often turned wooden balusters with corner posts which are each capped by an ornament such as an urn. Now and then a central cupola rests on top of the roof.

Most Federal Revival houses have very low-pitched roofs, commonly hipped, which are hidden behind a roof balustrade.

MAINTENANCE AND REPAIR

Few individuals have the skills to carry out major repairs of the roof or flashing. No matter how sound the roofing materials, the roof is only as durable as the quality of the workmanship. Besides, hazards such as the sharp pitch of a roof, the fragility of many roofing materials, and the disconcerting distance to the ground from the roof on a two- or three-story home make roof work difficult.

SAFETY PRECAUTIONS

Before repairing a roof, especially a steep or high roof, or walking on it to inspect it, become familiar with safe practices to avoid accidents. Knowing about ladders and using them properly are essential. Purchase a sturdy, well-made ladder. If you already own a Type 3 extension ladder (the cheapest type of extension ladder, approved to hold 200 pounds) be extremely cautious or, better yet, replace it with a Type 2 commercial-grade ladder. Weight that is not centered on the rungs of a Type 3 ladder may bend the side rails, forcing the rungs to twist and anyone on the ladder to fall. Check every ladder each time it is used for defects like weakened rungs or cracked rails. To be sure that flaws will be noticed, not cov-

ered up, never paint a wooden ladder. Once the job has been completed, store the ladder in a dry place.

Setting up the ladder safely and being careful as you work are easier than recovering from a broken back. Be certain the extension ladder always overlaps in the center by at least 3 feet. Take time every time you move the ladder to position it properly — locating a firm, level surface to support the legs and top of the ladder. Place the bottom of the ladder away from the wall a distance equal to about one-quarter of its height, but not in front of a door where there is a chance someone will open it. Never stretch from a ladder to reach the farthest inch of surface. When moving the ladder, keep well away from power lines, for a ladder striking a line can cause a fatal accident.

If you feel you are taking a chance, you have not set up the job properly. Extra precautions may be called for. A stabilizer bolted to the top of the ladder will make it more secure. To maneuver on a steep roof, hook a ladder over the ridge or tie a rope to a ladder placed on the roof, throw the rope over the ridge, and attach it to a tree or other sturdy object. A lifeline, or rope such as a ½-inch nylon rope in good condition, fastened to the worker, extended over the ridge, and tied on the other side to a tree, a porch column, or something else strong enough to hold will prevent a fall. Tying the top of the ladder to a sturdy object, possibly through a window to a radiator, is another way to avert an accident. For greater safety and ease of working, consider renting scaffolding to reach high portions of the house.

Other measures to keep the individual safe and preserve the roofing materials as well include:

- Wear sneakers or other soft-soled shoes.
- Work only on warm (not hot) days when there is little wind and when the roof is dry.
- Learn the weaknesses of the roofing materials. For instance, slate, tile, and wood shingles break easily. Using ladders and planks on the roof when working with these materials will save them. Do not assume that painters, someone repairing a TV antenna, or other workers who must get on the roof know how to protect the roofing material and the flashing. Before they set foot on it, discuss with them ways to safeguard the roof.

INSPECTION

Good roof maintenance demands a semiannual inspection and the knowledge of where trouble is likely to occur. There is no substitute for a nose-to-nose examination of the roof. If possible, walk around it for a close view. Otherwise, stand at the top of a ladder, look out of the house windows permitting a scrutiny of the roof, use binoculars, or hire a competent professional for help.

Figure 4-7. Queen Anne roof's crenelations.

Where should you look for problems (Figure 4-8)?

- Examine the places where the roof changes pitch or direction, such as at the curb on a gambrel roof or in the valleys, for disintegrating materials or for gaps where water might enter.
- Investigate the joints where the roof and the siding meet for any cracks.
- Look at the flashing for cracks and holes and for looseness where it joins another material.
- Pay particular attention to the flashing and the roofing material enclosing windows in a mansard roof.
- Find out if the covering over the ridge or the hip of a roof is tight and without gaps.
- Be alert for signs of clogging, inadequate slopes, or defects in the gutters and downspouts. Check with special care the condition of gutters built into the roof surface.
- Search the roofing materials for deterioration, such as cracks, blisters, or curling, and for any loose or missing parts.
- Watch for evidence of decay in the rafter ends and of water damage on the cornice.
- Inspect the interior walls and ceilings for dampness and moisture.

Also, check the ridge line to see if it is straight. If not, the reason might be sagging rafters or a foundation that is settling. An uneven roof may indicate that the sheathing beneath the roof has drooped. Inspect as much of the understructure of the roof as possible from inside the house. Look for water stains. Probe the rafters with a knife for any signs of rot. Another way to determine the condition of the underlayers is to examine them when removing any deteriorated roofing material.

Try to learn whether condensation occurs on the underside of the roof. Vents in the roof, gable, or eaves may be the solution to this problem. During your roof investigation, notice the trees nearby. Their shade can prevent the roof from drying out adequately, and branches that fall on or rub against the roof can cause damage.

When evidence of moisture in the interior of the house arises, measure the distance to the stain from an inside wall or a spot which can be identified from the outside. Transfer this measurement to the exterior of the roof for an idea where the trouble may arise. Be alert, for water may enter some distance from where you found dampness on the inside.

Once a problem with the roof is discovered, never delay the process of repair. Minor trouble soon becomes a disaster. If you wait, water trickling through the roof will damage the structure of the home.

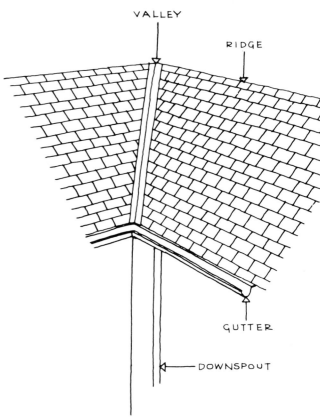

Figure 4-8. Parts of a roof.

Finding a qualified roofer is not always easy. A number of shysters call themselves roofers. Beware of becoming their victim. Chapter 15, Calling in a Contractor, explains how to track down competent professionals. Learn whether the roofer has experience working on older buildings and with the particular material on the roof. Not all roofers are skilled in working with slate, tile, or the more unusual materials on the roofs of many older homes. Sometimes, too, an aging roof may require a diagnostician, an uncommon individual who is able to analyze the problems arising from the quirks of construction or the peculiarities of design and to devise a remedy.

ROOFING MATERIALS

Different roofing materials protect a home in distinct ways. That is why a mansard roof may have slate on the lower, sharply pitched portion and metal on the flatter roof on top. A steep roof requires a material such as shingles, slates, or tiles to shed the water. A flat roof calls for an unbroken defense against the weather. In-between roofs that are too steep to hold tar or asphalt and too shallow for rigid shingles demand materials like metal, asphalt shingles installed by a cementing-down process, or special applications of built-up roofing for this purpose.

Today examples of most of the early roofing materials still exist. One exception is a thatched roof. The type of roofing material initially placed on an older house depends on when and where it was built, what materials were available at the time, and what was considered suitable for the style. If a home requires a new roof and replacing it with the original material is not feasible, try to duplicate as closely as possible the texture, scale, and color of the earlier roof, especially on a conspicuous roof.

Wood Shingles. About 1650, wood shingles began replacing thatched roofs. Wood shingles had the advantages of being lightweight, relatively easy to install, and cheap because wood was plentiful. The earliest wood shingles were hand split, but by 1802 the first patent was issued for a shingle-making machine. By the middle of the 1800s shingle sawing had become a large business.

The shape, size, and detailing of wood shingles, as well as the kind of wood, varied at first according to local customs and the availability of certain woods. For instance, native white pine was prevalent in the Delaware Valley and New England, oak and cypress in the South, and redwood and red cedar in the West. Common in the 1700s were shingles with square exposed ends, called square-butt shingles. Round-ended shingles, which helped to stop warping and gave the appearance of tiles, were also used. In the early 1800s ornamental patterns for roof shingles became popular for certain styles such as Gothic Revival. By the 1870s builders could choose from numerous shapes: square, diamond, cove, segmental, half circle, or octagon (*see* Figure 8-9).

During the closing years of the eighteenth century some cities, including New York and Boston, began to outlaw shingles because of the fire hazard, and builders turned to other materials. At the end of the nineteenth century wood shingles made a triumphant return on the large, sweeping roofs and siding of Shingle Style homes. Later, Georgian Revival houses employed shingles on hip, gable, or gambrel roofs. Today, however, many municipalities still do not permit wood-shingled roofs.

Because wood rots, splits, and warps, the life expectancy of a wood shingle is relatively short. Pine tar was a preservative in the late 1600s. Subsequently, shingles were painted, for protection, with oil in red or deep-brown shades, or sometimes in green to resemble slates. At present other preservative and fire-resistant treatments are available for shingles.

Care of Wood Shingles. Now most of the wood-shingle roofs are red cedar and will last about 20 to 30 years if properly installed, although some can do the job for 100 years or more. Wood shingles are graded from 1 to 4, Number 1 being all edge-grain heartwood, the most resistant to moisture. To ensure durability, Numbers 1 and 2 shingles are the only grades to consider for a home. Wood shakes, which are logs split or sawed into tapers, have been a popular roofing material in the past, and their care is similar to that for wood shingles. For more durable wood shingles or shakes, purchase those pretreated with a wood preservative.

When installing shingles or shakes, drive the nailhead flush with the wood. To allow for expansion, place shingles about ¼ inch apart and leave about ½ inch between wood shakes. When nails have worked their way loose, hammer them in and cover the nailheads with roofing cement. If the shingle ends have lifted up, try nailing them down, although this process may split the shingle. Drill a hole for the nail first before hammering it in, and apply roofing cement to the nailhead. For splits or holes in the shingles, wedge a piece of aluminum or galvanized steel under the deteriorated shingle far enough to extend beyond the crack. Nail through the shingle and the patch into the lath or sheathing underneath. Cover the crack and each nailhead with roofing cement.

Replace shingles too far deteriorated to patch, a process which can be unwieldy enough to require a roofer. To do the job yourself, begin by carefully loosening the shingle above. Then remove the old shingle by pulling or cutting away as much of it as possible. Cut off the nails holding the damaged shingle by maneuvering a hacksaw blade or a nail cutter beneath the shingles located directly above. Work a new shingle of the same size into the opening, if necessary using a block of wood and a hammer to drive the shingle into place. Nail down the replacement shingle with good-quality zinc-coated roofing nails. Coat the nailheads with roofing cement.

A wooden roof will last longer if kept free of moss, fungi, and debris, which hold moisture and can destroy the roof. Shade from nearby trees also prevents the roof from drying out. Once many deteriorated shingles have been discovered, the time for a new roof has arrived. Large areas where the shingles are a darker color, sponginess when probed with a knife, and warping are all signs of weakened shingles.

Slate. Slate stands at the top of the list of enduring roofs. The quality of slate varies and, of course, the better slate lasts longer. Other assets are its low maintenance and its fire resistance. Slate does have some drawbacks: It is expensive and subject to cracking and peeling, particularly if it is poor-quality slate, and it demands unusually sturdy framing underneath.

Only a few early settlers used slate as a roofing material. Because most slate was imported from

Figure 4-9. Slate roof pattern.

The nailhead should barely touch the slate, but the point must penetrate the sheathing.

Although durable, slates crack easily under the weight of a person, and they become more brittle with age. Never walk on a slate roof unless you use ladders and planks or know how to distribute your weight on the slates. For a cracked slate, try roofing cement over the crack as a remedy. To replace badly damaged or missing slates, start by removing the old slate using a nail cutter or a hacksaw blade. As a replacement, use a slate of the same size, shape, thickness, color, and texture. Finding a duplicate may be difficult, and if you are successful, purchase extras for future replacements. If locating a matching slate is not possible and the one to be replaced is in a highly visible part of the roof, remove an old slate from an inconspicuous section of the roof as a substitute. Put the new slate in the hidden location.

Wales, it was high priced and scarce. Not until the end of the eighteenth century did slate quarries operate in America. The development of railroads and canals made shipping easier and cheaper, and slate became popular in the mid-nineteenth century. In addition, building ordinances calling for fireproof coverings encouraged slate roofs in the larger eastern cities. Before the establishment of public water supplies, slate roofs were noted for collecting pure rainwater.

Slate is desirable for its decorative value—for its texture and color. The presence of minerals imparts colors to the slates ranging from blacks and grays through purples, reds, and greens. Slates from certain localities also have ribbons of color through them. On the high-pitched, visible roofs on Gothic Revival and Mansard homes, slates of various colors often form intriguing patterns resembling checkerboards, zigzags, and horizontal stripes (Figure 4-9). Shapes may differ, too, with several rows of square-ended slates, for example, alternating with a wide band of octagonal slates (Figure 4-10).

A standard slate roof is composed of uniform square-butt slates about ³⁄₁₆ of an inch thick. Slates of rougher texture, varied sizes, uneven butts, and often of several shades form what is called a textural roof. In a graduated roof slates similar to those found on a textural roof are arranged with the largest slates at the eaves and with gradually smaller slates rising to the ridge.

Care of Slate. A slate roof may last anywhere from 50 to 100 years—some say indefinitely. The key to its longevity is the quality of the material, flashing, nails, and installation along with persistent maintenance. Nails should be copper or the highest-quality zinc-coated roofing nails—never iron because it rusts and allows the slates to fall. The nail's size depends on the length and thickness of the slate.

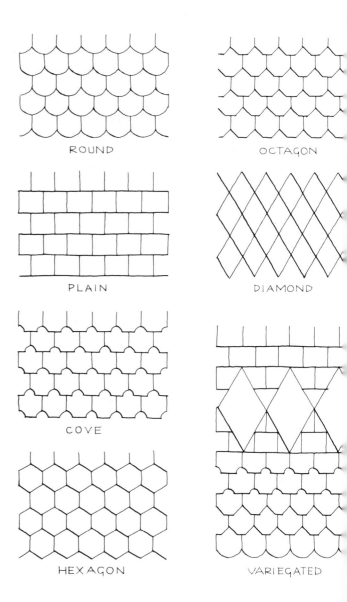

Figure 4-10. Slate shapes.

One way to add a slate is with a strip of copper to hold it in place. Use a piece of copper flashing cut 1½ to 2 inches wide and long enough to reach under the slate above and below the replacement slate 2 or 3 inches (Figure 4-11). Fasten the copper between the slates with copper or the highest-quality zinc-coated roofing nails. Hammer carefully to protect the slates. After coating the nailheads with roofing cement, slide the replacement slate in place. Bend up the end of the copper strip to hold the slate.

If many slates are either loose or falling out and the cause is poor installation, hire a roofer to lift all of the slates and re-lay them properly with the correct roofing nails. This procedure is worthwhile only if the slates are in good condition, for the cost could equal the price of a new roof of another material.

Asphalt Shingles. Asphalt shingles, made of felt saturated with asphalt and covered with a layer of ceramic granules, have protected numerous homes since the 1890s. Their low cost and relatively high fire resistance make them an attractive material. Their life span depends on their weight and the quality of felt and asphalt in the shingles. Grades of asphalt roofing range from 210 pounds per square (100 square feet) to about 400 pounds per square for double-layered, laminated shingles. The lowest grade that is good for roofing, however, is 250 pounds per square. Count on asphalt shingles to last from 15 years to a maximum of 25 years for the top grade. Houses in a windy location may require asphalt shingles manufactured with spots of adhesive underneath for greater wind resistance.

The most common type of asphalt shingle is the square-butt strip shingle available in different weights and fire ratings, 1 foot wide and 3 feet long, installed with 5 inches exposed to the weather. A visit to a roofing wholesaler, however, will reveal asphalt shingles in different textures, with irregular butt lines, and in numerous colors and mixed tones.

Investigate shingles made of fiberglass, a good new material that is lighter, easier to cut, more fire resistant, and somewhat longer lasting than asphalt shingles.

Care of Asphalt Shingles. A frequent fault of asphalt shingles is curling—an easy-to-solve problem if the roof is accessible. Using a putty knife, apply a coat of roofing cement under the curled end and press the shingle down onto the roofing cement. For a torn shingle, use roofing cement beneath the place where the shingle has split. Hammer roofing nails along the edges of the crack until the nailheads barely touch the shingle. Cover both the nailheads and the crack with roofing cement. Always use roofing cement sparingly. Too much is as bad as too little.

Replacing a missing asphalt shingle can be a troublesome task, possibly a job for a roofer. When doing the work yourself, begin by gently lifting the shingles above the missing or badly damaged one. With a chisel or pry bar, remove the nails from the shingle or shingle strip to be replaced or raise that shingle or strip from underneath with a flat spade until the nails pop out. Check the roofing felt and patch any tears with roofing cement. Next, slide the new shingle or shingle strip into place. Nail it down with roofing nails and coat these with roofing cement.

The loss of mineral granules from the surface of many asphalt shingles is a serious problem, indicating the need for a new roof. Installation costs are similar for all grades of asphalt shingles. When choosing the weight of the new material, remember that it is less expensive in the long run to apply a good-quality asphalt shingle rather than a lesser-grade shingle requiring replacement sooner.

Metal. Metal was an effective roofing material in the nineteenth century for those architectural styles with very low-pitched roofs. By experimenting with various kinds of metals, builders found the best ma-

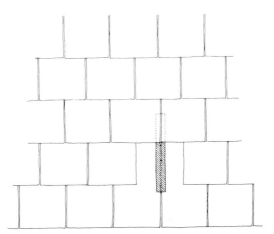

Figure 4-11a. Nailing a copper strip between the slates.

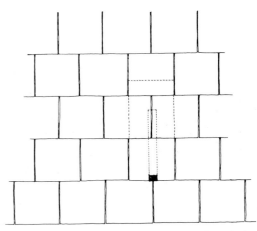

Figure 4-11b. Bending the copper strip over the end of the replacement.

terials for a reliable waterproof covering (Figure 4-12). For a few early roofs, soft lead or copper was used. Sheet copper was scarce and expensive, however, because it was imported from England until manufacturing facilities were opened in the United States at the end of the eighteenth century. By the 1850s it was more common. The seams between the copper sheets usually were upright on large roofs and flat on curved roofs such as the roofs found on cupolas.

The most popular nineteenth century metal for roofing was tin-plated iron. Its light weight made tin plate easy to install, and its reasonable cost and durability added to its appeal. Only when it is painted regularly to prevent corrosion is it long lasting. Reds or browns were the most common colors, although tin plate was sometimes painted a dull green to imitate copper. Look for tin-plate roofs on Greek Revival and Italianate homes, on the low-pitched top portion of mansard roofs, and on many porches. Often these roofs have bold standing seams. You will also see tin shingles embossed to create decorative designs or to resemble tile or wood.

A variation of tin roofing, called terne plate, has a duller finish. Manufacturers of terne plate dipped sheets of iron in an alloy of 80 percent lead and 20 percent tin. Other metals, including sheet iron, galvanized iron (coated with zinc to prevent rust and used primarily on commercial buildings), and rolled sheets of zinc, were employed less frequently for roofing.

Care of Metal. Generally, a metal roof is long lasting, fire resistant, and relatively easy to maintain,

but metals are susceptible to chemical pollutants in the air; to acids in rainwater, moss, red cedar, and oak; and to certain materials found in lime mortar or Portland cement. The electrolytic action from mixing different metals, whether in nails, flashing, patching material, or roof decorations such as cresting, will corrode metals.

To repair a small hole, put a drop of solder in the hole unless the roof is aluminum. A larger crack or hole will require a patch of the same metal as the roof. First, clean the area with steel wool. After using an acid flux on the roof and the patch, cover both with a thin coating of solder. Then attach the patch to the roof with solder. If the standing seam of a metal roof leaks, solder the hole or lift up the sheet and put a piece of metal underneath and solder. When this technique does not solve the problem, hiring a roofer may be necessary. To repair a leak at a flat seam, clean the area around the leak, use acid flux, and solder.

Built-Up Roofing. Built-up roofing is the customary covering for flat roofs, and it is also effective on shallow-sloped roofs. The idea of layering roofing materials was first experimented with in the mid-1800s. Today this type of roof consists of layers of saturated roofing felt unrolled into layers of mopped-on tar pitch or a similar viscous material. To help reflect the sun and prevent cracking, slag, gravel, or marble chips are often spread onto the top coat. Built-up roofing rests on top of a dry layer of roofing felt which is nailed over sheathing.

Care of Build-Up Roofing. Depending on the quality of the material, built-up roofs may last from 10 to 30 years. Two common problems are blistering and cracking. To repair a crack, clean out the crack and the surrounding area. Spread roofing cement over the crack and the cleaned area. Press a patch of roofing felt into the roofing cement, and cover it with more roofing cement. Push gravel lightly into the surface.

Taking care of a blister on a built-up roof is a similar process. Begin by cutting through the blister with a knife. Put roofing cement under the blistered area and press the layer flat. To hold it down, nail along the cut on both sides. Cover the area with roofing cement. Next, place a patch of roofing felt over the roofing cement. For extra protection, nail down the patch. Apply more roofing cement. Arrange gravel over the patch and press gently into the roofing cement.

FLASHING

Leaky roofs are most often the fault of loose, corroded, or cracked flashing. Flashing is a water-resis-

Figure 4-12. Metal roof.

tant material which protects the joints where the roof meets chimneys, walls, plumbing or attic vents, skylights, dormers, or another roof on a different plane. An inspection of the roof should always include a complete examination of the condition of the flashing.

Flashing materials include roll roofing, sheet plastic, and metals like aluminum, copper, galvanized iron, tin, terne, lead-coated copper, stainless steel, or zinc. When choosing flashing material, remember that dissimilar metals must not touch each other. Also, investigate the durability of various flashing materials. Galvanized iron, for example, will rust if not well protected. When replacing a portion of the flashing, try to match the existing material. Never use copper flashing with cedar shingles because the acid in the cedar will eat away the copper.

Flashing at the roof valley, the angle where two downward sloping roofs meet, is handled in one of two ways: open or closed. With the open method the roofing material stops before the valley, exposing the flashing and any deterioration. When the roofing material joins at the valley, covering the flashing to present a continuous roof surface, the valley is described as closed. A leak in a closed valley may require the removal of part of the roof at the valley to mend or replace the flashing, a job which is a likely candidate for professional help.

At the intersection of a lower roof with a wall or of a roof with a steeper roof and at the curbing on a gambrel roof, the flashing fits under the upper course and over the lower course. If the flashing is defective, the siding and roofing material around the flashing must be removed by a qualified roofer or a skilled amateur. When the leaking occurs at the joint between the flashing and the roofing or siding, caulking the entire joint may be sufficient.

A special technique has been developed for protecting the area where the roof meets a vent. A metal sleeve covers the pipe and reaches down into the inside. A sheet of metal with a circular opening in it, called an apron, is placed over the sleeve and is soldered to the sleeve at the bottom (Figure 4-13). Any leaking where the apron meets the roofing can be fixed by nailing the apron into place, if it is loose, and coating the joint between the two surfaces with roofing cement. If the sleeve and apron must be replaced, consider purchasing a plastic fitting manufactured for this purpose.

A roof is only as sound as its flashing. Even the tiniest hole demands an immediate dab of roofing cement or, for metal flashing, solder. Never apply roofing cement directly to bare metal, but coat the metal first with a paint thinner or a metal primer. Fill any larger gaps with roofing felt before covering the felt with roofing cement. For metal flashing, use a piece of compatible metal flashing cut 1 inch larger

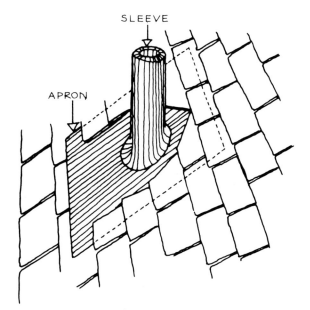

Figure 4-13. A vent apron.

than the hole on all of its sides. Cover the hole and area around it with roofing cement and push the metal patch into the roofing cement. If the flashing has moved away from the roofing material, roofing cement or caulking may seal the opening. Clean rusty spots with a wire brush and coat them with a metal primer.

SPECIAL CONSIDERATIONS

Other techniques exist to remedy roof problems.

Snow Guards.   In colder climates roofs need special care. In areas of high snowfall, snow guards can combat ice and snow slides and prevent damage to a steep roof. Different types of snow guards are available for various roof materials. The guards line up just above the roof edges sometimes in rows, the number determined by the pitch and size of the roof.

Electric Heating Tapes.   Ice buildup may form on roofs during freezing weather, holding water which can back up under the roofing material and seep through the sheathing into the house. One solution is clipping electric heating tapes to the roof edges. During a winter storm, connect the heating tapes to a convenient outdoor electric outlet or through a window into an outlet inside.

Gutters and Downspouts.   Gutters and downspouts that do not flow freely can allow ice and water to back up under the roofing material into the cornice and interior structure. Make certain the gutters and downspouts are clean and work well. To prevent freezing, install an electric heating cable in the gutters.

Eaves Flashing and Attic Ventilation. Wide metal flashing at the eaves (or a drip edge) is one way to direct water away from the house. By eliminating condensation problems, adequate attic ventilation will also help to keep a house dry.

MODERN ATTACHMENTS

Contemporary appendages, such as TV antennas, vents, and skylights, detract from the appearance of a house. When there is a choice, place them in an inconspicuous section of the roof such as at the rear.

REPLACEMENT

In time all roofs wear out. Untended roofing problems will lead to costly and extensive damage to a house. Widespread deterioration of the roof material, such as rotting wood shingles over large areas of the roof or mineral granules missing on numerous asphalt shingles, indicates the need for a new roof. A new roof may also be called for when the understructure is in poor condition. Sagging between the rafters, deteriorated rafters, rotted wood, and an uneven ridge line are signs of this problem. The lower edges of the roof are particularly vulnerable. Frequently checking the rafters, by removing the fascia boards if necessary, is always a good idea.

Before making the decision to replace a roof, seek the advice of several competent roofers. They can point out problems not obvious to an untrained eye and suggest alternative solutions. Obtain written cost estimates from different roofers when selecting one to do the work.

Placing a new roof over an old one is controversial. Some architects warn against it, and some roofers refuse to overroof. Hard, thick, or uneven materials, such as tile, slate, and wood shakes, do not lend themselves to overroofing. Generally, two new asphalt shingle layers on top of an original asphalt layer are acceptable if the old asphalt shingles are flat and unbroken. One asphalt layer can go atop a wood shingle layer. It can be put directly on the wood, but it is advisable to use horsefeathers, long, triangular wood strips which feather out the surface. Without horsefeathers, the new shingle surface has distinct ripples and is somewhat more subject to wind uplift. Usually with a built-up roof the old materials are taken off before the new ones are installed.

Additional factors enter the decision about overroofing. A strong, sound understructure is essential. Evidence of rot on an old roof always demands its removal before proceeding with a new roof, for the moisture in the old roof will eventually harm the new material. Also, building codes may not permit more than one layer of roofing.

The advantages of a double roof are easy to imagine. Extra insulation and added protection from a storm are two benefits. Also, in the process of reroofing, a house is not exposed. On the other hand, locating a firm surface for nailing is more difficult when the old roof remains, and the finished roof may be somewhat irregular.

When selecting new roofing material, the first consideration will probably be cost. The prices of slate, tile, and metal are forbidding. Always compare the durability of the materials, for the most expensive ones are frequently long lasting. Their cost over their life span may be less than the cost of a material which is cheaper initially, but short lived.

A convenient time to improve attic ventilation and insulation is when a new roof goes on. Check these components to be sure they are adequate. Also, examine the overhang of the roof, and think about enlarging it if it does not provide good protection for the siding. On this question the advice of an architect may be sought because adding an overhang or increasing the size of one already existing greatly changes the house's appearance.

Often, the roof is an outstanding feature of an older home, enhancing its character. When replacing a highly visible roof, closely imitate, if possible, the color, texture, and size of the original roofing material. Keep in mind that white and pale shades may suit a contemporary building, but not an older house. Darker colors such as deep brown, black, or gray and blends of these hues complement an older home and most likely resemble closely the original colors of the roof.

GUTTERS AND DOWNSPOUTS

Water is the relentless enemy of a home. Gutters and downspouts have the task of directing water from the roof away from the walls, foundation, and basement and away from any planting next to the house. If they do their job well, they prevent rot, decay, flooded basements, eroded soil, and stained building materials. Protect a home and prolong the life of gutters and downspouts by inspecting them in the spring and fall and making the required adjustments and repairs. If many large trees surround the house, however, you will have to perform this task more often.

Where should you look for problems (Figure 4-14)?

- Check the gutters, downspouts, and any leaf strainers for leaves, seeds, twigs, and other debris.
- Find out if the pitch of the gutters allows water to flow quickly into the downspouts.
- Investigate the downspouts for any clogging.

- Look for loose joints between the various parts of the gutters and downspouts.
- Notice whether the gutter supports and downspout straps are detached or broken.
- Examine the gutters and downspouts for cracks, holes, corrosion, and missing pieces. Check any existing patches for cracks or gaps between the patch and the gutter.
- Learn whether the paint is in good condition.
- Observe the fascia and soffits for peeling paint or rotting wood. These problems may result from water leaking from the gutters or downspouts.

During a storm, discover whether the gutters, downspouts, and other provisions for drainage successfully divert water away from the house. In cold climates in the winter, watch for the buildup of ice in the gutters.

MATERIALS

Gutters and downspouts come in many different materials with varying prices and degrees of durability. Galvanized steel, a common material for gutters and downspouts, is the cheapest and the least durable. Aluminum is a popular material because it is lightweight and resists corrosion. Aluminum, however, dents easily. Copper, one of the longest-lasting materials, is also the most expensive. Never use copper with wood shingles, for the acid in cedar shingles will quickly eat away the copper. Vinyl, a new material, for proper maintenance requires only regular cleaning and protection of the metal supports against rust.

Wood for gutters and downspouts is no longer popular. Wood is particularly susceptible to rot where the gutter joins the downspout, and wood replacement gutters are hard to find. In many cases they must be custom made by a carpenter. Either decay-resistant woods, like heartwood of red cedar or redwood, or wood factory-treated with a preservative is the longest-lasting replacement.

If you have inherited wooden gutters with an older home, they may last a long time with continual care. Maintain wooden gutters by painting the insides frequently, perhaps as often as every 3 years. First, clean the gutter well and sand or wire brush the surface. Apply a primer and paint. In the same way, paint the exterior of the gutters and downspouts as required. Before painting, apply new caulking to any joints where the caulking is loose or cracked.

TYPES OF GUTTERS

The two most common shapes for modern gutters are the half-round eavetrough and the K (also

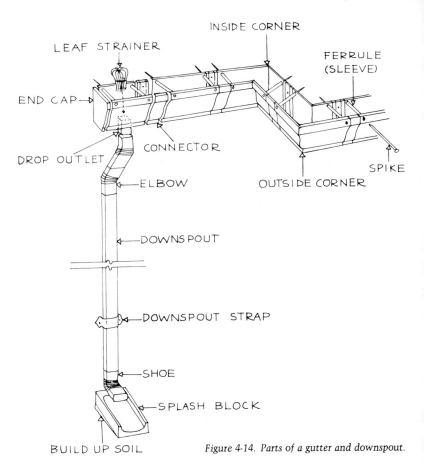

Figure 4-14. Parts of a gutter and downspout.

known as the box or ogee) gutter, which is in widest use today (Figure 4-15). The choice of gutter and downspout diameters depends on the square feet of roof each must handle and the amount of rain in the area.

Older homes sometimes have pole gutters formed of metal wrapped around a piece of lumber, either a two-by-four or a three-by-four. They sit on the roof near the edge, and the water runs from the pole gutters into downspouts (Figure 4-16). Finding a roofer who knows how to work with pole gutters is difficult.

Another type of gutter found on older homes is the built-in gutter, which is built into a cornice (Figure 4-17). The main advantage of built-in gutters is their inconspicuous appearance. They require great vigilance, however, for a leak can run through the cornice into the structure of the house, causing much damage. Take care of any loose joints or

HALF-ROUND

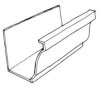

K GUTTER

Figure 4-15.
Half-round eavetrough
and K gutter.

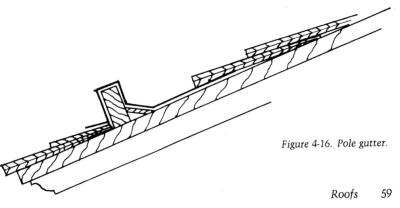

Figure 4-16. Pole gutter.

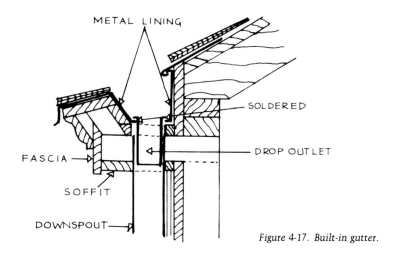

METAL LINING

SOLDERED

DROP OUTLET

FASCIA

SOFFIT

DOWNSPOUT

Figure 4-17. Built-in gutter.

cracks and holes in the metal lining as soon as they are discovered. Soldering the joints and tiny cracks and patching larger holes with metal patches will solve these problems. Unless you are experienced with metal work, professional help is advisable.

GUTTER SCREENS AND LEAF STRAINERS

Gutter screens or leaf strainers are well worth the investment, as they keep out twigs, leaves, and seeds and prevent deterioration of the gutters. Gutter screens are strips of wire or plastic mesh which fit under the roofing material and cover the gutter. Shaped like a small cage, leaf strainers sit in the tops of downspouts. Clean out the gutter screens and leaf guards when they have become clogged, and inspect them regularly, especially after storms, to be certain they are in place.

MAINTENANCE AND REPAIR

Many homeowners clean and repair the gutters and downspouts.

Cleaning. At least twice a year — in the spring to clean out seeds and in the fall to take out leaves — remove all debris from the gutters. Not only can twigs and seeds clog gutters and downspouts, but their weight can wrench the gutter hangers from the house. Also, any acids in the debris can consume the metal. With a stiff brush, remove mud and anything else that sticks and then brush out the gutters. Never sweep anything into the downspouts. For safety on a ladder, move it rather than reach too far.

Suppose you have noticed during a hard rain that the downspouts are clogged. What is the remedy? If possible, shoot water upward from the bottom of the downspout to dislodge the material. Be cautious about running water downward into the downspout because you may only pack the material tighter.

Often the trouble is at the elbow. Try removing the elbow and cleaning it out. A plumber's snake run through the downspout from the top may also free the material blocking the downspout.

Sagging Gutters. The cause of sagging gutters may be loose hangers. Renail any that are not tight. Adjusting strap hangers by bending them with pliers may bring the gutters into correct alignment. If the sagging results from an insufficient number of hangers, add new ones.

Cracks and Holes. Caulk any cracks at the seams where the various parts of the gutter meet. Either butyl-rubber or silicone caulking compounds will seal cracks in metal gutters. If the surface has been painted, choose a caulking compound that adheres to paint. Before caulking, clean dirt or corrosion from the area.

When a hole is found in the gutter, check the entire gutter for more holes. If there are many, replace the gutter rather than attempt to patch it. One way to patch a metal gutter is to use asphalt roofing cement. Clean all dirt from the area. With a wire brush or coarse sandpaper remove all evidence of corrosion. Never apply roofing cement directly to bare metal. Cover the area well with either a paint thinner or a metal primer. Then coat with asphalt roofing cement. Also, for small cracks you can solder metal gutters, except aluminum, to close the gap.

For larger holes, carry out the procedure described above for repairing smaller cracks using roofing cement. Place a piece of sheet metal or heavy-duty aluminum foil over the roofing cement. To avoid electrolytic action, use the same kind of metal as the material of the gutter. Extend the metal patch at least ½ inch beyond the hole on all sides. Cover the patch with a coat of roofing cement.

Replace any rotted wood in wooden gutters with a piece of wood the same thickness. For this patch, purchase wood pressure-treated with a preservative or saturate untreated wood with a preservative. Caulk the joints and cover them with aluminum or galvanized steel nailed on both sides before painting over the metal and the wood patch.

Rotting of the Fascia Boards and at the Roof Edges. One way to prevent deterioration of the fascia boards, rafter ends, roofing material, and sheathing is to install a metal drip edge under the shingles at the eaves (Figure 4-18). Nail between the edges of the first course of roofing material through the starter course and drip edge into the sheathing. Apply roofing cement to the nailheads and cover them with a narrow strip of flashing. The drip edge guides water away from the edge of the roof into the gutter.

REPLACEMENT

Homeowners may decide to replace badly deteriorated gutters and downspouts themselves. Although they may choose not to work on the highest areas of their homes, porches and other low sections are good candidates for installing and caring for gutters and downspouts. Aluminum, galvanized steel, and vinyl are easier than other materials to work with because they can be joined by connectors which are caulked with a special compound to make them watertight. The task, however, is not as effortless as advertisements for new gutters and downspouts proclaim. Copper will probably require a roofer because the joints must be soldered.

Never mix different metals in the gutter and downspout system. Electrolytic action will cause the metals to corrode. Supports, straps for the downspouts, screens, leaf strainers, replacement gutters and downspouts, and even metal patches must be the same metal as the gutters and downspouts already in place. Plastic, on the other hand, is safe with any kind of metal.

Gutters and downspouts should not touch the house, and the top edge of gutters should be below the roof line. Otherwise, ice can cause water to seep into the house or back up onto the roof. When installing gutters and downspouts, be sure their placement and joints allow room for expansion and contraction caused by temperature changes.

The correct pitch prevents water from standing in puddles in the gutters. Gutters should slope down toward the downspouts at the rate of 1 inch for every 16 feet of gutter. A very long gutter may slant from the center to downspouts at both ends. Check the flow by pouring water into the gutter. Plan on one support for every 30 to 36 inches of gutter and probably one on each side of the corner. Make sure the supports are loose enough to permit expansion and contraction of the gutter. One downspout is necessary for every 35 running feet of gutter, although this figure can vary depending on the area of the roof to be drained. Either straps or hooks will secure the downspouts to the wall—use two to a 10-foot section of downspout.

The color of the gutters and downspouts affects the appearance of a house, and it should blend with the walls to be less noticeable. If the house is brick or stone, the color should match the trim. Copper, of course, will oxidize to a darker, duller finish.

DRAINAGE

What happens after the water flows through the downspouts demands special attention. Rainwater conductors may run into a public sewer. If not, a number of choices exist; whichever method you choose, be certain water does not stand near the foundation of the house and find its way into the basement. Downspouts can be connected to underground pipes which run to the street, to a driveway, or to a low area on the property. Also, you can purchase splash blocks or make them out of bricks or cement to carry the water at least 4 to 5 feet from the house. Splash blocks tend to settle into the ground, and periodically building up the soil beneath them may be necessary to let the water run away from the house. If the downspout runs into a paved area, a splash block is not essential. Be careful, though, that the water does not freeze in the winter where people are likely to walk.

Another simple solution for drainage is to fasten a length of perforated hose manufactured for this purpose to the downspout. The hose will uncoil in a storm and harmlessly discharge the water.

A more complicated solution is to connect the downspout to the underground drainpipe that flows into a dry well. Before constructing a dry well, find out whether the soil will absorb the water. The dry well can be a 55-gallon steel drum with both ends removed and holes punched in the sides for the water to seep out. Fill the drum with broken stones or gravel and cover it on top with straw or roofing felt, then topsoil. The drum must lie at least 18 inches underground and 10 feet from the foundation wall. One dry well is required for each of the main downspouts. Whichever method you select, always be certain that the soil slopes away from the foundation for good drainage from the house.

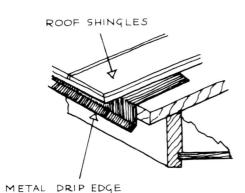

ROOF SHINGLES

METAL DRIP EDGE

Figure 4-18. Metal drip edge at eaves.

CHAPTER FIVE

CHIMNEYS

Chimneys can be simple, functional components of an older house or striking works of art, sculptured in unusual shapes or enlivened with pilasters, panels, arches, or lavish clay pots. Some are stately structures, adding dignity to the house; others are playful, poking out above the roof where least expected. Their height from the ground, their location, the roof balustrades, or the roof's shape may make the chimneys inconspicuous. More often they are prominent features, contributing to the individuality of an older home.

Chimneys deserve special attention to avoid the danger of fire. Regular inspection to identify possible problems and meticulous maintenance are essential. Chimney troubles include cracks and deterioration of the chimney material and the mortar; looseness or holes in the flashing; gaps in the joints between the cap and both the shaft and the flue; cracks, obstructions, or dirt and soot in the flue; or a slanting chimney shaft.

Continual exposure to sun, wind, rain, sleet, and snow makes chimneys particularly susceptible to damage. If rebuilding is necessary, as often occurs in an older house, duplicate the size, shape, proportions, and materials of the original chimney and try to retain any decorative details. Chimneys are an integral part of the overall design of a home, and careless alterations will only disfigure the house.

DESIGN

Countless versions of chimneys appear on older homes. Chimney designs were partly determined by the available building materials, local construction practices, the chimney's function, its location in relation to the fireplaces, and the style of the house. Occasionally, too, the personal preferences of the initial builder, architect, or owner are evident in the chimney's design.

Variations from style to style, from locality to locality, or from house to house within one style occur in the number and placement of chimneys, their dimensions, their materials, and their details. An older house often has several chimneys piercing the roof's silhouette. They may spring from the center of the roof's ridge, rise from partway down the slopes of a hipped roof, extend upward from the outside walls, stand against the exterior walls, jut out at the intersection of two roofs, or thrust up through a dormer. In the more formal styles chimneys are positioned to add to the overall symmetrical effect. In houses with more irregular layouts and asymmetrical exteriors, their placement seems random. The height and width of chimneys also differ markedly. Some are tall, narrow, and graceful; others are short, wide, and robust. You will discover a rich assortment of stonework and brick patterns, as well as a few stuccoed and plastered versions. Many older chimneys are plain, but a large number are painstakingly detailed with slanting shoulders, molded corners, or ornamental caps.

How can you tell if a chimney is original or suitable for the style of a house?

- Check the construction of the chimney on both the inside and the outside for evidence of rebuilding. Is there any new masonry? Are there any clues about age near the opening in the roof or in the chimney's foundation?

- Examine the mortar joints and mortar materials. You will find a soft mortar commonly composed of lime or crushed oyster shells and sand on many older homes. Harder cement did not come into use until after 1850, but some builders continued to apply lime mortar throughout the nineteenth century.

- Notice the position of the chimney on the house. Does it seem to be an integral part of the house's original design?

- Observe whether there are any fired-clay chimney pots and if they have generous decorations. Clay chimney pots were inaugurated around 1820 and were favored in many nineteenth century styles.

- Search for old photographs of the house showing the design and location of a chimney.

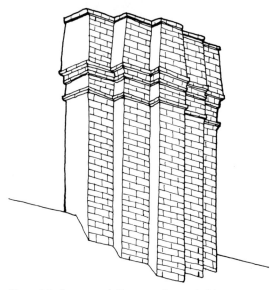

Figure 5-1. Seventeenth Century pilastered chimney.

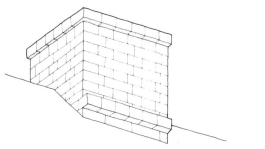

Figure 5-2. Seventeenth Century chimney with a drip course.

- Find other houses in the neighborhood in the same style and look carefully at the chimneys. Do they resemble the ones on your house?
- Study the following sections about the types of chimney designs appropriate for various architectural styles.

SEVENTEENTH CENTURY

Throughout the colonies chimneys were prominent features of most Seventeenth Century homes. Practical considerations came first, but from the beginning striking differences appeared between chimneys in the North and in the South, and variations occurred among localities as well. The earliest wood and clay chimneys proved to be fire hazards, and the more durable masonry chimneys soon took their place. New England preferred stone; Virginia chose brick.

In New England a Seventeenth Century house commonly had a massive, wide, and squat central chimney sitting parallel to and slightly behind the roof's ridge. These chimneys added rigidity and strength to the houses' wooden frames, and many were immense enough to include five fireplace flues built into the central stack. Later versions were taller rectangles straddling the ridge, and a home might have two of these chimneys on the ridge or on the gable ends.

Early New England chimneys were stone, either fieldstone or quarried stone, and later ones sometimes combined stone and brick. In these cases stone may have been laid to the upper floor or perhaps as far as the ridge, with brick employed on the top portion. Occasionally earlier stone tops were later removed and replaced with brick. A brick-topped chimney at times assumed a complex form with narrow protrusions, like pilasters, or a series of planes receding on both sides from the center (Figure 5-1). Copied from English prototypes, pilastered chimneys were especially common on larger homes in Massachusetts and Rhode Island. This type of modeled chimney often represented a cluster of several flues inside, creating cross sections in L or T shapes, or it resulted from an additional flue from a lean-to kitchen fireplace in the back.

Clay or clay and hair mortar was generally used from the chimney's base to the attic with the more expensive and scarce lime mortar applied in the stack above the roof. Preceding modern metal flashing, a drip course, or a single row of stone or brick projecting slightly beyond the chimney face just above the roof, helped prevent rain from running into the chimney's juncture with the roof (Figure 5-2). Caps were simple brick or stone courses.

Seventeenth Century homes in Virginia often have elaborate brick chimneys at the gable end walls. Exterior chimneys have wide bases which narrow to straight stacks as they rise by sloping offsets, or weatherings, at the sides. The offsets help shed rain and protect the bricks and mortar. In some examples, the upper portion of these chimneys stands a few inches away from the gable end.

Exterior end wall chimneys of a unique design called chimney pents were popular in Maryland and other southern colonies in both the seventeenth and eighteenth centuries. A chimney pent is a small structure with a pent, or shed, roof built between large, tall, double end chimneys (Figure 5-3). Constructed of wood or brick, chimney pents extend one or two stories, may project beyond the chimney face or be flush with it, and may either occur as single central structures or protrude from the sides of the chimneys.

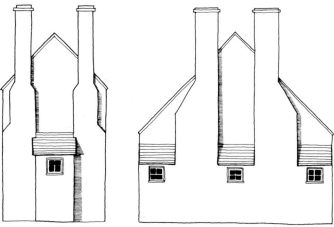

Figure 5-3. Seventeenth Century chimney pents.

EIGHTEENTH CENTURY— GEORGIAN, 1700 TO 1780

Brick was the favorite material for Georgian chimneys on brick, wood, or stone houses because bricks were plentiful by the eighteenth century. These chimneys almost always had plain rectangular shafts, now and then with molded, slightly curved brick caps. Stone chimneys in rural Pennsylvania and central stone chimneys in New England continued to be built.

Throughout the Georgian period chimneys were carefully situated to add to the house's symmetry (Figure 5-4). Builders of early houses usually placed two chimneys on the ridge several feet in from each gable end. After 1750 chimneys were frequently located in the gable end walls on both sides, a cost-saving procedure. Some paired end chimneys do occur, at times connected by a brick parapet, or low wall, rising above the roof line (Figure 5-5). A larger home with a hipped roof may have four chimney stacks, one placed at each corner of the hip's top portion or partially down the sloping sides. If a balustrade encompasses a flat top deck, the chimneys may be nearly invisible inside this enclosure.

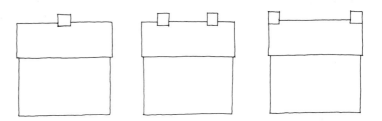

Figure 5-4. Georgian chimney placement.

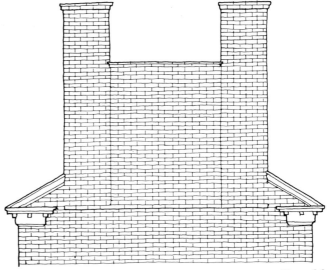

Figure 5-5. Georgian parapeted chimney.

FEDERAL, 1790 TO 1830

Federal houses usually have tall, slender brick chimneys, many times extending far above the roof (Figure 5-6). A stack may be plain or subtly accented with a protruding row of bricks near the top. Chimney caps are simple. When there are two chimneys on a pitched roof, they are located on the ridge at both ends or placed on one side. If four chimneys occur, they rise above the end walls of a pitched roof or sit at the juncture of the slopes on a hipped roof. Stone homes have stone chimneys. Once in a while a house has double brick chimneys on one end wall with a parapet linking the two stacks.

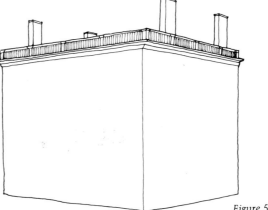

Figure 5-6. Federal chimneys.

GREEK REVIVAL, 1820 TO 1860

Chimneys on Greek Revival homes tend to be simple, thin, and moderately tall. Generally, they are built of brick and are found in various locations. A house designed in a temple form frequently has lower, inconspicuous chimneys positioned toward the middle of the roof (Figure 5-7). Sometimes four chimneys are symmetrically placed at the front and back, or two chimneys rise from one slope of a double pitched roof. A townhouse may have one or two end chimneys. In rare instances, double chimneys on the end wall of a house with a pitched roof have a low brick parapet wall joining the chimneys.

Figure 5-7. Greek Revival chimneys.

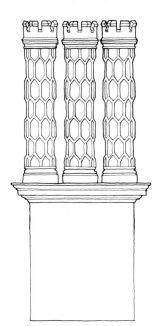

Figure 5-8. Gothic Revival chimney.

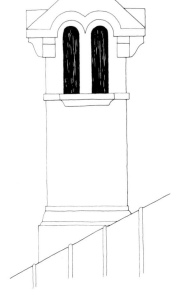

Figure 5-9. Italianate chimney.

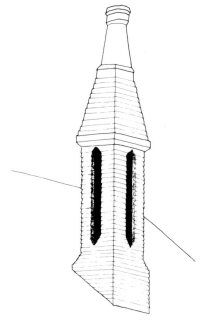

Figure 5-10. Stick Style chimney.

GOTHIC REVIVAL, 1820 TO 1860

Gothic Revival chimneys are works of art as well as functional parts of a house. Their carefully conceived designs ask to be appreciated.

Guidebooks promoting this style suggested a chimney would be more interesting if it was clearly divided into a base, shaft, and cap, similar to the parts of a column. Most designs follow this prescription. Chimneys are set on a small platform rising above the ridge. Occasionally the tall, narrow shafts are plain, but more often they are round or octagonal with curved or diagonally sloping lower portions. Patterns of diamonds, flowers, or sensuous interlocking curves enliven many surfaces (Figure 5-8). Caps are usually molded brick or terra-cotta with curves or diagonals flaring outward from the shaft. Most chimneys of this type are fired clay and have single, double, or triple stacks. Shorter and less graceful sculptured brick chimneys also occur, possibly with protruding shoulders near the tops.

Chimneys emerge in various locations. There may be paired chimneys at either end of a pitched roof or two about one-quarter of the way in from each side. They almost always sit on the ridge.

ITALIANATE, 1845 TO 1880

Italianate chimneys may be simple or elaborate, depending on the degree of formality of the house. Quiet versions sometimes are short and squat, stuccoed to repeat the wall material, and capped with a plain piece of brownstone. Taller, rectangular brick chimneys are perhaps adorned with slightly shouldered projections near the top. Molded terra-cotta chimney pots are also seen.

The more richly embellished chimneys on larger houses can be quite imposing structures. Certain ones resemble small towers: tall and narrow with arched openings near the tops echoing the round-headed windows below (Figure 5-9). These versions are stuccoed and capped with bracketed tile roofs. Other less fancy examples may be brick enlivened with recessed side panels and bands of dentils. Look for one or two chimneys generally located at either end of the roof or, on a hipped roof, near the center.

STICK STYLE, 1855 TO 1900

Stick Style houses have either low, plain, unobtrusive brick chimneys or tall, stately ones. The more dramatic versions may have ornate terra-cotta chimney pots, wide flared shoulders tapering to narrower bottoms, pyramid-shaped caps, or pierced shafts (Figure 5-10). Every once in a while the bricks are laid in layers resembling dripping frosting. Other decorative brickwork includes molded bricks and herringbone patterns. Depending on the size of the house, one, two, or three chimneys may be randomly located on the ridge, on the roof, or at the juncture of two roofs.

MANSARD, 1860 TO 1880

Expect to find bold chimneys on Mansard homes (Figure 5-11). A few hide behind iron crestings outlining the curbings around the roof's top edges, but most are striking features.

Often these chimneys are divided into bases, shafts, and caps. The bases are usually substantial platforms serving as transitions between the roofs and the shafts. The shafts may be plain, pilastered, broken by round arches, or enriched with classical details such as fluting. Ornamental caps with shoulders, sloping sides, or curved edges are common. Look, also, for fired-clay chimney pots. Some chimneys are tall and slender, but most are heavy and

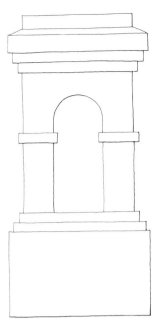

Figure 5-11. Mansard chimney.

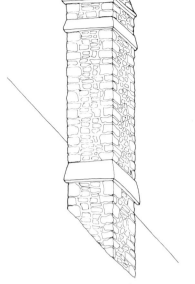

Figure 5-12. Romanesque chimney.

ample. Generally, the chimneys are brick, although stone homes have stone chimneys. A Mansard chimney almost always is situated above the roof's curbing. One may sit on either side at the front, or two may exist on one side.

ROMANESQUE, 1875 TO 1895

Watch for two distinct kinds of chimneys on a Romanesque house: short, simple ones or tall versions, perhaps with subtle ornamentation. The plainer types, usually made of rough-faced stone, sit squatly on the ridge. Often without a protruding cap, the top is accented instead by a stone slab. The more dominant chimneys may be brick, crudely cut stone, or sandstone similar to the house's walls (Figure 5-12). Wedge-shaped or rectangular stone quoins at times mark the edges of the bolder stone chimneys. Brick ones may have engaged round columns, pierced round arches as caps, or layers of shouldering at the tops. Sandstone chimneys occasionally have beaded moldings. In most instances the placement of the chimneys is unpredictable.

QUEEN ANNE, 1876 TO 1900

Queen Anne chimneys are extraordinary. They are imaginative creations assuming unusual shapes, boasting fanciful embellishments, and cropping up where you least expect them (Figure 5-13). Probably, you will see many chimneys, making the roof's already complex silhouette even more complex. Sometimes no two are alike on the same house.

A few simple, inconspicuous brick chimneys occur, but most are highly visible and extravagantly treated as though they were pieces of sculpture. Look for modeled brickwork with protruding shelves, or shoulders, raised or recessed panels, variegated patterns, and molded bricks with curved

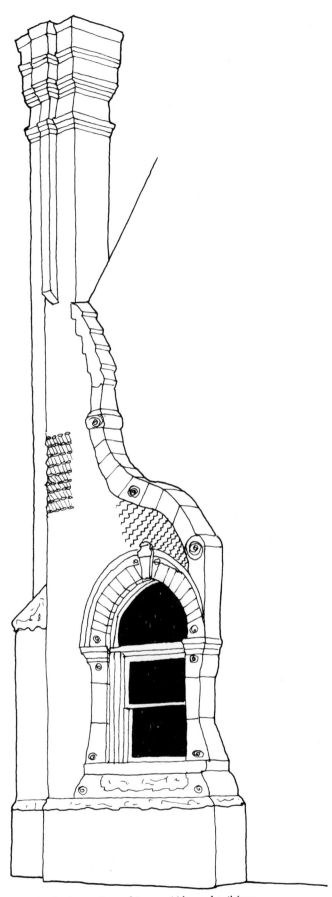

Figure 5-13. Queen Anne chimney. (After a detail from a photograph of a house in Calvert, Texas, by Todd Webb for the Texas Architecture Survey, courtesy of Amon Carter Museum, Fort Worth.)

Figure 5-14. Shingle Style chimney.

Figure 5-15. Georgian Revival chimney.

Figure 5-16. Georgian Revival chimney.

edges. The rectangular or curving shafts are often dressed up with pilasters, stringcourses, or terra-cotta panels incorporating sunbursts, sunflowers, or leafy designs. The caps may be pyramid shaped, boldly flared like trumpets, rounded similar to clay pots, or, rarely, plain stone slabs. Many-sided chimney pots and wider, squatter versions usually rest on substantial platforms. Some chimneys sit on the ridge; others rise from the roof, nestle against two dormers, or extend all the way to the ground. A few even shoot up through a dormer's roof or sweep down around a first-story window (*see* Figure 5-13 and *see* Figures 7-11 and 7-12).

SHINGLE STYLE, 1880 TO 1900

There are no standard chimneys on a Shingle Style house. Some are tall and massive; others are short and stocky (Figure 5-14). Still other, more slender ones rise only a few feet above the roof. The stacks are ordinarily rectangular, although their edges on larger, more sculptured versions may include some curves and tapered slopes. At times the stacks are decorated with recessed arches, plain panels, pilasters, bricks layered in contrasting patterns, molded bricks, or terra-cotta panels with sunbursts. Simple stone slab caps are common, but you will also discover widely flared or pyramid-shaped caps, several rounded flues, or small slanted roofs on top.

The chimneys are either brick or stone, with taller ones tending to be brick. Stone chimneys are likely to appear on a house having stone on the first story or on a veranda or tower. The stonework repeats the rough rubble or small boulders found elsewhere in these houses, adding to their rustic appearance. Chimneys may straddle the ridge, tuck into the roof line, spring from the roof, or rise from the ground. In most instances, when there is more than one chimney, their designs are similar even though one is a dominant chimney and any others are minor, smaller ones.

REVIVALS OF GEORGIAN AND FEDERAL STYLES, 1885 TO 1940

Chimneys on a Georgian Revival home may be high and imposing or low and unobtrusive, depending on whether the house is elaborate or simple (Figures 5-15 and 5-16). Most are made of brick, but stone occasionally was used. Chimneys on more pretentious houses may have molded bricks, recessed panels, corner pilasters, or flared shoulders. Caps are commonly plain stone slabs.

Chimney placement adds to the symmetry of the house — one on either end of a hipped or pitched roof. Sometimes they rise from the eaves when they are located on the front. In a home with double gam-

brel roofs, the chimney usually sits in the center at the juncture of the two ridges.

Federal Revival chimneys closely resemble the earlier prototypes. They are tall, slender, and rectangular with simple slab caps or short projecting flues. In most instances one chimney is placed on each corner of a hipped roof.

MAINTENANCE AND REPAIR

To work efficiently, a chimney must be correctly designed and well maintained. An improperly built chimney, or one that has not been attended to, can permit water to enter the house or present a fire hazard (Figure 5-17).

CONSTRUCTION GUIDELINES

By following certain guidelines, you will ensure a safe and efficient chimney. These practices also help to explain why chimney problems occur or whether a chimney is risky to use. Local building codes frequently regulate the construction of a chimney or the installation of a woodburning stove.

Recommendations for chimney height often suggest that the chimney extend at least 3 feet above a flat roof and at least 2 feet above the highest part of the roof. A chimney that is not tall enough may receive drafts deflected from the roof. To prevent these downdrafts, a hood or a terra-cotta chimney pot are ways to add the necessary height. A hood can be a flat stone or a reinforced concrete slab raised on brick piers 6 to 12 inches above the chimney top. Other reasons for installing a chimney hood are to keep out rain and to exclude any drafts from nearby trees or hills. Metal hoods are available, but they are less attractive. To prevent deterioration within, consider covering unused flues.

Guidelines for chimneys include measurements for the thickness of the chimney walls. They should be at least 4 inches thick for a brick chimney with a flue lining. For a brick chimney without a flue lining and for a chimney in a location exposed to strong winds, the thickness increases to no less than 8 inches. The walls of a stone chimney should be at least 12 inches thick. Because of its great weight a chimney requires a strong foundation. Some chimneys have their own foundations and their own footings. The bottom of the footings should be below the frost line, the lowest point below the surface at which the soil freezes.

The flue is the passage in the chimney through which smoke and hot gases move to the outside. To reduce the risk of fire, each fireplace or other heating unit demands an individual flue, although hot-water heaters often share a flue. If the flues are sep-

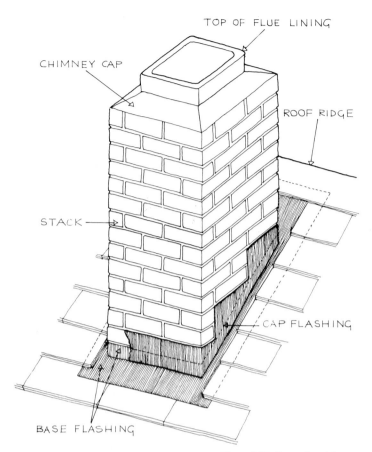

CHIMNEY CAP

TOP OF FLUE LINING

ROOF RIDGE

STACK

CAP FLASHING

BASE FLASHING

Figure 5-17. Parts of a chimney.

arated by a masonry divider at least 3¾ inches thick, called a wythe, two flues can be placed within the same chimney.

A flue often works better and is always safer with a lining, preferably of sections of fire clay at least ⅝ inch thick, with smooth joints between sections. Many chimneys on older homes do not have this kind of lining; in fact, Seventeenth Century and numerous Eighteenth Century chimneys had no lining originally. Burning wood in a fireplace with an unlined flue is an invitation to a house or chimney fire unless the flue has been found to be in sound condition after a careful inspection by an expert. In addition, unprotected bricks and mortar are apt to crack and disintegrate in such a chimney. Sometimes it is possible to install a steel flue lining in an old, unlined chimney.

Flues come in different shapes, but a round flue, not having corners where cold air and soot can collect, is most effective, although more difficult to install in brick or block chimneys. A vertical flue and one the same size from the bottom to the top provides a better draft. A change in direction should never exceed 45 degrees, with 30 degrees or less even more satisfactory.

A good practice is to leave a firestop of 2 inches between the chimney and all wood framing such as

beams, joists, and studs. One-half inch is an acceptable distance between the chimney and the framing only when chimney walls are at least 8 inches of solid masonry. This space should be filled with an incombustible material. Where the chimney cuts through the roof, a 2-inch space should exist to help prevent fires and to permit movement or expansion of the chimney.

Metal flashing installed in two layers seals the opening between the roof and the chimney. The bottom, or base, flashing extends under the roofing materials at least 4 inches and rests flat against the chimney side. The cap flashing, or counterflashing, laps over the base flashing on the chimney wall with its top embedded in the mortar of a brick or stone chimney or attached with nails and roofing cement to a stucco chimney. Joints are soldered except where the cap flashing extends over the base flashing.

To keep water from collecting at the back of a chimney located on a sloping roof, a cricket is set at the rear of the chimney (Figure 5-18). A cricket is a small double-pitched roof covered with metal flashing which reaches under the roofing material and stands against the back of the chimney under the cap flashing.

A chimney cap slopes away from the flue to shed water swiftly. An extension of the flue at least 4 inches above this cap is recommended. Another addition to the chimney top may be a spark arrester, nothing more than a rust-resistant wire mesh with openings between ½ and ⅝ inch. The wire mesh completely covers the flue, extending 12 inches or more above the chimney cap. Its purpose is to diminish the chance of sparks reaching a combustible surface, and it also keeps out birds and small animals.

CARE

Chimney repairs may not be possible for many owners of older homes because of the dangers of working on high or steep roofs and the special skills needed. Structural defects in a chimney also demand expert assistance. These include a leaning chimney stack, pipes or wires entering the flue, or two uses converging on one flue. Another serious problem is smoke flowing out of cracks in the chimney stack. In this case do not use the chimney until the trouble is eliminated.

The homeowner should inspect the chimney every fall. If this cannot be done from the roof, use binoculars for the task. To inspect the chimney:

• Examine the condition of the chimney materials for soundness and for cracks. For interior chimneys, investigate the condition of chimney materials from the attic and look for signs of leaks.

- Learn whether the chimney is vertical. It should not lean perilously.
- Search for cracks in the joints between the chimney stack and the cap and between the cap and the flue.
- Check the material of the cap for cracks and disintegration.
- Look at the flashing for rust, holes, and looseness.
- Notice whether the spark arrester is clean, securely attached to the chimney, and in good condition.
- Find out whether the inside of the flue is intact and sufficiently clean. Use a flashlight or an electric light lowered into the flue from the top to help you see, or look up the chimney from the fireplace opening. These methods will work only for straight flues. For slanted flues, try lighting a fire with a crumbled sheet of paper, gradually placing more sheets on the fire. You will learn whether the flue is clear, but not whether it is clean.

Flashing. Chimney problems are often problems with the chimney flashing. Flashing defects can cause water to run into the interior of the house. Repairing the base flashing may require removing some of the roofing material—a job for a professional. The cap flashing can separate from the mortar. For this repair it is necessary to clean out the old mortar, put back the flashing, and fill the opening with new mortar. For small gaps in the metal flashing, use a drop of solder; for larger holes, a metal patch.

Cracks. Water working its way through cracks in the chimney can lead to disintegration of the chimney materials or condensation on the inside walls of the house. When there is no flue lining, cracks in the bricks and mortar are especially dangerous. As soon as you notice a crack, take steps to repair it. If the problem is loose, crumbling, or missing mortar, repoint the problem area. Use the same type of mortar as the original mortar. Chapter 8, Walls, tells more about repointing masonry. Caulk any cracks found in the joint between the cap and the flue and between the top of the stack and the cap. Use mortar to fill gaps within the cap or stack. Cracks may arise from the stress of a television antenna strapped to the chimney. Be sure this situation has not produced the problem.

With the aid of a helper or two with strong lungs, you can carry out a smoke test to learn the location of leaks. Build a fire of paper, straw, or wood at the base of the flue above the damper. Light the fire. Once the fire is burning strongly, close the damper until the opening is about 1 inch. Placing a wet blanket over the fireplace opening will prevent smoke from entering the room. The next step is to cover the outlet at the top of the chimney with a wet blanket or wet burlap. Search for smoke escaping from the exterior of the chimney and into the attic and the rooms behind which the chimney passes.

Cleaning. Soot, dirt, creosote, and other matter can clog the chimney. Annual inspections will inform you of the condition of the flue or flue lining. When a woodburning stove is in frequent use, the interior of the chimney may call for cleaning several times a year. You may be able to reach the inside with special chimney brushes on extension handles, although a complete cleaning by professionals may also be necessary. Cleaning should be done with care to protect both the flue lining and the mortar joints.

REPLACEMENT

Uncorrectable defects in a chimney and repairs too substantial to be practical require chimney replacement. Sometimes, too, chimney stacks were altered in the past to accommodate a stove or to conform to the current architectural fashion. In these cases, hire a chimney expert to duplicate the original shape, proportions, placement, and materials when the chimney is a highly visible or a prominent feature of the house. A simpler version of the initial design without elaborate ornamentation is an acceptable alternative for an inconspicuous chimney or for one with decoration too costly to replace. A metal stack is out of place on an older home.

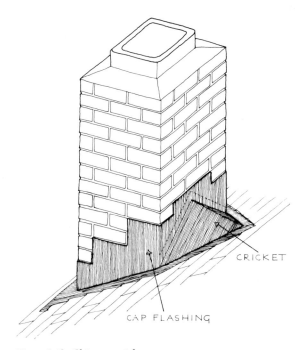

Figure 5-18. Chimney cricket.

CHAPTER SIX

GABLES

Gables may be major or minor features of an older house, or they may be totally absent. Whether gables appear and what form they take depends upon the type of roof, the architectural style, local building customs, and the preferences of the initial owner or builder.

A gable is the upper portion of a wall at the end of the roof extending from the eaves or the cornice to the ridge. For a double-pitched roof, the gable will be the shape of a vertical triangle with the slopes of the roof line determining the steepness of the angles. Gambrel roofs have gambrel-shaped gables. Jerkin-head gables are rare. (Chapter 4, Roofs, describes the different roof types.)

The simplest gables are on the end walls under a pitched or a gambrel roof, but gables can assume different forms. Some project beyond a wall below; others sit sideways, interrupting the main roof's eaves. Gables may top turrets and bay, bow, or oriel windows, and they may break the roof's smooth silhouette with their pointed peaks. In some homes a gable dominates the front or even encloses the entire side in a sweeping triangular shape. You will find small, medium, and large gables and quiet and ostentatious ones. Some have windows to light third floors; others are mostly decorative. The variety is seemingly endless.

When gables occur, chances are they are original because gables are usually constructed as an integral part of a house. They provide a clue to dating an older home. The windows, wall materials, or decoration, however, may have been altered. Occasionally, too, gables were added if an early roof line was changed to update the house.

Aside from providing light or additional head clearance inside, gables are pleasing components of older homes. They may even be their most noticeable feature. By retaining the original gables and properly renovating any deteriorated or unsuitably altered ones, you will be respecting the important contribution gables make to the house's appearance.

DESIGN

A gable may have undergone radical surgery in the past and now looks significantly different from the initial design. To help ascertain if the gables are original or modified:

- Examine the exterior and interior construction for any evidence of alterations. Is the construction material new? Are there old nails?

- Inspect the wall materials. Except for some masonry homes, gables are commonly sheathed in wood clapboard or wood shingles. Finding asbestos or other synthetic siding is a sure sign that a gable has been changed.

- Look at other homes of a similar style in the neighborhood. Do they have gables? If so, where are they located and how are they treated?

- Search the windows for hints, such as mortise and tenon joints, uneven glass, or small panes, that they are old.

- Study the decoration. Gables can be the most highly ornamented component of an older home. If there is ornamentation, does it resemble any found elsewhere on the house?

- Hunt for evidence that the house's main roof has been altered or raised by looking at the roof's understructure. A roofer, contractor, or architect may help determine if the main roof was modified. Sometimes to add more floor space or to make a house more fashionable, original roofs were changed. An alteration of this type could affect the presence, absence, location, or design of gables.

- Analyze the layers of paint on a wooden gable. The more coats of paint, the greater the probability that a gable is old.

- Scrutinize any old photographs of the house to see if gables are present.

- Review the following sections on architectural styles to learn whether gables are appropriate for the house.

Figure 6-1. Seventeenth Century Flemish gable.

SEVENTEENTH CENTURY

Most New England Seventeenth Century homes have steeply pitched roofs with simple gabled end walls. A third-floor casement window is often included. These gables may overhang slightly, projecting above the second story. At times decorative brackets support the overhanging gable, or carved drop ornaments accent each side.

Occasionally, one or more cross-gables appear on the front roof of houses built around 1700. These gables spring from the roof's eaves and have long sides reaching to the ridge. Cross-gables add usable third-floor space and usually have a casement window.

Every once in a while, especially in Salem, Massachusetts, gabled dormers are seen. These are dormer structures with tall, narrow gables stretching from the roof's eaves to the ridge. Another type of gable found in a few brick homes, particularly in Virginia, is the Flemish gable. Flemish wall gables are curved, rise above the main roof, and commonly incorporate tall chimneys (Figure 6-1).

EIGHTEENTH CENTURY— GEORGIAN, 1700 TO 1780

Early Georgian houses have plain gabled end walls when the roofs are gambrel or double-pitched, usually including one, two, or three windows. Ordinarily the gabled end walls of double-pitched roofed homes will have a horizontal crosspiece connecting the ends of the roof line, creating a triangular shape in the upper portion of the wall (Figure 6-2).

In a later Georgian home this triangle becomes a full pedimented gable, invariably resting on a cornice, with ornamental moldings, such as dentils, along the edges. A semicircular or other decorative window typically appears in the center. A later home may also have a central, projecting two-story pavilion capped with a pedimented gable, especially if the house has a hipped roof. Again, look for an ornamental porthole or fan-shaped window in the center and dentil moldings.

Figure 6-2. Georgian gable.

Figure 6-3. Greek Revival gable.

FEDERAL, 1790 TO 1830

Gables are not a common feature of a Federal house because the roof's slope, particularly on a hipped roof, in most cases is too low. Homes with pitched or gambrel roofs, however, will have gabled end walls. When windows appear in these gables, they line up with the windows below and resemble their designs.

GREEK REVIVAL, 1820 TO 1860

Pedimented gables are a hallmark of the Greek Revival style. These low triangular gables are formed by the roof slopes on the top and by a cornice or other horizontal crosspiece on the bottom (Figure 6-3). They are highly visible features on an end wall facing the street or as the top portion of a columned portico on a Greek temple. Townhouses are about the only type of home in this style lacking pedimented gables.

Predimented gables perched on the top of end walls most often rest on tall, two-story flat pilasters framing both sides of Greek Revival houses. Complete triangular shapes are common, but gables may spring up directly from the pilasters without the bottom crosspiece. The two sloping sides are invariably accented by a vertical facing band, called a fascia, and rake moldings. In other instances the roof slopes may jut out beyond the wall, decorated underneath with moldings or dentils which are also repeated on the horizontal crosspiece. Windows, when they appear, are placed in the center of the triangle. Look for oval portholes, semicircular fan-shaped windows, or a horizontal window with small rectangular panes.

GOTHIC REVIVAL, 1820 TO 1860

Enjoy the flamboyant, lavishly ornamented gables on Gothic Revival houses. Almost every home has at least one gable and many have several. Sometimes the entire roof seems like a series of intersecting gables.

Gothic Revival gables are steep and pointed, contributing to the vertical feeling of the house. Bargeboards with gingerbread embellish most gables, and if they are missing, a previous owner probably removed them. Bargeboards, also called vergeboards, are vertical boards which face the gable's roof edges or sit back slightly from them. Like lace ruffles, they are sheerly decorative, but their fanciful designs add a whimsical charm to these houses. They come in an astounding variety, with ideas inspired by guidebooks or created by local carpenters. Carved scallops, scrolls, trefoils, quatrefoils, garlands, and foliage are popular motifs (Figure 6-4). Also, look for repetitive

Figure 6-4. Gothic Revival gable.

cutout patterns. Bargeboards are always wood which could be easily carved or sawed into the desired shapes. Sometimes they adorn only the front gables, or they may also border end wall gables.

Pinnacles, or slender vertical pieces, often grace the gable's peak with one end rising above the roof and the other usually hanging below the bargeboard perhaps as a tassel-like pendant. Smaller finials shaped like spires may also perch above the gable's point.

Gabled wall dormers are a favorite feature of Gothic Revival homes. These hybrids have certain dormer characteristics, such as sharply pitched roofs and windows, but they are larger, taller, and more imposing than dormers and their ridges may intersect with the main roof's ridge. Often gabled dormers highlight the entrance by ascending directly above it.

Figure 6-5. Italianate gable.

ITALIANATE, 1845 TO 1880

Gables are rare on Italianate houses because low-pitched hipped roofs are prevalent. Sometimes, however, the edge of a hipped roof rises in the center to form a shallow angular gable which looks like two sides of a triangle (Figure 6-5).

When an Italianate home has a pitched roof or interlocking pitched roofs, gables with gently sloping sides occur on the end walls. The deeply projecting eaves are supported by lavish brackets, at times repeated in a series of twos or threes, or by modillions, horizontal scroll-like brackets.

STICK STYLE, 1855 TO 1900

Stick Style houses with steeply pitched roofs usually have gables on the end walls, possibly protruding over the second story. Sometimes this gable overhang is supported by braces, or slender brackets with little ornamentation. If the roof projects deeply, it, too, may have braces. Gables invariably have exposed framing echoing similar framing elsewhere in the house. Horizontal and vertical crosspieces as well as Xs and herringbone designs overlay the clapboard surface. In addition, any gable windows are outlined by this skeletal stickwork (Figure 6-6).

MANSARD, 1860 TO 1880

Do not expect to find gables on Mansard houses because their roofs are almost vertical on all four sides.

An unusual variation of a gabled wall dormer, however, occasionally appears when the roof line at the eaves surges upward in the center to form a gable with sweeping curved sides or a curved gambrel shape (Figure 6-7). These gabled dormers are usually on the third floor above the entrance with the wall extending into the roof area. An ornamental window, such as a porthole, often accents this type of gable.

Figure 6-6. Stick Style gable.

Figure 6-7. Mansard gable.

ROMANESQUE, 1875 TO 1895

Gabled wall dormers are prevalent on Romanesque homes (Figure 6-8 and *see* Figure 2-11). These extensions of the exterior wall rise to a sharp peak and have roofs joining the main roof either at the ridge or somewhat below it. They may be broad and wide or tall and narrow. Whether paired, grouped in a ribbon of windows, or recessed under a semicircular arch, the windows usually rest on a stone belt course and have another belt course along the top. Because belt courses are used elsewhere in most Romanesque homes, the gables closely relate to the design of the entire house.

Any decoration tends to be subtle. Small circles with delicate designs inside may accent the windows' corners, or dark-colored stones contrasting with the lighter-colored masonry walls may outline the windows. Finials now and then top the gables. Sharply pitched end wall gables are seen in a few homes. When they occur, the roof will probably be edged with stone.

Figure 6-8. Romanesque gabled wall dormer.

Figure 6-9. Queen Anne gable.

QUEEN ANNE, 1876 TO 1900

Queen Anne houses are teeming with gables. They are exuberant features, so much so that the style itself might be better named "Gabled." Rarely was a house designed without at least one eye-catching gable, and most often a single house is adorned with several different kinds (Figures 6-9 and 6-10).

Gables may appear almost anywhere. Look for them dominating steeply pitched end walls, projecting from the attic or second story, turning diagonally toward the main roof's ridge, crowning a two-story bay window, resting over a bow window, topping a turret, jutting out at the corners, peeking out shyly beneath another gable, or nestling against a chimney. Some gables are generous and expansive; others are moderate in size or even quite small. They also assume varied shapes. Expect to see sharp peaks, shallow triangles, deep pediments, curves, jerkin-heads, interlocking forms, or some with their corners cut. A few even have dormers on the sides.

A similar delight in surprises is seen in the gables' decorations. They may be plain—which is rare—or profuse. Simpler gables usually are bordered by a fascia or by moldings and are covered by a single type of wall material. More elaborate gables include all sorts of fanciful ornamentation: carved or cutout bargeboards, sunbursts, spindles, braces, brackets, half-timbering, strapwork, wood panels, plaster garlands, scrolls, flowers, pendants, dentils, or beading. Graceful finials or somewhat larger pinnacles sometimes accent the points. The small triangle at the gable's top is a target for special plaster or wooden embellishments. Wood shingle siding abounds with shingles cut in fascinating shapes: circles, squares, rectangles, and fish-scale, saw-tooth, diamond, or herringbone patterns. Frequently several varieties of shingles are combined in one gable, creating a richly textured surface.

Windows appear in most gables. There may be one, two, or three, generally smaller versions of the windows below, or a band of several windows. Occasionally the windows are recessed or they may hide behind a balcony.

The imaginative designs for Queen Anne gables came from many sources. Guidebooks showed ideas which were copied or modified. Catalogs offered different parts, such as fasciae, bargeboards, or plaster ornaments, to be combined at the builder's or owner's whims. In a neighborhood with many Queen Anne homes a local carpenter's personal stamp often is seen in the gable's design.

Figure 6-10. Queen Anne gable.

Figure 6-11. Shingle Style gable.

SHINGLE STYLE, 1880 TO 1900

Shingle Style houses incorporate gables in inventive ways. No matter what their size, shape, or location, shingles always cover all gables, subtly blending them into the overall design of the house. The gables tend to be broad and expansive, although some are sharply peaked. Long bands of horizontal windows appear frequently (Figure 6-11). Now and then a single window or a pair will be recessed with the shingles curving around from the wall's surface to meet the window's edge (Figure 6-12).

Because most homes in this style have pitched or gambrel roofs, or even both types combined, simple end wall gables are common. Third-floor gabled end walls with supporting brackets sometimes project boldly beyond the second story. In other cases, a wide, gently sweeping gambrel gable may reach out to enclose the second story. You may also find two interlocking gables—a larger one embracing a smaller one—nestled against a long front roof or twin gables perched above two adjacent second-story windows.

Gables can assume dramatic forms. Triangular end wall gables may sweep down to cover both the third and second floors, almost hiding the first story. At times the first floor may be reduced to a small central section with a massive peaked gable above it and single columns at the corners. An even more spectacular gable may cover the entire front, starting close to the ground and gently rising to the third floor, making the whole house front look like a long, shallow triangle snuggled against the ground.

Figure 6-12. Shingle Style gable.

Figure 6-13. Georgian Revival gable.

REVIVALS OF THE GEORGIAN AND FEDERAL STYLES, 1885 TO 1940

End wall gables appear on Georgian Revival houses when there are gambrel or pitched roofs (Figure 6-13). Sometimes on hipped-roofed homes the central portion of the front wall projects slightly, capped with a pedimented gable perhaps above a Palladian window. This type of gable may rest on two-story pilasters or engaged columns. Look for heavy dentils and moldings outlining the gable. Except for Federal Revival homes with pitched roofs and end wall gables, it is rare to find gables in these houses.

MAINTENANCE AND REPAIR

Before making any major changes, use your ingenuity to find ways to save the parts of a gable. Although gables are often high off the ground, making repairs difficult, the homeowner can accomplish some work from the inside. Knowing when repairs are necessary and possible will help you retain an original gable.

Regularly inspect a gable to be certain there are no problems (Figure 6-14). Look especially at the rake edges, windows, wall materials, paint, mortar on masonry walls, ornamentation, and the juncture of the wall and the gable if the materials are different.

The area where the rake edge meets the wall is often subject to moisture. Several measures are used to keep it dry. One is to place metal flashing at the rake edges, extending four inches beneath the roofing material and away from the gable's rake to form a drip edge. For bulky roofing materials, such as slate, pay special attention to the openings occurring at the rake between the courses of the material. One means of closing these gaps is to use separate pieces of metal flashing at each course bent over the rake edge (Figure 6-15). Also, check all joints at the cornice to be sure they are tight and caulked. To reduce moisture condensation, be certain the attic has adequate ventilation.

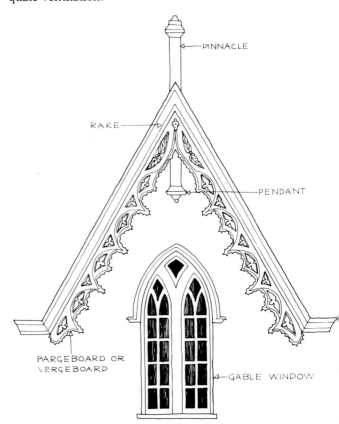

Figure 6-14. Parts of a gable.

Tight joints between different materials, parts of windows, various parts of the wall material, and the windows and the wall help prevent water from entering. At least once a year, inspect all these joints and caulk those needing a new sealant. Before applying the caulking, remove the old caulking and clean the area with a solvent. For added protection, keep all paint in good condition.

High gable windows are not always noticed. Make an effort to check them often to be sure they are closed. Inside storm windows and weatherstripping will help to keep out drafts and moisture. When a new window is needed, select one which is similar to the initial window in size, shape, number and arrangement of panes, materials, and decorations.

The wooden sections of gables are vulnerable. Examine these periodically. Without delay, caulk any small cracks. Fill larger cracks in the wood with oakum or another filler and caulk over the filler. Epoxy consolidants for strengthening the wood and epoxy fillers for cracks or small holes are other products useful for wood repair. A deteriorated portion of wood may be a candidate for a patch. Cut out the damaged portion of wood and with durable waterproof glue attach a new piece of the same size. For the patch, use wood treated with a wood preservative. Caulk the joints and paint or stain the new wood to match the wood already in place. The sections Small Cracks in Woodwork and Large Cracks and Rotting Wood in Chapter 11, Windows, describe more about wood repair.

If any parts of the gable require replacing, try to duplicate the color, texture, dimensions, and ornamentation of the original part. Rather than tearing off decoration with missing pieces or damaged materials, search for a new piece. For instance, stock molding may match the old wood molding. Sometimes you can create a good substitute from stock wood pieces of the same dimensions, but without the elaborate features of the original. Always treat any wood replacement with wood preservative.

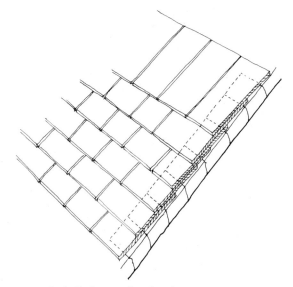

Figure 6-15. Flashing at the rake edge.

You may be able to reproduce a rotted or missing piece of bargeboard or other decoration with new wood of the same dimensions and shape. Trace an outline on cardboard of the required design. Use either a scroll saw, band saw, or hand sabre saw to cut the design on wood of the same thickness as the decoration to be replaced. Glue the new piece in place, caulk the joints, and paint to match the existing ornamentation. When the replacement is on the edge, screw a metal plate behind it to hold it tightly.

Manufacturers producing high-quality polyurethane architectural parts may sell decoration similar to the original embellishments on the gable. Another solution is to locate a craftworker with the skills to reproduce the ornamentation. It may be possible, too, to move original ornamentation from a little-seen location of the house as a replacement for visible decoration. This procedure is risky because ornamentation is often difficult to remove, and it may break in the process.

CHAPTER SEVEN

DORMERS

Dormers are not just a flourish, but a major component of many older homes. Even though they perch high on the roof and are not as obvious as other features, dormers enhance a house if their design harmonizes with its architectural style. Dormers are useful, too, providing light and ventilation to third floors and attics, increasing the interior head clearance, and transforming unusable sections of the house into extra space.

A dormer rises vertically out of the roof and has walls, one or more windows, and a separate roof of its own. Some dormers are bold; others are quiet. They come in all sorts of sizes and shapes: rectangular, round-headed, oval, eyebrow, or square. Dormer roofs most often are peaked, or gabled, but gambrel, hipped, jerkin-head, and flat roofs also appear. Dormers may be plain, or they may be richly ornamented with pediments, decorative shingles, pilasters, colonettes, brackets, scrolls, keystones, and gingerbread.

Once you are certain the dormers on a house are original features, appropriate reproductions, or suitable additions, take care not to disfigure them or allow them to deteriorate.

DESIGN

The type of dormer suitable for an older home depends upon its architectural style, when it was built, and the locality. Even though the general design of dormers, especially their shape and window type, is usually consistent within a style, local craftworkers often created their own variations in construction and ornaments. To discover these special local characteristics, look carefully at the dormers in other similar style homes in the neighborhood and compare them with yours and with the dormer designs described in this chapter.

The presence or absence of dormers and their types are not always accurate clues for dating a house. Dormers were never, or rarely, found in certain styles and in simpler homes. In some instances dormers were added long after the house was built to make an attic into a room, or dormers were sometimes embellished later to update an unfashionable style.

There are several ways to tell if a dormer is original or an appropriate addition:

- Examine the interior and exterior structure of the dormer. Compare the materials or building methods with a part of the house you are certain is original. Are they the same? Is there evidence the dormer is newer?

- Inspect the window or windows. Are there mortise-and tenon joints connecting the rails and the stiles? Does the glass have imperfections such as waves or bubbles? Is the style of the windows like the windows below? Dormer windows may not be an exact duplicate of others in the house, but they should bear a family resemblance.

- Look carefully at any decoration. Is it similar to ornamentation found elsewhere in the house?

- Check the roof. Is the roofing material the same as the main roof? Does the roof pitch and shape relate to the primary roof line? Roof shapes are not always exactly alike. Mansard roofs never have mansard-roofed dormers, but it is common, for example, to find gable dormers on gable roofs.

- Study the dormer's sides, or cheeks. Often cheeks are covered with the same material as the roof. Wood clapboards or shingles like the clapboards or shingles found on the body of the house may sheath other dormers.

- Analyze the layers of paint. If they are the same as the number of layers on a part of the exterior you have identified as original, the dormer was most likely constructed when the house was built.

- Search the area around the dormer on both the outside and the inside for hints that the dormer may be new or altered. For instance, is the roofing material near the dormer newer than the rest of the roof?

- Observe where the dormers are placed on the roof and how their location relates to the windows below. Symmetrical styles tend to have regularly placed dormers while irregular locations occur in the freer, more informal styles.

- Compare one dormer in the house with another. There are some exceptions, but dormers in the same house usually resemble each other.

- Review the following sections which describe the type of dormer suitable for a particular architectural style.

SEVENTEENTH CENTURY

Dormers, first used in England and later copied in America, almost never occur on Seventeenth Century homes. Instead windows in the end gables bring light and air to the third floors. If there are dormers, particularly in New England, they were likely added later.

A few exceptions are seen in certain localities. You may find shed dormers, the oldest type, on Flemish gable roofs on homes in northern New Jersey and New York and on Long Island (Figure 7-1). Occasionally shed dormers appear on early gambrel roofs and on a few Southern houses. Shed dormers are simple vertical structures with flat sloping roofs extending from the main roof. These dormers pop up through the main roof and look as if someone could snap them shut again. Windows are without decoration and either wood shingles or the roofing material usually covers the sides. Sometimes only one shed dormer sits in the center of the roof front, or there may be two, three, or four dormers.

The stair dormer is unique to Southern homes, especially in Maryland and South Carolina. Stair dormers occur in the rear of one-and-a-half story houses having a staircase in the back to give access to the half story above. Their dimensions are wide to accommodate the upper portion of the staircase. Usually stair dormers have pitched roofs with a triangular gable end and no ornamentation. On clapboard homes this same material covers the dormer's walls.

EIGHTEENTH CENTURY— GEORGIAN, 1700 TO 1780

Dormers made their grand entrance in the eighteenth century. At first they were small, narrow structures projecting timidly from the roof, seemingly tacked on almost as an afterthought. Gradually, throughout the century, they became more significant, even elaborate, features, jutting out from hipped, gabled, or gambrel roofs. Only the simpler Georgian homes, houses with very low hipped roofs, or ones with windows in third-floor gable ends did not include dormers.

Resembling a doghouse (a Southern name for this dormer), an early Georgian dormer usually has a simple peaked roof and a rectangular window with a low-pitched gable above. In certain areas, particularly in the South, these early dormers have small hipped roofs.

Around 1740 the gable above the window became a small, shallow triangular pediment. At first the pediments had no decoration except a simple molding along the edges. Later, dentils, or a band of miniature rectangles that look like teeth, echoing the dentils of a cornice under the eaves, often accented the pediments.

By the 1750s arched dormers appeared (Figure 7-2). The window usually has a shallow, arched top, a shape repeated above in the dormer's roof line. Sometimes this is the only arched window in the house. Larger homes frequently combine arched and pedimented dormers, either alternating them or having two pedimented dormers flank each side of an arched central dormer.

Late Georgian dormers are even more ornate and imposing, often adorned with either pilasters or engaged columns, and topped by semicircular heads or scroll pediments (Figure 7-3). Although narrow proportions are still found, late Georgian dormers tend to be wider and less fragile in appearance than earlier ones. The dormers are carefully aligned with the windows below. At times five dormers line up exactly above five windows across the front. When there are three dormers, they are evenly spaced on the roof with the central one over the entrance. Houses with hipped roofs may have dormers just on the front, on the front and back, or on all four sides.

FEDERAL, 1780 TO 1830

Whether or not dormers appear on a Federal home depends on the type of roof, the size of the house, and where it is located. Houses with nearly flat roofs rarely have dormers because there is little usable attic space. More numerous are dormers on rural homes, houses with sharply pitched roofs, and townhouses. Most often these dormers are tall and narrow with gable roofs, graceful pediments, or shallow arches (Figure 7-4). The windows have slender muntins and generally repeat the six over six panes of the windows below, although the panes may be smaller. Sometimes a round-arched window will have arched muntins at the top. In many cases the sides are covered with wood clapboard.

Federal dormers relate to the symmetrical placement of all windows in the house. A single dormer, for example, will be centered on the roof of a simple townhouse. On houses with pitched roofs two or three dormers may sit on the front roof directly above or in between the windows below.

GREEK REVIVAL, 1820 TO 1860

Dormers on Greek Revival houses are rare. Instead frieze windows or windows in end gables customarily light the upper floors.

There are at least two types of Greek Revival homes where dormers may occur. In townhouses dormers are occasionally placed on pitched roofs. These dormers usually have unpretentious pediments and simple decoration with classical motifs. Dormers may also be seen on columned Southern plantation homes with hipped roofs. Again, these are plain, and they often resemble the doghouse dormer.

GOTHIC REVIVAL, 1820 TO 1860

Whimsical creations, Gothic Revival dormers are plentiful, often appearing in unexpected places. Most dormers have sharply sloping roofs with deep overhanging eaves (Figure 7-5). On rare occasions they have very steep shed roofs. The windows, whether pointed, round-headed, or rectangular, are always narrow, reinforcing the house's vertical emphasis. When the house has vertical board siding, the same type of siding may cover the dormer's cheeks and frequently the front, too.

Decorations are most inventive. Bargeboards abound. These richly ornamented vertical boards edge the peaked roof line or hang slightly behind it. Typically, bargeboards are wide and bold, commanding attention and displaying all kinds of imaginative designs: scrolls, circles, lobes, swags, scallops, foliage, flowers, or cutout patterns. A central pinnacle, tapering upward to a point, gracefully accents the peak of many dormers. It may also pierce through the roof and bargeboard below, ending in a knoblike pendant suspended above the window.

Gothic Revival dormers do not always sit on the main roof. Sometimes the second-story windows, capped by tall peaked roofs, protrude above the roof line. Because this kind of dormer is an extension of the wall, it is called a wall dormer. Gabled dormers, described in Chapter 6, Gables, also appear on Gothic Revival homes.

ITALIANATE, 1845 TO 1880

Italianate houses rarely have dormers because the roofs are generally low pitched. When dormers do appear, they are usually on large homes with more sharply sloping roofs. Look for dormers with deep overhanging eaves supported by imposing carved brackets, echoing the main roof (Figure 7-6). Paired round-headed windows are commonly used.

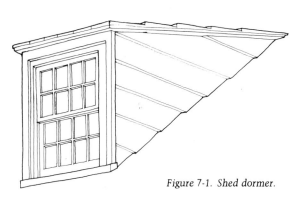

Figure 7-1. *Shed dormer.*

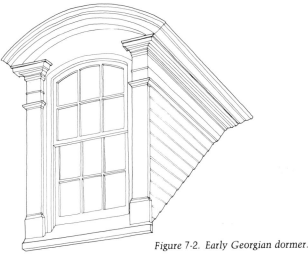

Figure 7-2. *Early Georgian dormer.*

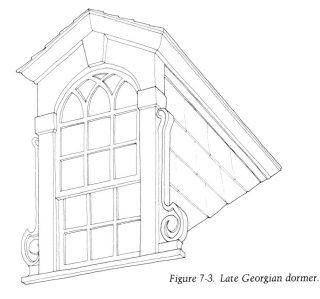

Figure 7-3. *Late Georgian dormer.*

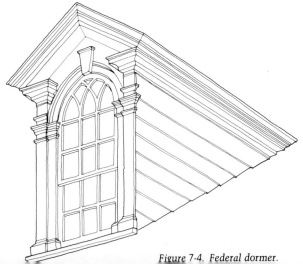

Figure 7-4. *Federal dormer.*

Figure 7-5. Gothic Revival dormer.

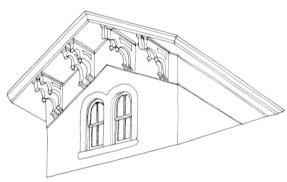

Figure 7-6. Italianate dormer.

Figure 7-7. Stick Style dormer.

STICK STYLE, 1855 TO 1900

Dormers on Stick Style homes are striking features (Figure 7-7). Most often they are wide and quite large. A bisected triangle, called a "king-post truss," marks the peak of many dormers. In simple versions the triangle's base is a horizontal crosspiece connecting both sides of the roof line near the top. A vertical post reaches from the center of the crosspiece to the roof's peak, dividing the triangle into two sections. Intriguing variations of this motif occur, often adding other vertical or diagonal pieces. A "king-post truss" pretends to brace the dormer's roof, but it is more decorative than structural.

Diagonal boards on top of the clapboards are another characteristic of larger dormers. This exposed skeleton resembles similar stickwork seen elsewhere in the house.

Many different kinds of roofs appear on these dormers, often several varieties in one house. Look for peaked, shed, and jerkin-head roofs as well as roofs that are tall and pointed like a witch's hat and end in a gentle flare resembling the edges of the hat.

Stick Style dormers have one, two, or three windows with the number of panes similar to other windows in the house. Often the windows are recessed under a broad overhanging roof. These dormers frequently have diverse decorations: brackets, pinnacles, cutout designs, narrow grooves, and finely chiseled small circles. Horizontal clapboards usually cover the sides, repeating the siding on the house. Generally the dormers line up with the second-story windows below.

MANSARD, 1860 TO 1880

Dormers are exuberant parts of Mansard homes. They are lavish, vibrant accents on the roof, clamoring to be seen and enjoyed (Figure 7-8).

A standard Mansard dormer does not exist. All sorts of shapes occur: triangular pediments, rounded or segmental arches, drip hoods, ovals, circles, and wide-shouldered caps with arched or triangular peaks (Figure 7-9). The windows may be rectangular, round-headed, eyebrow-headed, oval, or, more rarely, circular. Single windows are common, but paired windows sometimes add special emphasis to a dormer. Several types of dormers may occur on the same house.

Occasionally dormers are simple, but usually they are opulent, richly sculptured structures exuding ornamentation. Many layers of moldings may be piled one upon the other on the top to resemble a bonnet. Embellishments include finials, small urns, keystones, garlands, circles with radiating foliage, and scrolls. Pilasters, engaged columns, or curved decorations may outline the window's sides, and every once in a while a small balustrade adorns a dormer.

Often dormers appear on all four sides of a mansard roof, and only rarely are they absent. Frequently dormers are directly over the lower windows. Sometimes, however, Mansard dormers seem out of keeping with the house. In these circumstances it is probable the mansard roof and dormers were added later to provide more light, space, and ventilation to the third floor and to make an earlier house more fashionable.

ROMANESQUE, 1875 TO 1895

Romanesque dormers are often wide, imposing structures sitting firmly on the main roof, or they may be wall dormers. The windows of wall dormers are flush with the exterior wall's surface and rise above the eaves into the main roof (Figure 7-10). Usually these wall dormers are topped with a steep triangular gable which may also be flush with the wall. They frequently rest on a belt course, with another belt course appearing above where the dormer meets the roof line.

Roof dormers may have steeply pitched gables quite likely decorated with a rounded arch and sun rays. Their one or two windows may be flanked by colonettes or several small, squat columns. Graceful finials, like tiny spires, occasionally rise from the dormer's peak. Yet another kind of dormer encloses a band of three horizontal windows. You will also see tall dormers with a window placed in the gable above the lower window as well as hipped-roof dormers. A single house may include various dormers, and the location of the dormers may be random although some align with other windows.

QUEEN ANNE, 1876 TO 1900

Most often dormers on Queen Anne houses are ingenious structures put in surprising spots (Figures 7-11 and 7-12). They nestle against one or both sides of the chimney, perch on the roofs of corner towers, or spring up from the second-story wall. Only a small number line up with the windows below.

These dormers nearly always have unusual shapes and abundant ornamentation. They may be small triangles with deep overhanging roofs hiding a fan-shaped window, broad rectangles with peaked roofs, or tall and narrow versions. A few are wide and quite large, sometimes surrounding a Palladian window or a broad round-arched window, and perhaps boasting a balcony. Now and then you may

Figure 7-9. Mansard dormer.

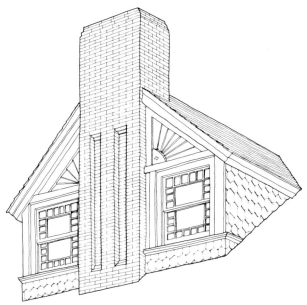

Figure 7-12. Queen Anne dormer.

Figure 7-10. Romanesque wall dormer.

Figure 7-11. Queen Anne dormer.

even find small dormers shaped like eyebrows. Wall dormers, often with steeply pitched roofs, also appear with either the top of a second-story window paralleling the roof line or with the bottom of the window cutting through the eaves. Besides the single or paired front windows, windows may dress up the cheeks.

Queen Anne dormers are rich in delightful decoration: sunbursts, cutout patterns, floral motifs, scrolls, circles, shingles, a ruffled crown, and, more rarely, a "king-post truss" bisecting a triangle at the peak. Lavishly carved brackets may support an overhanging dormer roof. Some homes have dormers on all four sides of the roof, frequently mixing designs. Not all houses have dormers, however, especially when there are many gables.

SHINGLE STYLE, 1880 TO 1900

Shingle Style dormers tend to be unadorned and to fit snugly into the main roof. Shingles envelop the dormers everywhere—on the roof, cheeks, front, and gable—and the dormers do not seem to be separate structures (Figure 7-13). Some dormers line up with the windows below; others do not; and not all houses have them.

Various designs occur. Some have moderately pitched roofs; others are more sharply peaked. Some have gambrel roofs; others have extensive overhangs hiding their windows. Shed roofs and roofs with four or more slopes are more rare. Under one dormer roof there may be one window, twin windows, or a band of three windows. Every once in a while, two dormers are paired, with their roofs touching each other.

Two types of dormers are characteristic of these homes: an eyebrow dormer and a gently curved convex dormer. In an eyebrow dormer the window

Figure 7-13. Shingle Style dormer.

Figure 7-14. Shingle Style eyebrow dormer.

peeks out shyly from a slight undulation in the roof (Figure 7-14). Often eyebrow dormers occur in unexpected places, quietly interrupting a long, unbroken roof. Convex dormers bulge out from the roof with shingles covering their curved vertical sides and with flat or low sloping roofs.

REVIVALS OF THE GEORGIAN AND FEDERAL STYLES, 1885 TO 1940

Dormers on Georgian Revival homes are bold, opulent structures, differing markedly from the more refined earlier versions of this style. Occasionally simple pedimented dormers appear, but elaborately ornamented, heavy-handed interpretations of classical dormers are more usual (Figure 7-15).

Among the pediment designs are scrolls, round-arched and gambrel shapes, and pediments separated, or "broken," in the center (Figure 7-16). They tend to be wide and heavy, seeming to overpower the window underneath by their size. Look for urns at the pediment's peak and for scrolls, swags, garlands, and floral designs as embellishments. Dentils may accent the juncture between the pediment and the walls. Fluted pilasters or engaged columns often flank the windows. Dormer windows may repeat the shape and number of panes seen elsewhere in the house, or they may differ. Six or nine rectangular panes over one single pane was popular. At times the upper sash has curved muntins or a geometrical pattern.

Georgian Revival dormers usually fall into line with the windows below. They may, however, cluster together with, for example, three dormers connected by a decorative railing. Less pretentious Georgian Revival houses have no dormers, and they rarely appear on Federal Revival homes.

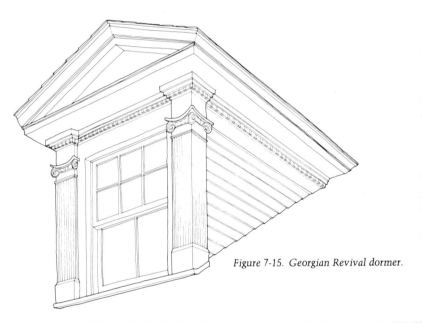

Figure 7-15. Georgian Revival dormer.

Figure 7-16. Georgian Revival dormer.

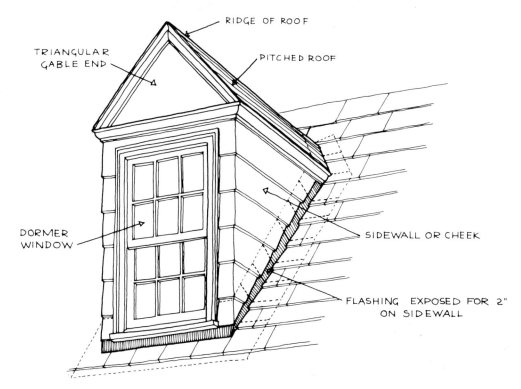

RIDGE OF ROOF

TRIANGULAR GABLE END

PITCHED ROOF

DORMER WINDOW

SIDEWALL OR CHEEK

FLASHING EXPOSED FOR 2" ON SIDEWALL

Figure 7-17. Parts of a dormer.

MAINTENANCE AND REPAIR

The key lifesaving procedure to perform on dormers is an inspection every time you examine the roof of the house, or at least once a year. Dormers are in the advance line of the weather's attack, and they are especially vulnerable. Their rapid deterioration is not unusual.

Where should you look for dormer problems (Figure 7-17)?

- Examine the roofing material and the siding for deterioration.
- Investigate the flashing where the dormer sides meet the main roof for looseness, cracking, or missing pieces.
- Check the window sash, frame, sill, and decoration for rotting or degenerating wood and the condition of the glass and putty.
- Be alert for cracks between the window and the wall of the dormer.
- Study the paint on the window, siding, and any ornamentation for indications that repainting is needed.
- Be aware of any evidence of weakness within the understructure such as sagging ridges or rotting rafters.
- Inspect the inside for stains, peeling paint, and other signs of leaks.

Homeowners can do some minor repairs to dormers. When the dormers are on a high or steep roof and when the repairs are major, professional assistance may be necessary. In Chapters 4, 8, and 11,

Roofs, Walls, and Windows, read the Maintenance and Repair sections for ways to solve particular problems. By making all possible repairs from the inside, you will avoid the hazards of working on the roof.

ROOFING AND FLASHING

A common source of leaks is loose or cracked flashing where the dormer sides join the main roof. On dormers the flashing interweaves with the roofing material and turns up under the siding, extending for a minimum of 8 inches for sound protection. In areas of heavy rainfall, keep the dormer siding 2 or 3 inches above the house roof, exposing the flashing. Seal the edges of the siding with a wood preservative, or use wood already treated with a preservative. Flashing should also shield the joint between the dormer roof and the main roof. Trouble with the flashing may be tricky for the amateur to solve because it often requires removing part of the siding and roofing. Professional help may be needed.

If the dormer roof is in poor enough condition to demand a new roof, match the material of the main roof and keep the pitch and shape of the original dormer roof when these suit the design of the house.

SIDING

In cases where the dormer siding must be replaced, try to discover the original siding, perhaps by poking through several layers of old material. Dormer siding usually duplicates either the roofing materials or the wood siding of the house. Avoid asbestos and imitation bricks and stones which do not belong on older houses. A good choice of dormer siding will enhance the house. For instance, vertical boards on a Gothic Revival dormer will reinforce the vertical effect of a house with similar wooden siding.

WINDOWS

Dormer windows are often forgotten because they are out of sight. Look at them frequently to be certain they are closed tightly against the cold, rain, and snow. Installing storm windows, easily done on the inside, will keep out drafts and water. Weatherstripping also helps insulate the top floor.

Dormer windows should resemble the dormer's original windows. When installing new dormer windows, remember that modern awning, picture, and jalousie windows are not acceptable. In general, new dormer windows should match the width of the windows in the house and the type of sash. The number of panes and the window's height may differ from the other windows in the house. Often dormer windows are shorter and have fewer panes.

CONSISTENCY OF DESIGN

When repairing a dormer on a house with several dormers of the same design, consistency is important. These dormers were meant to look alike. For instance, if one dormer requires a new window, roof, or siding, be certain these match the window, roof, and siding of other similar dormers in highly visible locations. It may be necessary in some circumstances to make changes on all the dormers at the same time to ensure their uniform appearance.

ORNAMENTATION

With a little investigation you may be able to match badly worn or missing pieces of ornamentation. First, check the extent of the damage, for a possible solution is replacing only the necessary portion of the decoration. Manufacturers specializing in stock wood moldings or high-quality polyurethane decorations may have suitable products for dormers. Various catalogs are available listing these firms. Also, a craftworker may duplicate the part required. Decorations on dormers, even though they are far off the ground, enliven an older house, and you will miss them if they are not replaced.

REPLACEMENT

Adding or removing dormers, replacing an existing original dormer, and choosing the best dormer design for a home are major decisions when the dormer is in a conspicuous part of the house. Study the Design section of this chapter or seek a knowledgeable architect's guidance. When not doing the work yourself, hire a competent carpenter and roofer.

REPRODUCING AN APPROPRIATE DORMER

Suppose you have exhausted every possibility of repair. The entire dormer, an attractive asset to the house, is so far gone nothing can save it. What do you do next?

When the dormer is in a prominent location of the house, replace the hopeless, old dormer only with an accurate reproduction. Never let more up-to-date materials and modern styles tempt you. Make a pattern for the new design by measuring the parts of the old dormer. A skilled carpenter can then build a new dormer by following these dimensions. One way to create a less costly version of the dormer is to duplicate all parts and their dimensions, but not the details. Dentils, for example, could be omitted in the interest of economy.

Keep the new dormer in the same location as the one being replaced. Dormers are a considered part of the house's design, and their placement relates to the windows beneath. In many styles the dormers line up with the windows below, or they sit halfway between them.

REMOVING AN UNACCEPTABLE DORMER

Dormers which are original or suit the style of the house should never be removed or blocked off. Sometimes a dormer is a later addition that does not blend with the design of the house. Or, perhaps, it is in the wrong place, or it has awkward dimensions. In these cases consider removing the dormer, but only after talking to an architect or a competent builder to find out what, if any, structural problems will be encountered.

If you take out a dormer, adding a small window in an existing gable end is another way to bring light and air into the attic. Gable windows should resemble other windows in the house, although, like dormer windows, they may be shorter and have fewer panes.

ADDING A DORMER

A new dormer, you may have concluded, will increase the space, light, or air in an upper floor or attic. The best location for an extra dormer is in the back or on an inconspicuous side of the house. Do not place wide, modern dormers where they can be easily seen, for they will disfigure the appearance of an older home. If the dormer must be added in the front, match as closely as possible the roof pitch, the roof and wall materials, and the window style and decoration of the house. Keep in mind the position of the windows underneath when choosing the dormer's location.

CHAPTER EIGHT

WALLS

Exterior walls are a protective covering similar to skin. They prevent the weather from deteriorating the structure of the house and help to keep the inside warm in winter, cool in summer, and dry. They also support the building. No matter what size or style house, the walls are so pervasive that they quickly draw your attention. Neglecting regular maintenance and significantly changing the original materials will drastically alter the house's appearance.

Make every effort to discover whether the wall materials on an older house are original or similar to the initial walls. If they are, carefully preserve them, for they contribute to a home's individuality. Replace unsuitable or worn wall materials by duplicating the initial ones as closely as possible.

DESIGN

Most older houses are wood, brick, stone, stucco, or plaster, or combinations of two or more wall materials. The original wall material on a house was selected for several reasons: the availability of a certain material, how much it cost, whether there were local workers skilled in using it, how the climate affected it, whether the house was a city or country house, what the building codes allowed, and whether a wall material was considered appropriate for the house's architectural style. Sometimes, however, the choice was simply based on traditional usage in an area.

To determine if the wall material on an older house is the original material, an adequate replacement, or an ill-conceived substitute:

- Examine the exterior and interior wall construction. On wooden houses, are there short, narrow clapboards, wide, overlapping flat boards, flush horizontal boards, or vertical board and batten siding? Houses built before 1700 and many constructed as late as the mid-1700s have stone, clay, or brick infilling between the studs behind the

clapboard rather than the later sheathing underlayer.

- Observe the nails if the walls have wood siding. Until about 1800 nails were generally hand-wrought with wide flat heads, varying lengths, rectangular shanks tapered on all four sides, and hand-hammered points. Between 1790 and 1830 machine-cut nails began to be produced in factories, eventually replacing the handmade types. Cut nails taper on only two sides of their shanks as they were cut from plates, and the two cut sides show marks from the cutting machine. Their ends are usually squared off and not pointed. From about 1800 to the 1830s cut nails had irregular hammered heads, while nails made after the late 1830s ordinarily had level and regular stamped heads. Wire nails came into use for homebuilding during the third quarter of the nineteenth century (Figure 8-1).

Warning: Finding a certain type of nail may be a useful clue to the age of an older home, but it is unwise to rely on nails for dating a house. Hand-wrought nails, for instance, were employed by some builders years after the introduction of cut nails, particularly in rural areas, and cut nails were favored by many builders into the twentieth century.

- Look for synthetic siding materials such as asbestos, aluminum, asphalt shingles, foamstone, or vinyl (Figure 8-2). These are new materials never initially utilized on an older house. Most often, synthetic materials are a second covering applied over the older siding. If lucky, you may find the original siding intact underneath, perhaps requiring only minor repairs (Figure 8-3).

Figure 8-1. Old Nails

MODERN WIRE NAILS

HAND-WROUGHT NAILS

MACHINE-CUT NAILS

Figure 8-2. *Synthetic siding.*

Figure 8-3. *Clapboards found beneath synthetic siding.*

- Determine in other instances whether there are any layers of siding behind the outer one. In the late 1900s, for example, wooden shingles were sometimes applied over older clapboard.
- Count the paint layers on wood siding. If there are many layers, chances are the siding is old.
- Check the mortar on a brick or stone house. Early mortar was of soft lime or, now and then, crushed oyster shells mixed with sand. Harder cement came into use around 1850. Except for repointing, it is unlikely that the walls of an older brick or stone house have been tampered with unduly.
- Look at other architecturally similar homes in the neighborhood to discover their wall materials.
- Search for old photographs which might show the initial wall materials.
- Find the original property deed or the one first referring to a house constructed on the site. Deeds may mention the exterior wall materials in a general way.

- Ask a knowledgeable architect for an opinion on what type of wall material would be appropriate for the house.
- Study the following descriptions of wall materials which are suitable for a particular architectural style.

SEVENTEENTH CENTURY

The earliest settlers used several wall materials: brick, stone, and wood siding and shingles. Wood was the most popular because it was plentiful, inexpensive, and relatively easy to assemble. At first wood was split by hand, but sawmills were set up as early as 1625, making wood available in larger quantities. So much wood was produced for building that it was exported to England. Oak, a hard, durable wood, was commonly used in Connecticut, Rhode Island, the middle colonies, and the South, while cedar and pine were favored in Massachusetts.

Three types of wood siding, all left unpainted, were employed, especially in New England: clapboards, flat boards, and flush siding. An early clapboard was 4 to 6 feet long, about 5 to 8 inches wide, with a butt ½ inch thick tapering to a feather edge sometimes only ⅛ inch thick. Hand-forged nails fastened the thin beveled edges to the framework of vertical wooden timbers, or studs, behind. The horizontal clapboards overlapped about 1 inch leaving exposed the thicker bottom edge. Clay and straw, stone, or crude bricks filled the spaces between the studs and provided insulation.

The other two types of wooden siding were found in only a few homes. Flat boards, placed horizontally, gave a more regular, smoother surface than clapboards. These boards were wider, ⅞ inch thick, and were rabbeted, or notched, at their upper edges and often beaded at their lower edges (Figure 8-4). They overlapped and gave the appearance of wide clapboard siding. Flat boards were popular in the South and among the Flemish and Dutch. Houses with flush wooden siding have horizontal sawed boards 12 to 18 inches wide which are nailed directly to the studs. They have beveled or rabbeted edges, sometimes with a bead along the lower edge.

Although brick was prevalent in Virginia and in the Dutch settlements along the Hudson Valley in New York, the scarcity of lime for mortar hampered its use even though many early settlers were brickmakers, clay was available, and brick manufacturing began quite soon. Ground oyster shells proved to be a poor substitute for lime. Not until the end of the century, when better transportation made lime more available and when ordinances in several large cities prohibited new wooden frame houses as fire hazards, was brick used throughout the eastern seaboard.

Brick was usually laid in English bond with courses, or rows, of headers (or exposed brick ends) alternating with courses of stretchers (or exposed lengths) (Figure 8-5). Occasionally bricks around window openings were a harder consistency and a slightly different color. Brick walls were very thick, possibly 18 to 24 inches for larger buildings. Builders used brick in unique ways in Maryland where homes with brick end walls and wooden front and back walls are found. Sometimes the walls have an all header bond or decorative patterns of glazed bricks laid out as diamonds, hearts, diapers, or zig-zags—designs also seen on houses in southern New Jersey. Glazed bricks have a bluish black color and a glassy surface made by firing the brick to a high temperature.

Stone was not a common building material in the 1600s. Many early settlers had formerly lived in wood frame houses and were not familiar with stone building methods. Unless the walls were very thick, stone homes could also be quite damp inside. Lack of lime for mortar, however, was a major obstacle. In New England good lime was available only in Rhode Island. The few stone houses constructed tended to be large except for several smaller stone-enders, houses with stone end walls and clapboard front and rear walls, in Rhode Island and Connecticut.

Rough-textured, hand-riven wood shingles of oak, chestnut, white pine, or cedar were used on a small number of houses on Long Island, in New Jersey, and in New England. These shingles could be as long as 3 feet and were up to 10 inches wide with an exposed surface anywhere from 8 to 16 inches. At times their butt ends were curved.

EIGHTEENTH CENTURY— GEORGIAN, 1700 TO 1780

Houses were constructed of wood, brick, stone, and plaster in the eighteenth century. New England favored wood; stone was common in eastern Pennsylvania, northern New Jersey, and the Hudson Valley area of New York; and brick was prevalent throughout the colonies.

Wood was popular for both modest Georgian houses and grander residences. Clapboard siding resembled the earlier type except that around the middle of the century some builders graduated the clapboards by increasing the area of the exposed clapboard from the bottom row upward. Sometimes clapboard was used only on the front and shingles were placed on the other walls, or a house was totally shingled as happened often in Nantucket. About 1700 builders began changing the construction behind the clapboards by adding a layer of sheathing boards to the studs. The clapboard was in turn nailed to the sheathing. This method provided increased insulation, made the house more weatherproof, and allowed for the gradual abandoning of the clay, stone, or brick filling between the studs.

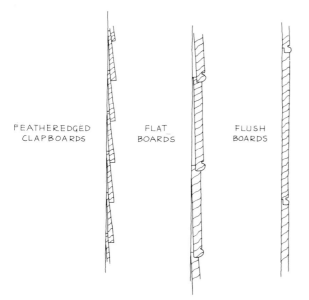

Figure 8-4. Clapboards, flat boards, and flush boards.

FEATHEREDGED CLAPBOARDS   FLAT BOARDS   FLUSH BOARDS

Figure 8-5. Brick bond patterns.

ENGLISH

FLEMISH

COMMON OR AMERICAN

DUTCH CROSS

Figure 8-6. Quoins.

Brick houses abound, especially in Virginia and in the larger cities. Often they were laid in Flemish bond with the headers and stretchers alternating in each course (*see* Figure 8-5). The headers may be glazed, creating a decorative checkerboard pattern of different shades and textures. A rich variety of brick colors is found: from soft orangish reds, warm roses, and salmon pinks through vermillions, darker wine reds, purple tones, and blue-black hues. An orangish-colored brick, poorly burned and less expensive, appears mostly in party walls between townhouses, on interior walls, and elsewhere where appearance and quality are not important.

The use of English bond continued primarily in the water table at the base of a Flemish bond wall. Sometimes, particularly on the rear walls, the bricks were laid in another pattern called common bond with stretcher courses punctuated by an occasional course of headers (*see* Figure 8-5). Early common bond ranges from a row of headers every third course to a row of headers every ten courses. In later houses the header courses may occur every seventh course, but no set sequence exists in most houses.

Early brickmaking utilized box molds for the rectangular bricks. Curved-edged bricks were also produced for water tables, belt courses, trim around doorways, and chimney caps. Rubbed, or gauged, bricks made by rubbing the brick with stone to create a smooth, reflective surface, accented windows and the corners of a house or served as other trim.

Stone houses were rare in New England and the South, but were common in eastern Pennsylvania, northern New Jersey, and New York's Hudson Valley where stone was used for both simple and pretentious homes. The type of stonework varied from rubble walls, laid in a rough, irregular manner, to increasing refinement. Carefully selected stones of about the same size and shape or hewn stone blocks were often laid in somewhat level courses, but with random heights. On more elaborate houses dressed stones with smooth surfaces and uniform size were laid in level courses with even joints. At times, to economize, the dressed stone was used only on the front of the house, and cruder stone was employed elsewhere. Cobble masonry, or small rounded boulders set in a thick mortar, was popular in the Mohawk Valley in New York. Fieldstone and quarried stone as well as innumerable local varieties of stone were also favorite construction materials. Of necessity the walls in stone houses can be very thick, varying anywhere from 18 to 36 inches.

Plaster or stucco sometimes covered stone or brick houses, particularly in Charleston and Philadelphia. In Charleston the stucco was tinted in pastel shades of pink, yellow, blue, or green.

Larger Georgian homes may have decorative quoins (interlocking slightly projecting corner blocks) (Figure 8-6) occasionally combined with rustication (ashlar walls with deep joint groovings). Because of their robust scale, raised surfaces, varying textures, and deeply recessed joints, quoins and rustication are prominent features. Quoins are properly an embellishment of brick or stone masonry construction, and rustication a form of dressed masonry, though both are patterned in stucco and fabricated in wood as an imitation of stone to make them look more grandiose. Trim and decorative details on Georgian houses—cornices, pilasters, and the framing around doors and windows—were often wood.

FEDERAL, 1790 TO 1830

Federal houses were built of brick, wood, or stone. Some were stuccoed and scored to imitate stone. In general, brick was favored for homes in the larger cities and for more elegant houses. Narrow wooden horizontal clapboard was common in New England, and stone was popular in Pennsylvania especially in rural areas.

Brick houses may have simple stone lintels above the windows, narrow stone belt courses dividing the floors, wooden cornices, and wooden balustrades edging the roofs. More pretentious clapboard houses may also have tall, slender wooden pilasters attached to the walls at the corners. Most ofter the pilasters, which are fluted or grooved, turn the corners to face both the front and the side walls.

GREEK REVIVAL, 1820 TO 1860

Most Greek Revival homes have horizontal wooden clapboards as siding, although townhouses and a few more elaborate homes are ordinarily brick which is, in rare instances, stuccoed to imitate stone. A wooden house with a front gable end generally has wide wooden corner boards (Figure 8-7), often with recessed panels or flat wooden pilasters. You will usually see a wood cornice and an exposed horizontal sill board just above the foundation. Look for stone lintels over the doors and windows in brick houses, stone window sills, and simple wooden cornices.

GOTHIC REVIVAL, 1820 TO 1860

Many types of wall materials appear on Gothic Revival houses. Earlier homes tend to be wood or stone; later versions often combine materials such as sandstone with a gray granite trim, hard, smooth machine-made brick with a sandstone trim, or brick and stone together in intricate patterns. Sometimes less expensive materials imitate stone: Matched wood boards are rusticated or brick is stuccoed. Imitation stone was considered fashionable as well as economical.

Because wood was a relatively inexpensive siding material, guidebooks for this style often recommended it. Numerous homes have vertical clapboards, vertical planks about 10 inches wide, or board and batten siding. In houses with board and batten siding, the edges of the boards are tongue-and-grooved to fit together and are nailed side by side in an upright position. Battens, or narrow vertical strips about 2 inches wide and possibly molded at the edges, are nailed over the joints of the boards to protect them from the weather. The boards and battens may rest on a horizontal wooden plank and extend to the roof or to a similar-size plank running under the eaves.

ITALIANATE, 1845 TO 1880

Italiante houses typically have horizontal wood clapboards with simple wood corner boards and wood sill boards. Larger homes may be constructed with brick and covered with a smooth stucco. On these houses the trim, such as window sills, lintels, and chimney tops, is often cut brownstone, a material also commonly found on townhouses. In addition, watch for stone Italianate houses with rusticated quoins at the corners or brick homes stuccoed and painted to look like stone.

STICK STYLE, 1855 TO 1900

As the name of this style suggests, wood sheaths Stick Style houses. Earlier homes commonly have horizontal clapboards, and vertical board and batten siding sometimes appears on later houses. Every once in a while wooden shingles, usually of the fish-scale variety, may cover a few gables and dormers, or the peak of a gable will have vertical clapboards.

Most houses have overlays of wooden boards, or stickwork, on top of the siding, suggesting the structural frames beneath (Figure 8-8). Builders of Stick Style homes considered this exposed skeleton to be an honest expression of how the building was put together. These various horizontal, vertical, diagonal, or X-shaped crosspieces, however, are not structural, but decorative. Besides creating interesting patterns on the wall's surfaces, they also accent windows, gables, dormers, and porches.

MANSARD, 1860 TO 1880

Mansard houses may have wood, stone, or brick walls. Homes with horizontal wooden clapboards often have tall, vertical corner boards and wooden sill boards. In a few instances, wider boards are placed flush with one another to create horizontal bands, perhaps including subdued rustication, or incised lines to make the wood look like stone. This technique was simply an inexpensive way of imitating the more costly stone. Townhouses are almost always stone, the favorite wall material at the time. Quoins mark the corners of many stone houses.

Figure 8-7. Corner board.

Figure 8-8. Stickwork.

ROMANESQUE, 1875 TO 1895

Almost every Romanesque house is masonry, commonly crudely cut or rock-faced stone, giving the home a rugged, massive appearance. A different texture and color of stone, usually smoother and lighter or darker than the body of the house, emphasizes arches, windows, lintels, doors, and stringcourses. For instance, the walls may be light sandstone and the trim a dark brown stone, or a light gray stone may outline various features on a deep red-brown stone house. Terra-cotta tiles and panels and brick inlay also embellish entryways, gables, and roof lines. Now and then several masonry materials combine in one house. Look for stone belt courses, arches, and corner quoins in brick townhouses. In other examples, the lower stories are stone with brick on the upper floors. Wood was rarely used as siding on Romanesque homes.

QUEEN ANNE, 1876 TO 1900

Queen Anne builders rejoiced in mixing many textures, shapes, sizes, patterns, and colors of wall materials in one house. Even in the few homes having only one type of siding, expect subtle changes. A brick house, for example, may have bricks laid in assorted patterns, darker-colored brick stringcourses, and embellishing terra-cotta panels.

You will discover intriguing combinations of wall materials. A modest multicolored stone house may have flamboyant wooden flourishes on porches, balconies, gables, and dormers. Homes with brick on the first floor and wood shingles of various shapes on the upper stories were prevalent. Look also for combinations of clapboard and wood shingles sometimes used alone or together with brick or stone.

The siding on Queen Anne gables inevitably differs from the rest of the house. Here you will find half-timbering, strapwork with vertical and horizontal crosspieces, bargeboards, decorative wooden ornamentation, square panels, and wood shingles. The entire gable may be sheathed in the same style of shingle, but more frequently a variety of shapes—round, square, octagonal, or rectangular butts, circles, fish scales, zigzags, or diagonal squares—are combined to create a lively, richly textured surface (Figure 8-9). Round towers and turrets usually have wood shingles as siding, especially in their upper portions.

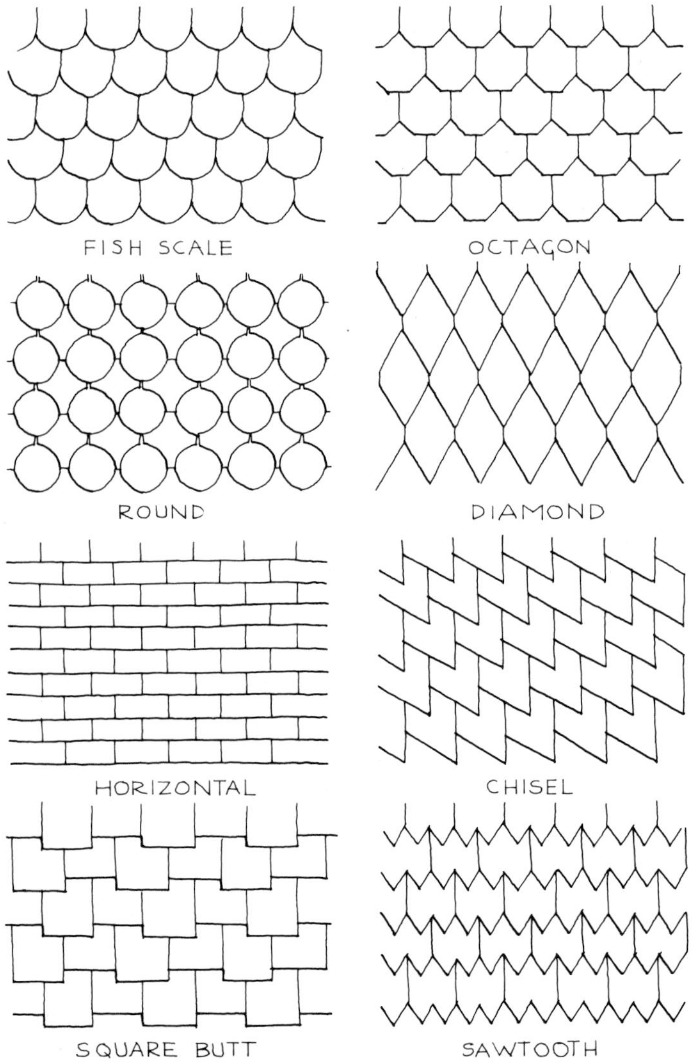

SHINGLE STYLE, 1880 TO 1900

Shingle Style homes are exactly what their name implies: enveloped by wooden shingles. Not only are the roofs made of shingles, but the walls and porches are also covered by shingles, unifying the entire house.

Shaggy, textured wooden shingles are favored, usually with square or rectangular butts, creating subtle horizontal lines. The shingles' overlapping may also be staggered, making the surface seem even more ragged. A few houses have shingles with smoother textures; different types of shingles occasionally cover the gables; and later houses may have round-butt shingle siding. Most often the wooden shingles are unpainted or given a natural stained finish.

Not all houses in this style were completely shingled. Every once in a while the first-story walls were stone: possibly random rubble of crude large stones or rugged fieldstone boulders to create a rough-textured surface contrasting with the wooden shingles above. The stonework may reach into part of the second story or cover the lower portion of a tower. Only a few later houses have brick walls on the lower floor.

A word of warning: Not all houses sheathed in shingles are Shingle Style designs. When this style came into vogue, owners of some earlier houses had shingle siding put on to create more fashionable houses.

FISH SCALE   OCTAGON

ROUND   DIAMOND

HORIZONTAL   CHISEL

SQUARE BUTT   SAWTOOTH

Figure 8-9. Wood shingle shapes.

Various wall materials appear on Georgian Revival homes, often depending on the formality of the house. Walls are frequently sheathed in wood clapboards with widths varying from about 3½ to 9 inches, or considerably wider than the earlier Georgian style. Tall corner pilasters, possibly with recessed vertical panels, and ornate cornices are popular features on larger wood houses. Other wall materials include stucco, fieldstone, wood shingles usually with rectangular butts, and brick which was favored for grander urban houses, often laid in Flemish bond.

Most Federal Revival homes are brick, inevitably adorned with stone lintels, although some stone houses are found.

MAINTENANCE AND REPAIR

Walls of old stone, brick, and wood are a treasure. Few builders today can afford to duplicate the care and materials that went into the exterior walls of an older home. The type of mortar and joint, the tool marks on the wood or stone, the bond of the brick, and the special patterns of the siding or shingles distinguish the older house.

After discovering a problem with the walls, the homeowner should explore all possibilities of repair. Even seemingly minor trouble such as a crack, if not attended to, can permit water to enter the walls and damage the structure of the house. To solve many wall problems, the homeowners' skills will be enough. Widespread deterioration or difficulties high on the side of the house may call for professional help.

Inspecting the walls each year is a good beginning to ensure their long life. Where should you look for problems?

- Search for gaps in joints where moisture might enter—between dissimilar materials, where the walls meet windows and doors, at the corners, around the juncture with the foundation, and between the various parts of the wall material.
- Look at wood siding for cracks, warping, splitting, and signs of decay.
- Examine bricks and stone for chipping, cracking, disintegration, and efflorescence.

- Notice whether stucco or plaster walls have cracks and holes.
- Check the mortar in masonry walls for cracks and crumbling and for missing pieces.
- Inspect the caulking for looseness and cracks.
- Find out whether walls that should be straight have bulged.
- Examine the condition of the paint for blistering, cracking, or peeling.
- Note where vegetation is growing on or too close to exterior walls and whether it is causing any damage.

STONE

Stone houses are likely to be either limestone or sandstone. Brownstone is a sandstone. Limestone is more durable, but it is particularly vulnerable to disintegration from sulphur in the air. Both types of stone range in their degree of hardness and in their color from very light or, for limestone, white to much darker shades such as brown. Limestone and sandstone are formed in layers, and for long-lasting walls more resistant to water penetration these stones should be placed in a building the same way the layers of sediment accumulated on the ground (Figure 8-10).

The textures, finishes, and shapes of stone vary. An undressed stone is one that is unchanged from its natural condition as it came from the quarry. Stones are semidressed when they have been cut to an approximate size; they are dressed when they have been worked to a specific shape. Stones, such as granite or marble, are often polished to a high gloss.

Stonework patterns in older houses range from informal to somewhat more precise to rigid and formal. Learning about these configurations can enlarge your appreciation of a stone house and, when required, help you to replace sensitively a portion of a wall (Figure 8-11).

COURSED Masonry is coursed when it is laid in mortar in horizontal layers to make a wall, and it is uncoursed when it is not set in level rows.

RANGEWORK Rangework describes coursed masonry in which all stones within a course are the same height. The height of the courses may vary.

Figure 8-10. Stone placement.

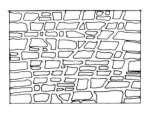
COURSED RUBBLE

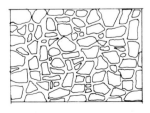
UNCOURSED RUBBLE

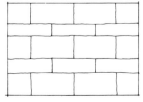
RANGE

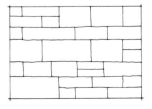
BROKEN RANGE

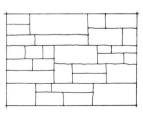
RANDOM RANGE

Figure 8-11. Stonework patterns.

BROKEN RANGEWORK Broken rangework is a variation of coursed stone. It is also set in horizontal layers, but any course may be broken at times into two or more narrow courses.

RANDOM RANGEWORK Random rangework is stonework placed in layers which are occasionally interrupted by a stone piercing the rows.

RUBBLE Rubble describes rough stones of various sizes and shapes. It may be laid in a casual, irregular manner or coursed in somewhat even rows.

ASHLAR Ashlar refers to dressed stones cut in rectangles with the faces that will be next to other building stones precisely shaped. The joints between the stones are smooth and even. The overall appearance of ashlar can be quite formal especially if it is laid in uninterrupted courses. A wall of ashlar stone may be constructed as rangework, broken rangework, or random rangework.

Stones are not impervious, but subject to a number of injurious forces. Wind and any nearby trees can damage them. Water flowing from a roof or a clogged gutter can dissolve parts of certain stones, an effect hastened by harmful chemicals in the water. Vines, such as ivy, can open up joints. The growth of moss or fungi on stones and any bushes near a stone wall can prevent the wall from drying out and may lead to serious deterioration.

When water is drawn into stone and freezes, the expansion of the water at the time of freezing may cause spalling, or the chipping off of small pieces of stone. Water, also, can work its way through the surface of the stone, carrying with it salts, which may come from soot on the stone, from the mortar, or from the ground. During crystallization the salts expand, breaking off particles of stone in the process. Sometimes entire layers of stone will fall off to expose a more porous inner surface. Salts can crystallize on the surface and form a whitish stain, called efflorescence.

Especially dangerous to limestone, acids from the atmosphere can also eat away the surfaces of other kinds of stones. Openings in the mortar joints, the settling of a building, and the expansion of rusting ironwork, such as railings or clamps set into the stone, may create even more problems.

What can you do about these difficulties? Locate the source of the trouble and try to find a remedy. Fixing the flashing or cleaning out a blocked downspout may be all that is required.

Small Cracks. One way to take care of any minor cracks in the stone is with one of the various epoxy adhesive products made for concrete repair. Clean the surface well by brushing with a bristle brush, and follow the manufacturer's directions for using the epoxy product.

Large Cracks and Deterioration. Rebuilding the damaged part of a stone is possible. To do this, chisel out the deteriorated portion of the stone, cutting more deeply into the inner edges of the hole to create a place for the patch to lock. Fill the hole with a mixture of 1 part sand, 2 parts cement, and a little lime. Match the surface and color of the stone. For this job you may decide to call in an experienced stonemason.

When you suspect that a large crack or a noticeable curving of the wall results from a serious structural flaw, consult a structural engineer or a competent contractor. One way to learn whether the wall is moving is to nail to the mortar two strips of metal overlapped in an X shape. Nail only at the top of each strip (*see* Figure 14-3). Scratch the starting position into the metal. Watch the metal over several weeks to learn whether the wall is moving and in which direction.

Replacement. The best source for replacement stone is the original quarry. Try to match the color, size, and finish of the stone. When a good substitute is not available and the problem area is in a conspicuous location, moving stones from another, less visible part of the house or, perhaps, from a retaining or decorative wall may be the answer. Add the newer stones to the little-seen location.

BRICK

In contrast to new brick, an old hand-molded brick seems quite irregular in size, shape, color, and texture. To accommodate this unevenness, mortar joints were often wide. The more uniform machine-made bricks made a thinner mortar joint possible. Examining the quality of the bricks on all parts of the house may be enlightening, for sometimes the front has better brick and the back or sides have a less durable, more porous brick.

Bricks experience many of the same problems as stones. They can break off or wear down from the impact of wind, trees, and water. Freezing within the bricks and salt crystallization can chip off pieces of brick. Efflorescence also appears on brick surfaces. To defend against these forces, the homeowner should investigate the cause of the problem and take immediate action before further harm results. Also, clear away any growth on the bricks or any vegetation that grows too close to the wall.

Cracks. Repair cracks, often found near windows and doors, by filling them with mortar of the same type found in the joints between bricks.

Replacement. Replace badly cracked or deteriorated bricks, but first try to discover the reason for the trouble and find a solution. Match the old bricks in size, color, and texture. You may be able to locate suitable old bricks at a wrecking-company yard, from a building supplier, or in a store specializing in architectural parts. When you are unable to find similar bricks, remove bricks from a less visible section of the house or from a garden wall on your lot and place them in the areas where you have taken out the damaged bricks. Put the new bricks in the inconspicuous locations. As a last resort, purchase new handmade bricks that are as close as possible to the color, texture, and size of the older ones.

Before beginning the task of replacing a damaged brick, put on goggles. Chip out the mortar around the brick and, then, pieces of the brick until all the brick has been removed. Take out as much of the mortar as possible from the opening. Use a wire brush to clean out the loose fragments of brick and mortar. Wet all of the surface within the opening. Put mortar to match the existing mortar along the sides and bottom of the cavity. Wet the new brick and apply mortar to its top surface before inserting it. Apply mortar to the joints and strike them to match the old joints.

REPOINTING

When mortar is crumbling, missing, or badly cracked, repointing is necessary, but only on the portion of the wall having the deteriorated mortar. Do this job only when there is no chance of freezing. With a chisel and a hammer cut out the old, loose mortar, being careful not to chip the bricks or stones. When working, wear safety goggles to protect your eyes. Take the joint back about 1 inch for brick and 1½ inches for stone. Clean out each joint thoroughly.

The new mortar should match the old in color, strength, texture, and the type of joint. Sending a mortar sample to a testing laboratory will elicit an accurate account of its composition. A simple test to learn whether you have an older lime-sand or a newer Portland cement mortar is trying to break the mortar in your hands. Portland cement mortar is hard and will not break; the lime mortar is relatively soft and weak and will split apart. The mortar must be softer than the stones or bricks it surrounds, or the joints may crack and the stones or bricks spall. One formula for soft mortar is by volume: 1 part Portland cement, 2 parts hydrated lime, and 9 parts sand. To adjust the color and texture, try various sands and use white instead of gray cement. Experiment by repointing a small section or applying the mortar to an unused brick to discover how well the new mortar blends with the old when dry.

Before beginning, check the form of the original mortar joint, both horizontally and vertically, for

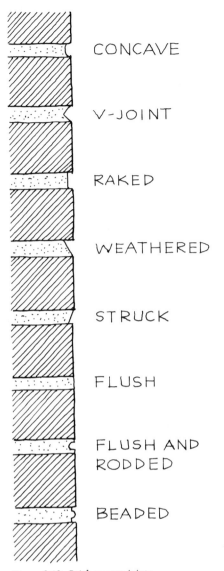

CONCAVE

V-JOINT

RAKED

WEATHERED

STRUCK

FLUSH

FLUSH AND RODDED

BEADED

Figure 8-12. Brick mortar joints.

these are not always the same (Figure 8-12). When repointing only a portion of the wall, you may decide to imitate the joint as it exists now, after weathering, not as it was when new. If the corners of the bricks or stones have worn off, recess the mortar rather than duplicate a flush joint, which will appear much wider than it was originally.

Moisten the joint and adjacent bricks or stones with water and keep them moist as you work. For a first-rate job, apply the mortar in two layers, letting the first layer dry before continuing with the second. Be meticulous. Keep the mortar in the joint. If you do spread mortar on the bricks or stones, brush it off with a stiff bristle brush after it has dried, but before it has hardened. For curing, keep the mortar damp with a fine spray from a hose for 2 or 3 days after the job has been completed.

Repointing is slow, tedious work. When hiring someone to do the repointing, be certain the individual is experienced and will do the painstaking job required. Carelessness and incompetence lead to seriously damaged masonry.

WOOD

Wood siding comes in a multitude of types and sizes. Among these are horizontal clapboards, vertical board and batten patterns, and red cedar shingles with square, octagonal, diamond, fish-scale, and sawtooth ends. Edge-grained rather than the flat-grained woods are increasingly used because they swell and shrink less and hold paint better. They split, cup, and warp less often, too, but they are more expensive than flat-grained woods.

Vigilance will keep wood sound. When trouble occurs, knowing what to do and preventing subsequent damage will prolong the life of wood siding.

Decay or Rot. "Decay" is a byword associated with wood. The more you know about decay, the better chance your wood has of steering clear of this debilitating attack by fungi. Brown rot and white rot are the two most frequent kinds of decay. Brown rot acquired its name from the resulting brown stain on the wood. Cracks, usually across the grain, and depressions in the wood are symptoms of brown rot. With white rot the wood appears lighter than normal, and dark lines may edge the discoloration. In both kinds of rot surface growth may be present.

A water-conducting fungus which spreads from damp to dry wood produces a severely destructive, but fortunately rare, type of rot known as dry rot. Dry rot in the basement has penetrated within the walls of a building to invade the sound wood on the roof. Dry rot advances swiftly and it may destroy all the wood within a building in as short a time as 2 years. One way to identify dry rot is by the white strands on the wood that develop into a wool-like covering.

When examining the wood for rot, check for rust around nailheads and for staining beneath any paint. To further test for decay, probe the wood with a sharply pointed object such as a screwdriver or penknife. When there is little resistance to the sharp object, the wood is in a weakened condition. Another technique is to press the screwdriver into the wood at an angle. Lift up a small section of the wood. Decayed wood will break into short, irregular pieces; sound wood will splinter into longer pieces.

For rot to occur, wood requires a moisture content of more than 20 percent. In areas with a significant amount of rainfall the following suggestions will help to forestall decay in wood siding. Use only dry lumber and, better yet, choose a naturally decay-resistant wood, such as a heartwood of cypress, red

cedar, or redwood, or wood treated with a wood preservative. Also, consider purchasing edge-grained lumber. Keep the roof in satisfactory condition. Make certain that gutters and downspouts are in good working order and that water drains away from the house. A wide roof overhang and sound flashing where the siding joins the roof will lessen chances of rotted wood.

Chapter 14, Foundations and Basements, describes how to keep ground moisture from entering the walls. Remember that horizontal ledges collect water which can soak into the wood. Where possible, surfaces should slope away from the house. A valued attraction of many older homes is a superabundance of wood decoration with many joints—all susceptible to water penetration. Watch joints carefully to be sure they are always tight, caulked, and well painted.

To defend against decay already in the wood, first find the source of the dampness. Common causes of wetting are wood that has not been either properly dried or stored; moisture arising from damp soil; rain penetrating through joints, splits in the wood, or cracks in the paint; or water splashing the walls from the ground or from a lower roof such as a porch roof.

After locating and taking care of the cause of rot, the next step, if you have serious decay from the water-conducting fungus, is to prevent further wetting of the wood and then to destroy the fungus completely because the survival of even the smallest amount will initiate the attack anew. The safest remedy is to replace all the infected wood with wood that is pressure-treated with a preservative, for the water-conducting fungus affects naturally decay-resistant woods. Some specialists suggest removing all wood about 2 feet beyond the attack. After removal, burn the rotted wood immediately or haul it away from your property.

For the less dangerous brown rot and white rot, use a fungicide on the wood under attack and on adjacent wood. Make certain the infected area has dried out and will stay dry. Badly rotted wood may require replacement, and in this case wood treated with a preservative is best.

Molds and Stains. Siding manufactured from the softer sapwood (not heartwood) and from wood with little natural resistance to decay are targets for molds and stains. Discoloration from a mold is generally on the surface; brushing or light planing will remove it. Certain stains such as sap stain, which is brought about by a fungus, may leave permanent staining. The various fungi responsible for molds and stains do not cause decay, but they make the wood susceptible to water penetration and they disfigure the wood.

Warped Boards and Shingles. The following technique may successfully straighten a board or shingle that is bulging outward if it is possible to screw into a stud or sheathing. Drill pilot holes for the screws in the center of the board or shingle. Drill larger holes partway through to countersink the screws. Gradually tightening the screws should straighten the warped board. When the board is straight, cover the heads of the screws with putty. Allow the putty to dry before painting or staining to match the board.

Small Cracks and Splits. If you notice a small crack in wood siding, caulking the crack may be a sufficient repair. Repair a split board or shingle by placing a piece of building paper under the split and between any existing nails holding the board or shingle. Use threaded aluminum or galvanized siding nails to nail along both sides of the split and countersink the nailheads. Cover with putty and, when the putty is dry, paint.

Large Cracks and Deteriorated Wood. One way to repair a large crack in wooden siding is to fill it with oakum or another satisfactory filler and then caulk over the filler. Epoxy consolidants for decayed wood and epoxy fillers for cracks and holes that are not too large are other means to take care of wood problems.

When a large area in a board is damaged, it is possible to cut out the deteriorated portion. Be careful to saw only the board you are repairing. For clapboard, insert small wedges under the board you are working on. With a hammer and chisel, splinter the portion you have cut and take out the small pieces. Sliding wedges under the clapboard above may help you to remove any remaining pieces. With a claw hammer, pull out any nails holding the pieces of wood. Check the building paper beneath for cracks or tears and patch these with asphalt cement. Replace the damaged portion with a piece of wood of the same size and kind, treated with a wood preservative. When using a hammer to tap in the new board, insert a small block of wood between the hammer and the board to protect the new wood. Use aluminum or galvanized siding nails to nail the board in place in the same way the original board had been nailed (Figure 8-13). Countersink the nailheads and fill the holes with putty. Caulk the joints between the original board and the patch. Paint or stain to match the siding.

If the decay is too widespread to patch, replace the entire board with a board of the exact size and type. Again, duplicate the nailing pattern of the original board.

Shingle Replacement. The process of replacing a shingle on the wall of a house is similar to replacing a roof shingle. Being careful not to harm any of the other shingles, cut the damaged shingle into small pieces with a hammer and chisel. Remove the pieces and the nails holding the deteriorated shingle in place. Try cutting the nails with a hacksaw blade slipped beneath the shingle above the one you are removing. Patch any tears or cuts discovered in the building paper, using asphalt cement for the repair. Slide the replacement shingle into place and nail with aluminum or galvanized nails. Putty the nailheads.

If you cannot locate new shingles to blend well with the old ones, move old shingles from a little-seen area of the house and then replace those shingles with the new ones.

Gaps in Joints. Joints ought to be checked frequently to be sure they are sealing the house against water, air, dust, and insects. Examine the joints between the frames of the windows and doors and the house, between the siding and any adjoining surfaces such as a porch floor, between the siding boards, between dissimilar materials, and at corners. To close any openings begin by removing the old caulking and cleaning the area with a solvent. Prime bare wood and other porous surfaces and wait for the primer to dry. You are then ready to caulk. Either a rope caulk or butyl caulking will work well.

Peeling Paint. Water entering a joint or crack in the siding and condensation in the walls are the two main sources of paint failure from moisture. If a leak is the problem, seal the joint or crack where the moisture is coming in. If condensation is the trouble in an insulated house, the solution may be a vapor barrier installed on the inside of the wall. Also inserting louvered metal vents in the siding or small wedges under the laps in lap siding are other ways to prevent the accumulation of moisture. Good ventilation in the attic or under the eaves will lessen the chances of condensation.

STUCCO

Early stucco contained lime or clay, sometimes both, mixed with sand and, at times, mingled with animal hair for strength. Usually the stucco on the walls of a house built through the end of the 1800s was applied over masonry. Subsequently, however, on houses with wood-stud framing, wood lath and, then, wire lath began to be used as the base, or ground, for the coating of stucco. The first, or scratch, coat penetrates the lath to create an anchor for the next application of stucco. The first coat is crosshatched to provide a bond for the second, or brown, coat. The third, or finish, coat may be smooth, more ruggedly textured, patterned, or pebbled.

Figure 8-13. Nailing pattern for clapboard.

Cracks and Deterioration. Use a lime mortar to fill narrow cracks. For larger cracks and for deteriorated areas, remove all of the loose stucco. Choose a time to work when the surface is not hot from direct sunlight; then the patch will not dry too quickly. Cut the opening wider on the inside surface than on the outside to lock in the patch. Make any repairs in the building paper or lath underneath. Thoroughly clean out any dirt and stucco before continuing. If you are repairing stucco that is put on over brick, cut out the mortar about ¼ inch for a good bond.

Mix a batch of stucco to match the color, texture, and degree of hardness of the existing stucco. A patch that is too hard may work loose from or crack or pull off the stucco already on the building. For a softer mixture, add only a little Portland cement to the lime and sand. Experimenting with different sands may lead you to the correct color. Before patching, wash the masonry or wet the wood lath underneath in the area to be repaired.

Apply the first, or scratch, coat about ½ inch thick. When the surface has become hard enough, scratch it with the point of the trowel to prepare a bond for the next coat. As soon as the surface is firm enough to hold another coat, dampen the scratch coat and put on the second coat to reach about ⅛ inch of the surface. Smooth out the second coat, and keep it damp for about 5 days while it hardens. Wet with a fine spray from a garden hose before applying the finish coat. When the stucco begins to set (after about 20 minutes), texture it to match the existing finish. Keep the final patch damp with a fine spray for about 1 week of curing time. If the patch differs in color, consider painting the whole wall after about 6 weeks.

CLEANING

A wall deteriorating because of dirt, salts, or pollutants may call for cleaning. Improper cleaning methods can produce great and permanent damage to a building. Abrasive methods, like sandblasting and cleaning with grinders or even wire brushes, are destructive, eroding part of the surface along with the dirt or stain. Although it is being promoted for cleaning wood, sandblasting is an injurious method for this material as well.

When considering cleaning exterior walls, consult a professional, such as a knowledgeable architect, for advice. Companies promoting various cleaning methods will only give a biased opinion. Even relatively gentle cleaning techniques, such as applying low-pressure water, using water with a mild, non-ionic detergent, or scrubbing with a natural-bristle brush, require extreme care. For instance, clean with low-pressure water only in warm weather when there is no chance of frost for several months, for the water may freeze and cause the masonry to crack or spall. In addition, take care that the runoff water is drained away from the building and that no water can enter open joints in the building.

To choose a satisfactory method, a cleaning test is mandatory. On different patches of the wall in a little-seen location, try each of the methods being considered, including the least harsh as well as other appropriate techniques. Before evaluating the test patches, wait a year through all kinds of weather. If a year seems a long time, remember that some problems, such as those which may be caused by chemical cleaners, take longer than a year to become evident.

These warnings suggest that the best action in many cases is not to clean at all. Cleaning is a risky procedure.

WATERPROOFING

Be cautious about coating a masonry building with waterproofing or water-repellant materials. Waterproofing can create new difficulties or intensify the problem you are attempting to solve. In the long run the best waterproofing method may be to trace the source of moisture and correct the trouble.

When you suspect, however, that the wall may require some kind of coating, possibly for a sandblasted brick surface now extremely porous or a wall subject to persistent staining, get advice from an architect or another qualified individual to avoid a mistake. A firm specializing in waterproofing may not always make an objective recommendation. The specialist consulted should suggest the product that will work best and how and where it should be applied. Sometimes only the area where the specific trouble occurs, not the entire wall, needs treating.

PAINTING

Never paint an unpainted brick or stone house unless you have been advised by a competent professional that painting is the only way to save a wall, perhaps one that has had a dose of abrasive cleaning. Paint is nearly impossible to remove completely from brick or stone, and the stripping process can damage these surfaces. Once painted, the building must be routinely repainted—an added maintenance cost. Read Chapter 13, Paint and Color, to learn which colors and finishes suit the style of your house.

REPLACEMENT

If deterioration is widespread or repair is impossible, replacing the old walls is the only choice. The following considerations are a guide to selecting a new material.

- The ideal is to locate material similar to the original. Quarries, wrecking-company yards, and businesses specializing in historic building materials are places to look.

- If the homeowner cannot find or afford a material like the original, an alternative is to approximate closely its dimensions, texture, and details.

- Retaining the emphasis, whether vertical or horizontal, is also a key factor, for any change in the direction of the materials distorts the overall impression of the style. The Design section of this chapter explains whether vertical or horizontal wall materials suit each style.

- Simulated stone and brick and aluminum or vinyl panels embossed to look like wood advertise themselves as counterfeits. They are never appropriate for an older house, and they may be expensive besides.

- No matter what a glib salesperson asserts, newer materials are not necessarily better than the stone, brick, wood, or stucco found on older homes. Nor are they problem free. For example, vinyl becomes brittle and may break in cold weather. It melts or warps when exposed to the extreme heat of a fire. Aluminum and vinyl dull over time and may require painting, steel siding rusts, hardboard and plywood split, and aluminum corrodes, scratches, and dents. In addition, if a portion of vinyl or aluminum siding requires replacement, matching exactly the existing siding may be difficult or impossible because certain styles and colors have been discontinued.

- Synthetic siding can hide rot or invading insects. Such problems proceeding unnoticed can seriously damage a building. Also, the owner must be alert that the siding is properly installed and the materials do not become damaged through use; otherwise, water may enter and harm the structure.

- Chapter 15, Calling in a Contractor, explains how to find someone to do the work. Never permit a door-to-door salesperson to pressure you into a quick decision.

Before putting on new wall material, certain steps are necessary. Discover the source of any dampness and take care of the difficulty. Covering up a problem can seriously hurt the structure of the house. Be certain the structure beneath the exterior walls is

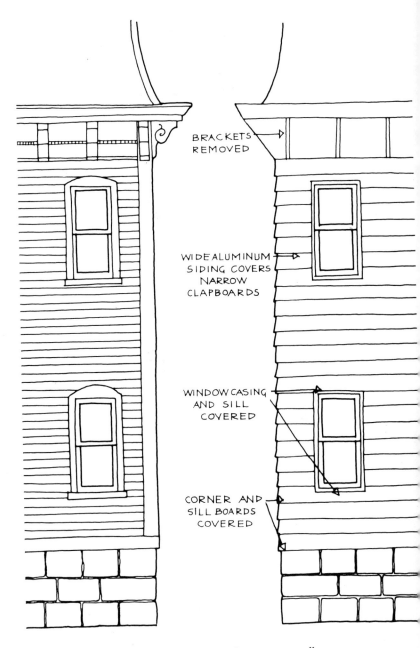

Figure 8-14. Appropriate and inappropriate replacements on walls.

sound. Proceed only after any deteriorated wall material has been removed and any extreme curves in the walls have been straightened.

A contractor may suggest cutting off, covering, or removing much of the window or door frames, moldings, corner boards, and ornamentation to facilitate the application of the new material. Do not let this happen, for these features along with the original wall material contribute to the value, economic and aesthetic, of the older home (Figure 8-14).

CHAPTER NINE

PORCHES AND PORTICOES

Older houses have a smorgasbord of porches and porticoes. Almost every older home has at least one portico or porch, and a few houses have both. As transitions between the outside and the inside, these structures shelter the entryways from the weather. A prominent one may announce the entrance, offering a gracious welcome. Others are quiet features tucked, at times, within the body of the house. Porches with more generous dimensions, sometimes called verandas, become spacious outdoor living rooms inviting leisurely relaxation.

Whether a portico or porch was intended for an older home depends on the house's architectural style and geographic location, the climate, and social customs in the area. Porches abound in warmer climates, in seashore or vacation places, and in today's urban neighborhoods which were yesterday's suburban locales. Less closely associated with warmer climates, porticoes are found on both rural and city homes.

Porches and porticoes are among the most vulnerable components of an older house. Usually wood, they are susceptible to rotting, sagging, and deterioration. They are also targets for modernization and for unsympathetic alterations using synthetic or contemporary materials. Because of changing tastes or disintegrating parts, many original porches and porticoes have not survived. Those remaining are a vanishing breed.

Porches and porticoes help to create the appeal of older homes. By making appropriate repairs, try to retain any initial versions or those which suit a house's style. If total replacement is necessary, attempt to duplicate the initial size, shape, materials, decoration, silhouette, and placement on the house. An accurate replacement is particularly important for porches or porticoes on the front of the house, on twin homes, and on street blocks where many homes are the same style with similar porches.

DESIGN

The original design of porches and porticoes springs from several sources. For some earlier styles, guide-

books and builders' manuals spelled out their exact dimensions. Beginning in the late nineteenth century, popular magazines illustrated various designs considered suitable for a certain style. A fancy porch or portico was often incorporated to dress up an otherwise plain house.

An architect's or builder's interpretation of a style or the homeowner's desires may have dictated the presence or absence of these features, their proportions, and ornamental details. Many times the personal artistic touch of a carpenter distinguishes a porch or portico, especially in its gingerbread flourishes. When mass-produced millwork, such as columns and balusters, became available, the design of porches gained greater freedom. By the late 1800s various parts of a porch could be selected from catalogs and imaginatively assembled.

You will find low one-story porches and porticoes, imposing two-story versions, balcony porches, and roof decks. Porch roofs are generally low pitched or nearly flat and are covered with the same material as the main roof or with a metal such as tin. Classical columns are common although some styles favor turned columns, ones with cut corners, or posts. Balustrades are also diverse, ranging from simple posts to elaborate turned balusters or, sometimes, Chinese latticework. Enjoy the decoration on porches and porticoes, for these are often the most embellished components of an older house.

Many times porches and porticoes were appendages, tacked on to the original house by a subsequent owner and possibly having a design inconsistent with the style of the house. Deciding whether to keep these later additions depends on how well they harmonize with the house's style, where they are located, and how much use they will receive. An architect can help to determine what to do.

How can you tell if a porch or portico is original or appropriate for the house?

- Examine its construction, particularly where it joins the wall of the house. Is there evidence, such as old nails and mortise and tenon joints, that the structure is old?

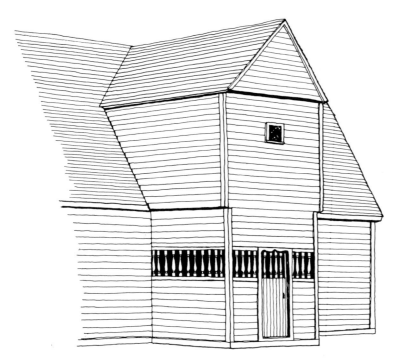

Figure 9-1. Seventeenth Century porch chamber.

Two types of enclosed porches do sometimes appear. A house built in New England often has a small interior vestibule behind the front door. This entry, called a "porch," has a steep staircase nestled up against the massive central chimney. A two-story enclosed porch projecting from the center of the house, an idea borrowed from England, occasionally occurs on homes in Maryland, Virginia, and New England (Figure 9-1). The second-story porch chamber and the gable on top may overhang slightly. Usually, the walls are solid, but turned wooden spindles may punctuate the side walls at eye level. Some projecting porches are later additions put on to help insulate the inside rooms and to provide a sheltered entryway.

EIGHTEENTH CENTURY— GEORGIAN, 1700 TO 1780

Porticoes made their first full-blown appearance around the mid-eighteenth century on the Georgian houses built by prosperous New England merchants

- Analyze the materials. Most older porches and porticoes are wood; a few are stone or brick. Modern materials, such as concrete steps, wrought iron columns, and plastic awnings, are a sign of recent alterations.
- Count the paint layers and compare these with ones on a section of the house you are certain is original.
- Search for old photographs to see if any porches or porticoes are visible.
- Check the neighborhood for houses designed in the same style. Do these have a portico or porch resembling yours?
- Study the following sections describing the porches and porticoes suitable for different styles.

SEVENTEENTH CENTURY

Seventeenth Century homes almost never have open porches or porticoes. Watch for a couple of local exceptions: the Dutch stoop and the piazza in Charleston, South Carolina, introduced around the end of the century. The Dutch stoop, found on houses in northern New Jersey and lower New York and on Long Island, is a low platform, reached by one or two steps, in front of the entrance with a bench on either side. Its use persisted into the 1700s. The piazza, an idea probably derived from the West Indies, is a long, one-story porch with plain wooden posts, well suited to the warm climate.

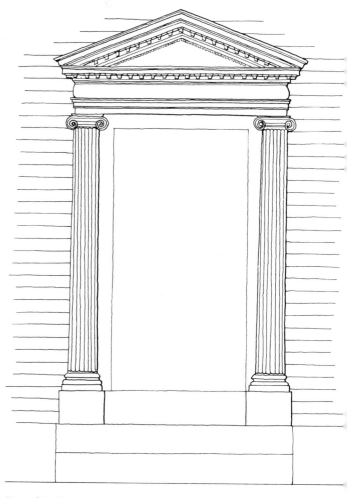

Figure 9-2. Georgian portico.

and by South Carolina plantation owners. Inspired by English prototypes and drawings by Palladio, a sixteenth century Italian architect, which were available in architectural handbooks, porticoes not only shelter an entryway but give it dignity and prominence and add to the classical character of a Georgian house. By the 1770s porticoes became a hallmark of New England coastal towns, were abundant in rural Vermont and Connecticut, and dotted the eastern seaboard.

A portico is a small porch with classical elements including a pediment and columns supporting decorative crosspieces (Figure 9-2). Its roof is gently pitched and it stands on a low or raised platform. In numerous ways the portico is a development of the ornate Georgian entrance with its pilasters carrying a pediment overhead, except in a portico free-standing columns support a small roof whose gabled end becomes the pediment.

Copied from Greek or Roman designs, the column is divided into three parts: a base, a tall shaft which generally tapers upward and may be plain or grooved with vertical channels called fluting, and a capital at the top (Figure 9-3). The ancient Greeks devised three major orders, or types of columns, distinguished most easily by the capitals. A Doric capital is two simple, narrow blocks, one resting on the other. The lower block curves gradually upward from the shaft to the wider block above. A necking, or plain molding, marks the capital's juncture with the shaft. An Ionic capital has rounded volutes on either side resembling spiral scrolls or ram's horns and connected by an ornamental molding. A Corinthian capital is the most elaborate, enlivened with overlapping acanthus leaves and, in rare instances, also accented with small volutes at the top (See Figure 9-3).

The Romans later used these three Greek orders in their buildings, often with taller shafts, and they added two orders: the Tuscan which looks like a simplified Doric order and the Composite which combines Corinthian and Ionic features. Although Georgian builders often diligently copied these five classically correct orders, they also formed their own hybrids.

The decorative crosspieces above the columns are together known as the entablature (Figure 9-4). The entablatures of the three Greek orders are slightly different, but the same three divisions occur in each of them: an architrave which rests on the capitals, a frieze above, and a cornice on top. Architraves on Doric porticoes are unadorned except for tiny drop-like pendants, or guttae, along the tops, but they may be layered on Ionic porticoes or enriched with decorative moldings on Corinthian examples. On a Doric frieze, look for triglyphs, or vertically

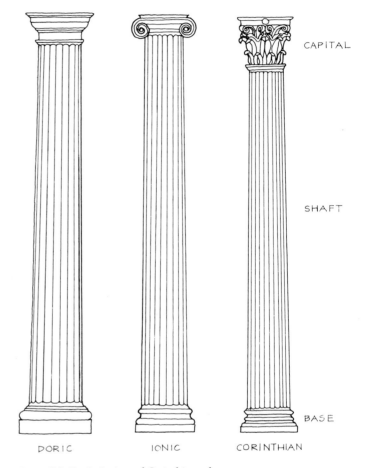

Figure 9-3. Doric, Ionic, and Corinthian columns.

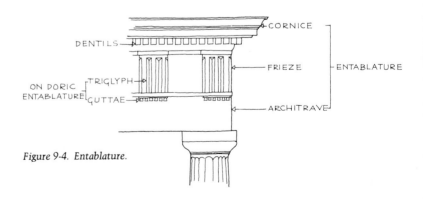

Figure 9-4. Entablature.

Figure 9-5. Georgian portico.

dentils. Similar engaged columns flank the door and carry the back corners of the entablature. The portico is reached by high steps on three sides. Variations of this portico sprang up all over New England with subsequent examples sometimes fancier and, maybe, six-sided. A few, however, were added later when porticoes became even more fashionable.

Two-story porticoes occur on South Carolina river plantations, in Charleston, and in other areas of the South. Certain imposing examples—perhaps with four Doric columns on the first tier, Ionic columns and a turned balustrade above, and a large pediment resting overhead—were taken directly from Palladio's drawings. Charleston, also, has some one-story houses featuring long shaded piazzas with rooms opening onto them. A house having a portico across the entire front with two-story columns was rare before the Revolution. Some of these colossal porticoes were built in New York, and rural versions were constructed in Vermont. After Mount Vernon included a portico of this type in the late 1780s, this design became increasingly popular.

Local builders developed other unique ways to shield the entrance. Hoods, with very low pitched roofs, narrow triangular ends, and wooden panels underneath, jut out over front doors in many Pennsylvania homes, especially in rural areas. Pent eaves, perhaps with a small pediment above the entry, are also common in southeastern Pennsylvania; they extend across the front and sometimes around the entire house (*see* Figure 4-3). By adding simple posts to the expansive overhanging eaves on their gambrel-roofed homes, Flemish builders in northern New Jersey and southern New York and on Long Island created spacious porches. Houses in North Carolina may have shed porches hidden underneath sweeping, low-pitched roofs, a form possibly borrowed from the West Indies. Outside enclosed vestibules are seen every once in a while in New England, although some are later additions. Often plantations in Louisiana and Mississippi have wide two-story galleries encircling four sides of the house.

FEDERAL, 1790 TO 1830

Porticoes are splendid features on many Federal homes, especially those built between 1810 and 1820 (Figure 9-6). Embellishing the central doorway, the portico is the focal point of the house, graciously inviting visitors to enter. Typically one-story high, some one-and-a-half story porticoes and a few exceptionally elegant three-story versions forming semi-circular central pavilions also appear.

In sophisticated city houses porticoes are usually accurate copies of the classical columns, entabla-

grooved, projecting rectangular blocks occuring in a series with plain or decorated panels in between. Friezes on Ionic and Corinthian porticoes tend to be simple. Cornices generally have decorative moldings with dentils appearing in Doric cornices, dentils and egg-and-dart moldings in Ionic ones, and both of these plus modillions and other floral or foliage moldings in Corinthian cornices. Variations in all three types of entablatures frequently are present in Georgian houses, as builders created their own interpretations.

The end gable of the portico's roof forms a triangular pediment with dentils and other moldings usually accenting the pediment's edges. Early Georgian pediments are quite steep, but later versions are most often shallow. The pediment may extend only a short distance from both sides across the bottom, or it may be entirely absent, with a low balustrade gracing the top of the entablature (Figure 9-5).

One common New England portico is rectangular with round, fluted Ionic columns one-story high, a simple entablature, and a low pediment edged with

tures, proportions, and ornamentation taken from Palladio's designs. They are graceful, dignified, and classically correct works of art. In contrast, porticoes on country homes often seem like cousins. Similar motifs occur, but the builders or carpenters interpreted them more freely. The architrave and frieze, for example, may be plain bands, the architrave may be exceptionally narrow, or a simple beaded molding may replace the architrave. Other ingenious individual touches are seen in the ornamentation. The result is a rich medley of porticoes echoing the classical themes in an informal, personal way.

Many porticoes are shallow rectangles or squares, but semicircular and semielliptical shapes are more typical on high-style houses. Occasionally in a larger portico the central portion projects forward, combining a square in front with a rectangle behind. Because the pediments are an elaboration of the end gables, their sloping sides correspond to the pitch of the portico's roof. Most are low pitched, although a few country ones are quite steep. Some pediments include three straight sides forming the standard triangle. Others eliminate the bottom side, extend the lower horizontal crosspiece slightly beyond the capitals leaving an open center, or have a gently curved underside springing from the capitals. The two diagonal sides on open pediments are usually paneled underneath on their soffits; the ones with the vaults, or curved undersides, are commonly plastered.

A number of Federal porticoes have entablatures or cornices without pediments, perhaps curved and topped with shallow sloping roofs. Later versions occasionally have flat roofs with horizontal entablatures carried around the two sides. Large city houses, such as those in Salem, Massachusetts, often have delicate wrought-iron balustrades running along the edges of flat-roofed porticoes. The light, almost fragile ornamental ironwork is enlivened with diamonds, hearts, circles, ovals, and tall urns. Some designs look like the contours of turned wooden balusters. Frequently the front stair railings repeat the balustrade's decorative patterns, or more ornate railings may also include arrows, fleur-de-lis, or tear-shaped designs.

On country houses and less ostentatious city homes, Tuscan columns are the most popular type, followed by Ionic columns and some Doric ones. Particularly on later, fancier houses, watch for Corinthian columns. In a few instances two orders, such as the Doric and Ionic, combine in a single portico with one type at the corners and the other in between. Now and then square Doric piers occur. Although the number and arrangement of columns vary, on modest and rural homes the two-column type is favored. A highly fashionable house may have four columns arranged in pairs at the corners

Figure 9-6. Federal portico.

or evenly spaced when the portico curves. The majority of porticoes have pilasters or engaged columns on the front wall directly behind the free-standing columns which support the back corners of the entablature and roof.

Almost all the columns are attenuated, or very slender compared with the original Greek and Roman proportions. As a rule of thumb, early Greek Doric shafts are five times their diameters, and the Roman Doric shafts are generally seven-and-one-half to eight times their diameters. Ionic shafts are usually nine diameters high, and Corinthian are ten diameters. By comparison, early Federal shafts of all orders were based on ten diameters. Later ones use eleven or twelve diameters and some reach the extreme of seventeen diameters, creating extraordinarily thin columns. To further accentuate their height, some columns are elevated on tall rectangular pedestals. Made from solid pieces of wood, the shafts of the columns taper gradually upward, although cruder versions have a pronounced slant. Many shafts are plain and smooth, some are fluted, and a few are grooved with thin lines which look like reeds.

Finely scaled ornamentation adds elegance to Federal porticoes. In the entablature, look for small modillions, petite dentils, narrow vertical grooves alternating with tiny blocks, beaded or egg-and-dart moldings, graceful festoons, rosettes, swags, circles, ovals, and elliptical shapes. This lovely decoration is subtle because of its delicacy and its low relief, or closeness to the surface.

Instead of a portico, the entrance is sometimes accented merely by the framing, allowing the fanlight, sidelights, and paneled door to be highly visible. Urban row houses may have simple stone front stoops, perhaps with plain wrought-iron handrails. Southern houses occasionally have sweeping verandas surrounding the houses at every story. Well suited to the warm climate, these galleries offer shadowed places for relaxation.

GREEK REVIVAL, 1820 TO 1860

Porches and porticoes adorn many Greek Revival homes. Variations abound. Carefully following the classical prototypes presented in architectural guidebooks, some are prim and proper. Others are less correct, their builders translating this style's formality in more modest or liberal ways. Whether imposing or subtle, they always add dignity and grandeur to these houses.

On large or small houses, luxurious two-story mansions or simple one-story homes, temple fronts were popular (Figure 9-7). A wide pediment extends across the top of such a portico with an entablature beneath supported by four, five, or six columns. Pilasters commonly stand against the wall behind the corner columns. This type of portico may cover the entire front, reach across three-quarters of the front, grace only the central entrance, or repeat itself in the back. Occasionally a two-tiered temple portico appears with the upper columns standing on top of an entablature below. A Southern plantation with a hipped roof often has a two-story columned front without a pediment, perhaps with the columns surrounding three or four sides of the house. Sometimes there is an ornamental wrought-iron balcony projecting from the second story behind the columns (Figure 9-8).

Greek Revival porticoes may take less elaborate forms. The doorway is often accented by a small one-story, two-columned portico topped by a shallow pediment or by only the entablature or cornice. Less frequently, a portico has two sets of twin columns or, more rarely, two groups of three columns. These simple porticoes are always square or rectangular (Figure 9-9).

Porches are tucked into some homes, possibly built on the front of wings extending from one or two sides of the house or placed underneath the second story running along half of the front and around the corner to one side. A few central doorways are deeply recessed in a wide niche with pilasters flanking the front wall edges and with two columns standing in front of the door in the opening. More elaborate recessed porches have wide wall projections on both sides of the opening, called antae, which may be embellished with recessed panels.

Figure 9-7. Greek Revival temple front.

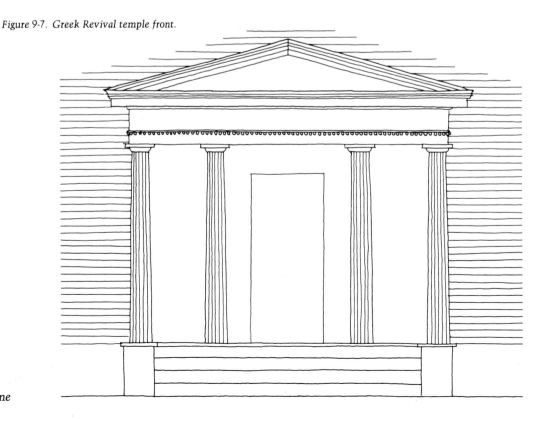

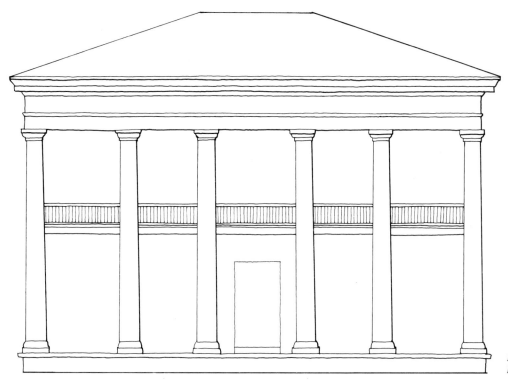

Figure 9-8. Greek Revival temple front.

Doric columns with the early Greek proportions are common. The most authentically Greek-inspired versions do not have bases. The Doric order, however, was freely interpreted, possibly without fluting, especially on rural houses. Some columns are square rather than round and include recessed panels—a characteristic unheard of in ancient Greece. Watch for Ionic columns, too, and for a few Corinthian and Composite ones on fancier homes. Occasionally two Greek orders mingle in a single house, perhaps with Ionic columns on an entrance portico and Doric columns on the side porch. Houses with two-tiered porticoes usually have Doric col-

umns on the first tier and Ionic above. The columns are generally wood and less often stone or brick.

The portico's entablature tends to be plain, in keeping with the prevalent Doric order. Except for a series of small teardrop-shaped guttae running across the top, the architrave is quite likely unadorned. Look for garlands, wreaths, or triglyphs, vertically grooved rectangular blocks, enlivening some friezes. You will also find simple moldings and dentils. When a cornice caps a portico, there may be a balustrade above.

A portico or porch does not grace every Greek Revival home. In some instances, porches from later

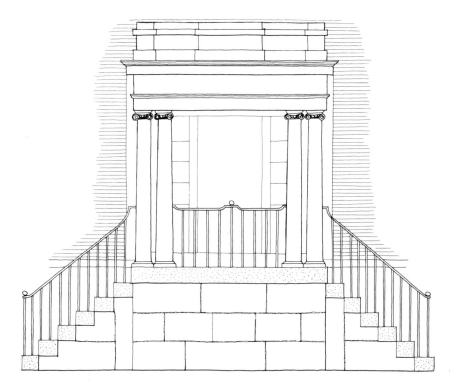

Figure 9-9. Greek Revival portico.

Figure 9-10. Gothic Revival porch.

styles, such as the Italianate, were added to Greek Revival houses. Occasionally homes built earlier were given temple porticoes to make them more fashionable.

GOTHIC REVIVAL, 1820 TO 1860

Almost every Gothic Revival home has a porch or open veranda. The majority are flamboyant and richly ornamented, echoing other fanciful designs in the house (Figure 9-10). Because they are wide and spacious, these porches invite you to lounge under their shelter. They crop up around the central entrance, across the front and two sides, along the back and partly down the sides, and at each side of a central projecting pavilion. Only a few small, simple versions resemble porticoes.

The proportions of the porches with their tall and slender columns or posts contribute to the vertical feeling of these houses. You will see many sharply pointed arches as well as elongated round versions and Moorish arches shaped like horseshoes. An elaborate porch sometimes has a higher balustraded central section accented with pointed knobs on the corner and center posts. Look for several different types of columns: modified round and slender Tuscan or Doric columns, a cluster of three delicate colonettes sitting on a pedestal, columns with a vertical block above their capitals, cutout columns with designs such as half-moons, and lattice posts with Xs and three-lobed trefoils at the tops and bottoms. Less frequently, there are plain round or flat posts.

Builders took advantage of the new machine-cut decorative trim to adorn Gothic Revival porches. Favorite targets for these embellishments were the edge of the porch roof, the arches and the spandrels, or the roughly triangular space between the curve of the arch and the enclosing right angle on the side. Among the decorations applied to spandrels are elongated trefoils, quatrefoils, circles, and circles with quatrefoils in their centers. Tiny spikes which look like icicles hang down from the inside of some arches, or small scallops outline them. The porches may have gracefully curved brackets at the tops of the columns or thin cross braces. Crenelations, or small square blocks alternating with an open space of the same shape, similar to medieval battlements on castles, may run along the edge of a flat roof. At times a series of miniature points like a crown borders the roof line. On a few porches balustrades with interlocking Xs or bisected triangles occur.

Many porches do not have railings, giving them a light and airy appearance. When balustrades do appear, they are usually quite decorative, having cut-out patterns with arrows or quatrefoils, interlocking Xs, bisected upside-down triangles, or lattice patterns. These porches generally sit on a low one- or two-step platform resting on the ground. For elevated porches, the area between the porch floor and the ground may be enclosed by a screen of simple vertical wooden pieces or with a lattice of multiple Xs or squares.

ITALIANATE, 1845 TO 1880

Italianate houses usually have prominent porches or porticoes, both occasionally on the same home. Many times, particularly when they are an arched loggia, the porches are an integral part of the house rather than an afterthought. Often as wide as 9 feet, these generous porches beckon the inhabitants to enjoy them (Figure 9-11).

Look for porches spanning the entire front, wrapping around only a portion of the front and part of a side, or reaching across the back. On a large front porch with a low-pitched or flat roof, another small projecting porch accented with a triangular pediment or a round arch may jut out over the entrance.

Porticoes most often have flat roofs, deep eaves supported by ornate wooden brackets, shallow segmental arches, and classical details. A less formal home may have a simple, bracketed protruding hood sheltering the front entry.

Expect to discover dozens of different columns: some resembling the Doric and Tuscan orders, Ionic or Corinthian versions on more elaborate houses, ones with widely flared capitals, and plain posts with lavish brackets instead of capitals (Figure 9-12). Every once in a while the columns in front of the doorway are more richly ornamented. Round shafts are thick and heavy or tall and slender. Some are fluted; a few are sculptured in several layers, square, or punctuated with recessed panels. Many times the columns have clearly articulated bases and stand on substantial paneled pedestals. The number and placement of the columns differ from house to house. An arrangement of single, evenly spaced columns is popular, although you will also find twin columns placed at the corners or bordering the entrance, columns clustered in groups of three, or columns spaced to echo the window positions above.

In general, early or more informal Italianate porches have less ornamentation than later or formal ones. Imposing curved brackets are always abundant except on a round-arched loggia. The

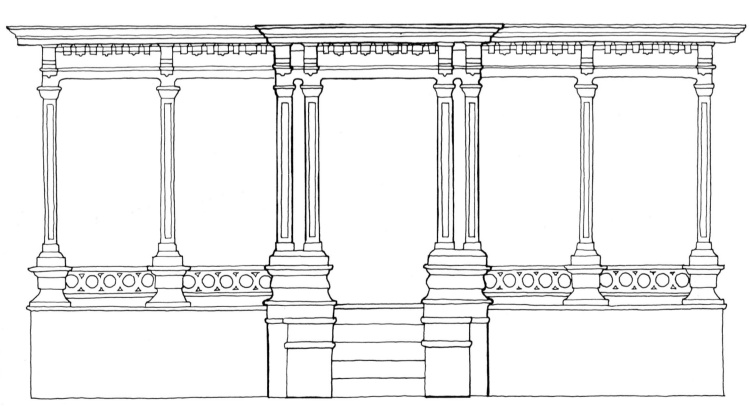

Figure 9-11. Italianate porch.

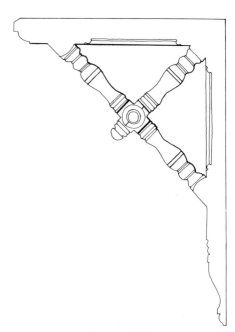

Figure 9-12. Italianate capitals.

brackets are occasionally pierced or bulbous, and the ones near the front door may be more massive. In a few instances, keystones or hanging pendants mark the centers of arches. Other decoration includes bold dentils, large modillions, and balustrades crowning some flat-roofed porches and porticoes. The roof balustrades usually have rounded forms such as interlocking circles or turned balusters.

Numerous Italianate porches and porticoes are entirely open, without any railings. When present, balustrades may appear only on the side porches and may have turned balusters or cutout patterns with circles, ovals, or teardrop shapes. Simple vertical posts or X crosspieces are less common. Porticoes and porches are frequently elevated from the ground with steps, although low platforms also occur.

Figure 9-13. Stick Style porch.

Raised porches have wooden lattices, cutout designs such as quatrefoils, or masonry beneath.

STICK STYLE, 1855 TO 1900

Expect to see generous porches spanning the front and sometimes one or more sides on many Stick Style homes, especially those along the seashore (Figure 9-13). Many times the first-floor rooms open directly onto these verandas, and second-story covered balconies provide additional access to the outside. A few houses have small entry porches, perhaps with an enclosed balcony or wide gable above.

Original porches are quite easy to identify by their striking stickwork in intricate patterns of wooden framing and ornamentation. Look for "king-post trusses," or bisected triangles, at the porch corners or in a series bordering the eaves (Figure 9-14). Corner "king-post trusses" are usually tipped on their sides with a diagonal crosspiece beginning at a block partway down the column forming the bottom of the triangle.

Plain diagonal or gently arched braces are another characteristic of these porches. Certain ones combine both types of braces, with the rounded ones at the corners and the more simple versions elsewhere. Whether thick or thin, these wooden braces, once in a while enriched by subtle carvings, spring from protrusions midway down the columns.

Most porches have tall, very thin round columns or simple stick posts. The columns may have a few spindle turnings, narrow rectangular blocks at the tops and bottoms, or flared capitals. Typically, the posts are evenly placed, and the columns are paired or, perhaps, clustered in threes especially at the corners. Some porches have railings; others do not. Porches which wrap around two sides may have plain balustrades with bisected Ys at the corners between horizontal crosspieces. Simple stick posts occur on unpretentious houses. Other balustrades include turned balusters, Chinese lattice grilles with interlocking squares and rectangles, Xs in a series, and cutout patterns with round-ended rectangles turned upright or sideways. Look for additional subtle ornaments such as delicate brackets topping posts, small turned spindles running under the eaves, exposed rafters, or, rarely, balustrades with X-shaped crosspieces above flat roofs.

Stick Style porches may be close to the ground or somewhat raised, reached by a few low steps. Vertical slats or diagonal lattices usually enclose the space between the porch floor and the ground.

MANSARD, 1860 TO 1880

Expect to see an open, spacious veranda on nearly every detached Mansard home. In keeping with the houses' style, these striking porches seem solid and substantial, often adorned with flamboyant ornamentation. Porticoes and bracketed door hoods are also found, particularly on townhouses.

When a portico accents an entrance, look for classical details, round arches, and a wide overhanging roof usually with supporting brackets (Figure 9-15). Less formal, small entry porches sometimes substitute for fancier porticoes, and either type may occur in the front or back of a home. Shallow porches frequently nestle directly against the main body of the house, although a few side porches project beyond. These porches occur in various positions: across the entire front or back; halfway across the front, perhaps with one end tucked beside a protruding two-story bay; around one or two corners; within the body of the house at one front corner, possibly sharing the same roof with a bay window; beneath the second-story corner as a front stoop; or off the first-floor windows as an open or covered balcony. In some instances, a porch and a portico appear on the same house.

Few columns follow the pure classical orders. The more authentic Ionic and Corinthian columns usually are on porticoes. Modified Doric or Tuscan columns may have altered capitals or added blocks. Other capitals include flat shoulders, flared edges, lush foliage, and ornate garlands. The shafts may be round, square, turned, octagonal with cut corners, or square with panels. In radical versions the shafts slant sharply inward from wide square bases. Many columns have blocklike bases and stand on wide, heavyset paneled pedestals. In general, the columns are evenly spaced across a porch, but look for paired

Figure 9-15. Mansard portico.

columns or clusters of three at the corners. A portico has two single columns or pairs of twins.

Mansard porches are commonly richly endowed with embellishments (Figure 9-16). Decorative bands of leafy designs, spindles, dentils, heavy modillions, or various cutout patterns may edge the eaves. Expect round or shallow segmental arches or curved ones with flat tops, often having keystones, small scallops, turned drops, or pendants at the centers. Circles, pendants, or flowers may enliven spandrels. Delicate brackets with curlicues, scrolls, or foliage typically spring from above the capitals. Fragile wrought-iron cresting, bold corner finials, or balustrades with circles, pierced panels, or squat turned balusters sometimes adorn porch and portico roofs.

When porch balustrades occur, you may find bulbous balusters or cutout patterns of ovals, interlocking circles, or quatrefoils. If present, stair railings may repeat the same design and terminate with substantial paneled newel posts with round knobs on top. Steps without railings are usually stone, at times with curved sides. The majority of these porches are elevated. Vertical slats, rectangular panels, solid masonry, lattices, or cutout patterns cover the space underneath the porch floor.

Figure 9-16. Mansard porch.

ROMANESQUE, 1875 TO 1895

Round arches are the most noticeable feature of most Romanesque porches and porticoes. At times, one stupendous arch springs directly from the foundation to become a wide cavelike opening with the doorway deeply recessed behind it. Other versions incorporate Syrian arches, or broad semicircular arches rising from low supports (Figures 9-17 and 9-18). In some instances, the rounded portion of the arch is enclosed with glass designed as a radiating sunburst. A series of short columns may sit on niched piers below. For emphasis, rusticated stones,

decorative bands, or stones of a color different from the body of the house often outline the arches. Keystones or pendants may crown the center of an arch.

Instead of these cavernous openings, Romanesque homes may have porches extending across full fronts, prominent side porches, porticoes, corner porches hidden beneath second stories, and covered arched balconies. Columns are usually squat and stout with flamboyant leafy capitals and sometimes foliage designs on the bases. Other versions, standing on tall pedestals, are shaped like round vases. A few are heavy square pillars.

The masonry walls below almost all porches and porticoes extend upward in some examples to form solid balustrades above the porch floors. Other balustrades are simple stick posts enclosed in arches, cutout patterns with round arches, or, less commonly, wrought-iron shaped as ornate leaves. The flat roofs above some porches and porticoes are occasionally adorned with balustrades having short, heavy balusters, perhaps combined in pairs, and wide paneled corner piers.

QUEEN ANNE, 1876 TO 1900

Eye-catching porches and porticoes on Queen Anne homes are like the icing on a cake. Abandoning any rigid design rules and making use of the countless machine-made accessories, builders and architects released their imaginations. These porches and porticoes come in a multitude of sizes and shapes, abound with fascinating decorations, and emerge in unexpected places. A few are serene, but most are exuberant features, asking for your applause (Figures 9-19 and 9-20).

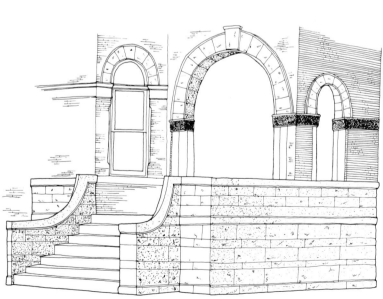

Figure 9-17. Romanesque porch.

Figure 9-18. Romanesque porch.

Look for large porches spanning all or a portion of the front, curving around the sides, or bulging out around a corner, possibly with a tower above. Broad two-tier porches may loom across the front or tuck into part of the front and bend around to one side. Sometimes a miniature covered porch or small open balcony juts out above the main porch. Recessed upper-story porches, perhaps hidden beneath a wide arch, were popular, especially in seashore homes.

In certain localities, such as San Francisco, tiny entrance porches on townhouses are masked by an extraordinary assortment of ornaments: round arches inside rectangular frames, cutouts resembling upside-down commas enclosed in squares with two defined sides, or tipped horseshoes surrounded by three-sided frames. When classically detailed porticoes occur, their proportions are exaggerated. Some porticoes even shelter two doorways on double houses. Porticoes with pediments are festooned with foliage, sunbursts, and garlands (Figure 9-21). Not surprisingly, several kinds of porches often combine in a single house.

A standard Queen Anne column does not exist. Some are spindly and skinny; others are short and stout. Most are wood, but certain ones are stone and brick. Countless types of turned wooden columns were created with various bulges and blocks. A turned column may expand and contract rhythmically up and down the shaft, flare out at the top or bottom, swell in the middle, twist around like rope, or resemble a vase. Most often, these turned columns have tall blocks at the bottom and sit on plain bases.

Other porch supports include round and square columns, slender stick posts, massive masonry piers, and square, paneled stone columns. Leafy capitals top some columns, delicate incised decoration may replace a capital, or there may be no hint of a capital. The columns sit directly on the porch floor or rest on pedestals. Arranged in various ways, single columns can be evenly spaced to create the same size bays (the space between the columns) or put closer together near the corners or by the entrance. At times, twin columns or a cluster of three columns stands on one substantial pedestal.

Most porches overflow with lively ornamentation. A band of spindles usually hangs under the eaves like a fringe (Figure 9-22). Some spindlework is similar to the turned columns or balusters, only in miniature. Other spindles resemble spools of thread, bobbins, or Christmas tree ornaments pierced with thin vertical spikes. The spindle border may be narrow or deep, and the spindles may crowd together or hang slightly apart. Look also for cutout patterns, crisscrosses, or pierced panels with sunbursts in the band beneath the eaves. Porticoes may have heavy dentils and modillions; beaded mold-

Figure 9-19. Queen Anne porch.

ings, wreaths, and garlands in the frieze; and central pendants. An inventive builder might even have placed a large upside-down open shell above a flat-corniced portico.

Many porches have flat-topped arches, occasionally varying in height and embellished with scallops or zigzags. Scrolls, circles, or spindles are found on some spandrels. Also, expect to see curved or bulbous brackets. Some radiate like sunbursts; others open like lacy fans. Delicate wrought-iron cresting adorns some porch roofs, and balustrades of turned balusters or Chinese latticework rise above a few porticoes.

Figure 9-20. Queen Anne porch.

Figure 9-21. Queen Anne portico.

Figure 9-22. Queen Anne porch's spindlework.

Gables are a conspicuous part of many Queen Anne porches. When porches have pitched roofs, the gable ends are often flamboyantly decorated, and the steps are placed at the end of the porch. In other instances, a wide gable, perhaps with a window, strapwork, and sunburst panels, crowns a second-story porch. If a portico intersects a porch at the entrance, the gable end of the portico's roof becomes a pediment, probably garnished with sunbursts, garlands, or foliage.

Porch balustrades are almost universal and delightfully diverse. Turned balusters are just as varied as turned columns. Plain stick railings occur, possibly enclosed in an upside-down arch or designed in two unequal levels separated by a crosspiece. Cutout patterns of scrolls, circles, flowers, or lyres are typical. Spindles appear either in two small tiers, as elongated bobbins, or between vertical dividers with rectangles above. Other railings include slender reeded posts, perhaps punctuated with a few panels, and Chinese latticework. As vertical extensions of the foundation wall, solid stone balustrades are common on brick or stone houses. A few porches and porticoes nestle close to the ground on one-step platforms. Raised ones have square or diagonal crisscrosses, vertical slats, horizontal clapboards, or masonry as enclosures beneath.

SHINGLE STYLE, 1880 TO 1900

A porch, either fitting comfortably into the body of the house or protruding from a side, almost always accompanies a Shingle Style home. In both instances the porch is an integral part of the house, blending with its design and interweaving the inside with the outside. Because most Shingle Style homes were built at the seashore and other vacation sites, these ample porches were well suited for summer outdoor living (Figure 9-23).

Do not be surprised to find a house sheathed in shingles boasting a Queen Anne porch. Some earlier homes were later covered with shingles to make them look like houses built in this style.

The most prevalent kind of porch is tucked underneath the main roof. It may extend across all or part of the front, occur at a corner, or wrap around one side. Smaller versions are located only near entrances. Because the roof sweeps down from the ridge to cover the porch, the columns and railing are flush with the exterior walls.

Projecting porches are wide and spacious. Their long, low silhouettes echo the horizontal lines of the house. Often these verandas stretch along the entire front, curve around a corner, or run along a side. Accenting a corner, at times, is a two-tier round or many-sided porch capped with a peaked roof (*see* Figure 9-23). Occasionally a house has a substantial

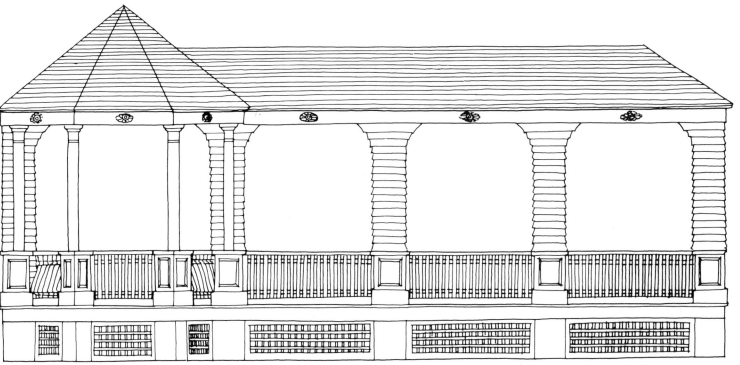

Figure 9-23. Shingle Style porch.

porch protruding forward at the entrance, possibly with a second-story room above or an elaborately decorated gable pediment.

Shingles completely sheath many porches, covering the piers, flat-arched openings, and balustrades, fusing them with the shingled house (Figure 9-24). Other homes have plain square posts or round wooden columns. The capitals are generally simple, perhaps gently flared, or they may be modified Doric and Corinthian designs. Thick stone pillars sometimes with massive boulders are found on houses having stone foundations and first-story walls. To emphasize the corners, every once in a while these porches include flared wooden posts sitting on stone pedestals.

Do not expect to see fancy decoration on these porches. When balustrades occur, they are subdued. In addition to the shingled balustrades, features to look for are stick posts, Chinese lattices, stone walls extending upward from stone foundations, and, rarely, turned balusters which may bulge outward. Many Shingle Style porches hug the ground on low platforms. Other, slightly elevated versions have pierced lattices or stone, if stone is used on the house, beneath the porches.

Figure 9-24. Shingle Style porch.

Porches and porticoes usually dress up Georgian Revival houses. In almost every example the porticoes are inflated versions of the earlier prototypes with wider dimensions and a profusion of classical details. Porches are seen only on Georgian Revival houses.

Placed in front of the central entrance, a Federal Revival portico is most likely a large rectangle with paired Ionic columns. Except for pronounced dentils, the entablature is generally quite plain, crowned with a wooden balustrade.

In contrast, Georgian Revival porticoes are much more prominent (Figure 9-25). More like porches in size, they appear in oval, semicircular, rectangular, and square shapes bulging out from the center of the

At times these porticoes are immense. When the central portion of the house projects forward as a pavilion, two two-story columns may support the top pediment. In some instances, a second-story balcony connects these two columns, or a two-tier porch may join two sets of one-story columns. A few examples have porches piled on top of one another for three stories.

On many Georgian Revival houses rectangular porches branch off from one or both sides. This type of porch may be one-story high, possibly with a balustrade above, or two-stories high with a glass-enclosed interior room on the second floor. Other porches may span the entire front. The space beneath these Revival porches and porticoes is closed in with wooden lattices or masonry.

Figure 9-25. Georgian Revival portico.

house. Look for tall Doric or Ionic columns, ones with flared capitals, and round smooth or fluted shafts. Frequently four evenly spaced columns form wide bays, although twin columns or a grouping of three may be used at the corners of square or rectangular porticoes. Swags, garlands, beaded moldings, and bold dentils may adorn the entablature. Porticoes with flat cornices often have wrought-iron or wooden balustrades overhead with turned balusters, wooden panels, and wide paneled corner posts topped with tall urns. Sometimes these porticoes have segmental arches creating curved vaults underneath, full triangular pediments, or pediments with the bottom open in the center.

MAINTENANCE AND REPAIR

Porches and porticoes are sheltering features, but often unsheltered themselves from the weather. Without watchfulness and care rapid decay is the almost inevitable result. By being near the ground, porches are also targets for insects. To be safe in wet climates, keep all porch wood well above the ground unless it is pressure treated with a wood preservative. As a further precaution, separate the porch from the rest of the house to prevent transferring to the house any trouble with the porch.

Wise and frequent maintenance is the key to a long-standing porch. When you see a problem, track down and eliminate its source; then take care of the symptoms. The list of places on the porch or portico where problems are likely to arise is long. Inspect them at least once a year (Figure 9-26).

- Examine the wood steps and posts, the underside of the porch, other wood near the ground, and the place where the porch joins the house for decay and for signs of termites and other insects.

- Check the area under the porch for excessive moisture.

- Scrutinize the columns and posts, especially at the bases, for decay.

- Look at the flooring and steps for cracks and deterioration and for the proper slope away from the house.

- Search the joints for any gaps, particularly where the porch joins the wall or another roof.

- Investigate any masonry, mortar joints, and wood for evidence of deterioration.

- Be certain the roofing material and the flashing are in sound condition. Check under the roof for dampness or moisture stains.

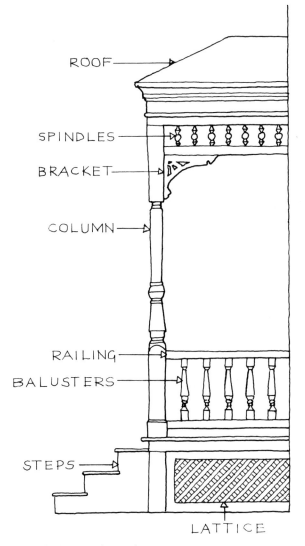

ROOF

SPINDLES

BRACKET

COLUMN

RAILING

BALUSTERS

STEPS

LATTICE

Figure 9-26. Parts of a porch.

- Notice whether gutters and downspouts work well and find out if water splashes any nearby wood.
- Study the paint for peeling, blistering, or cracking.
- Be alert for rust spots around the nails, pointing to a possible moisture problem.

WOOD CARE

Most porches and porticoes are constructed entirely, or in large part, of wood. To prolong the life of the wood, a homeowner can make a number of repairs. Fill small cracks in the wood with putty or caulk them. For larger cracks or holes, use plastic wood. For wide gaps in the wood or joints, insert oakum or another filler and caulk over the filler. Other products to lengthen the useful life of wood include epoxy consolidants for deteriorated wood and epoxy fillers for holes and cracks.

Another technique is to replace the rotted section of wood. Cut out the damaged wood and patch the wood with a piece of wood of the same dimensions. Glue the patch into place. Caulk over the joint and paint or finish to match the existing wood. The sections Small Cracks in Woodwork and Large Cracks and Rotting Wood in Chapter 11, Windows, explain more about wood repairs.

When replacing wood in wet climates, install either wood treated with a wood preservative or all heartwood stock of naturally decay-resistant woods such as cypress, redwood, cedar, white oak, or black locust. On areas of the porch or portico where the paint has peeled or deterioration has begun and where horizontal ledges occur, treat the wood already in place with a wood preservative. Remove the paint first to allow the preservative to soak into the wood. Before repainting, apply a primer compatible with the wood preservative.

MASONRY CARE

Use good maintenance procedures on brick or stone on or under the porch or portico. When needed, repoint the joints and repair any cracks or deterioration. Duplicate the kind of mortar, its color, and the type of joint initially put on the porch. Any new bricks or stones should resemble the color, size, and texture of the original masonry material. Chapter 8, Walls, describes more about masonry care and repointing.

ROOFS

The faster the water drains off the porch roof and away from the porch, the longer the porch will survive. There are several ways to direct water harmlessly from the porch. The gutters and downspouts of the house should work well and should not dash water onto the porch roof or other parts of the porch. The porch may require diverters to control where the water goes or gutters and downspouts located in inconspicuous locations, if possible. Also, the porch roof should slope away from the house.

Low porch or portico roofs were often originally metal, although many of these have been replaced with a different roofing material. Maintain these roofs in good condition. Not only can water get through a rusted or deteriorated roof to the sheathing or roof timbers beneath, but it can damage the entablature, capitals, columns, posts, and other parts of the porch or portico. Another place where trouble can occur is at the juncture of the porch or portico roof with another roof or the walls of the house. Check carefully to be sure the flashing does not have holes or cracks or is not loose. Make the necessary repairs at once, for water can permeate the walls of

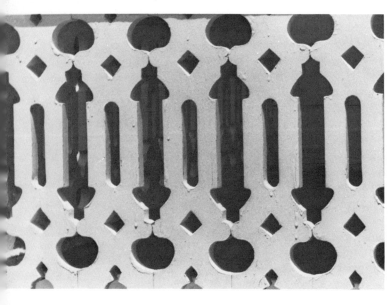

the house and cause serious structural damage. A drop of solder for a small crack or hole and a metal patch for the larger holes may take care of metal flashing. When the flashing has come loose and exposes a gap, put the flashing back and seal the joint with caulking compound. Removing part of the wall or roof material to reach the flashing may call for professional help. Chapter 4, Roofs, gives more information on roof repairs.

COLUMNS, BALUSTRADES, ENTABLATURES, AND BRACKETS

Porch or portico columns, balusters, entablatures, and brackets must be checked regularly and repainted whenever the house is painted, or more frequently, if necessary. Before painting, scrape off cracked or loose paint, sand and clean the surfaces, and apply a coat of primer to seal the wood pores.

Joints can provide a gap for water to enter. Tighten any loose joints immediately. If necessary, put a screw at an angle through both pieces of wood to hold the pieces together. Drill a pilot hole first, countersink the screw, and cover with plastic wood. Paint over the plastic wood. Keep the joints caulked and painted.

Railings will shed water better if the top slopes away from the center. Wood railings on the bottom will last longer if they do not touch the porch floor.

The base of a column often does not dry out and, consequently, it rots. A base resting directly on the porch floor increases the chance of decay. Vents inserted at the base and near the top of a column help to dry out a column. Adding a metal plate between the floor and a column's base is another way to resist rot. If any part of a column must be replaced, retain the sound parts and locate a similar part to take the place of the damaged capital, shaft, or base.

Balusters, also, are subject to rot at the bottom where moisture accummulates. The top portion may not deteriorate as quickly because it is protected from the weather by the handrail. If only one or a few balusters have rotted bottoms, carefully remove these, restore the rotted areas by one of the methods suggested in the Wood Care section of this chapter, and replace them. When many balusters have deteriorated, consider removing all of them, making the necessary repairs, and replacing them upside down with the stronger portion now on the bottom. Whether this procedure is feasible will depend on the extent of the rot and the baluster's design.

If the entablature and brackets are basically sound, a homeowner can replace small broken or missing pieces. Take a piece of cardboard and cut out a pattern of the piece needing replacement, copying an existing similar piece. Use a small saw, such as a bandsaw, to cut the design from wood. Treat the wood with preservative. Then glue or nail the piece in place. Prime and paint to match the existing color.

FLOORS

Check porch and portico floors periodically for loose or warped planks, protruding nails, and exposed or deteriorated wood. Any wide surfaces, such as flooring or treads on steps, wet easily and hold moisture, especially when there are depressions in the wood. Porch floors should not lie flat, but should slope slightly away from the house to shed water. To protect a wood floor in a wet climate when the wood is not treated with a wood preservative or the floor is not made of naturally decay-resistant wood, caulk the joints between the boards with white lead in linseed oil. Be certain, too, that the underside of the flooring is in satisfactory condition.

Figure 9-27. Porch steps.

STEPS

Wood steps are especially susceptible to rot or deterioration when they have concave areas and when they do not slant slightly away from the porch (Figure 9-27). Rot is more likely, too, if the steps or their supports are in contact with the soil. A 3- or 4-inch concrete strip placed between the bottom step and the ground is one way to separate wood steps from the soil. Caulk the joint between the step and the concrete.

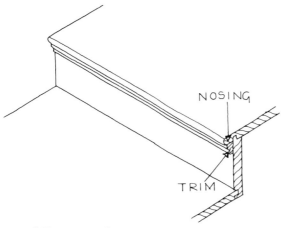

Figure 9-28. Nosing and trim on porch steps.

When steps are worn, it may be possible to turn over the treads and walk on the sturdy underside. To replace a tread or riser, try the following procedure. When the step has both a riser and a piece of trim above the riser under the nosing, or tread extension, remove this trim with a chisel or putty knife (Figure 9-28). Carefully hammer the underside of the tread at the nosing, releasing the tread from the riser. Lift the tread from the riser and from the stringers at the sides with the aid of the chisel or putty knife. Pull forward to remove the tread from the riser above.

If the riser requires replacing, release it from the tread above and saw off the exposed nails with a hacksaw. Cut replacements the same size as the treads and risers unless the old tread does not extend beyond the riser about 1 inch. In that case, add 1 inch to the width of the tread to form a drip cap

above the riser. Place the riser in position and nail it to the stringers. Nail the new tread in place. Put back the trim piece, if there had been one initially above the riser.

THE GROUNDWORK

Pay particular attention to the bottom of the porch — its supports, its foundation or crawl space, and the underside of the floor — as these less-visible areas can be the source of many problems (Figure 9-29). Sloping the soil away from the porch is a good practice. Adequate ventilation is essential, and if moisture seems to collect in this area, adding vents may help. When the porch sits over dirt, cover the ground with sheets of building paper or polyethylene overlapping about 6 inches to reduce moisture on the porch. If the ground beneath the porch is uneven, seal the edges of the covering with asphalt cement. Otherwise, hold down the edges with bricks.

Wood near the ground requires termite protection. Remember: Except in dry climates, only wood pressure treated with a wood preservative should touch the ground. Untreated wood should remain well above the soil. Concrete footings are one means of raising wood supports above the ground level.

Uneven settling of a foundation may cause a porch to sag. When both the porch roof and the floor sag in the same area, the cause of the problem may be in the foundation or footings. In these circumstances contact a competent general contractor for advice.

REPLACEMENT

For many styles the porch or portico gives the house its personality. If one part of a porch or portico has deteriorated beyond repair, replace that part. For example, install a new floor, replace a roof, or add another column for a rotted, split, or bowed column. In these situations, do not tear down the entire porch or portico.

Plan ahead when replacing parts. First, try to retain as many of the original pieces as possible. If a part cannot be saved, obtain exact copies of its materials, dimensions, and details. One exception could be balusters. Stick posts might be a substitute for turned balusters, if the latter are not available. Stock moldings or a series of moldings may serve to build a handrail or a cornice. For replacement parts, try suppliers of decorative parts, who carry an assortment of columns, capitals, pilasters, balusters, brackets, cornices, and friezes in many sizes. You may also order special designs from some of these companies. Other sources of duplicate parts may be wrecking-

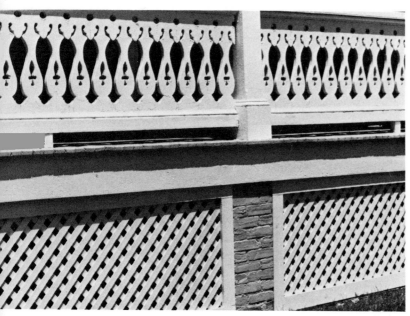

Figure 9-29. Porch lattice.

Figure 9-30. Metal or plastic awnings and wrought-iron columns and balusters.

company yards, stores specializing in architectural parts, lumber and millwork companies, and cabinet-makers, who will create replicas of the impaired pieces.

If a reproduction of the original is not feasible, copy the materials and dimensions without the details. In visible locations, always use similar parts. Simpler or slightly different versions may be hidden in less-conspicuous locations.

A special problem occurs when work is done on columns, posts, or other supporting members of the porch. During this work provisions often must be made for holding up the roof. You may decide to call on professional help for this task.

Some contractors and siding specialists tell homeowners that a porch or portico is a nuisance and out of date and attempt to persuade them to demolish it. Leisurely afternoons or evenings on the porch are events of the past: The automobile and television have seen to that. The porch or portico, however, has a role as a stage setting for a house, often defining and enhancing the style. Once these are gone, the house has lost a portion, sometimes quite large, of its value.

When many parts of the porch have deteriorated severely, major repairs and wholesale replacement of these components may be impractical. In these circumstances, the porch or portico must be torn down and a suitable new version constructed. Do not substitute concrete steps, metal or plastic awnings, and new wrought-iron columns or balusters (Figure 9-30). These materials clash with most older houses and are not maintenance free. Wrought iron, for example, will rust, and it seems flimsy in place of the sturdier looking wooden posts or columns. Plastic, metal, and concrete detract from the brick, stone, or wood in an older home and diminish its value. On early twentieth century residences that have original concrete steps or some initial wrought-iron porch parts, these features can be retained.

Consider removing any porch clearly inappropriate in style or materials. A competent architect can advise you about whether or not to keep porches

Figure 9-31. Twin house illustrating the value of retaining the original porch.

and porticoes that were added later and which are not designed in the same style as the house. Sometimes these newcomers enhance a home, and they reflect a portion of its history. When removing an unfitting porch, seek a qualified architect's advice about devising a sympathetic replacement, possibly using some of the materials in the house or echoing certain of its features. Be certain all new work meets the requirements of the community's building codes.

When adding more interior space to a house by enclosing a porch in a highly visible location, consult an architect. If well designed, an enclosed porch could become an asset to the house.

TWIN AND ROW HOUSES

If a home is a twin or row house with a prominent front porch or portico, try to duplicate the original design in any replacements (Figure 9-31). To retain the unified appearance of twin or row houses, coordinate necessary changes with your neighbors, always copying as closely as possible the initial porch or portico.

CHAPTER TEN

DOORS AND DOORWAYS

Have you ever really looked at your front door and doorway? The next time you enter your house, do not thrust your key into the lock and walk in hurriedly, already plotting your next five tasks. Pause. Look above you and smile at any exuberant scrolls. Turn to the side and pat a column. Admire the craftsmanship of the doorway. Think of the families before you who lived in and cared for your house. Feel the solidity of the door as you open it. Now walk inside.

Front doors in older houses are more than entrances and exits. They provide security, privacy, and protection from the weather. They are an invitation to visitors and a prelude of what they will find inside. But your door and doorway do something else. They always relate to the original design of the house. The size of the front entry, where it is located, and its decoration—all these aspects were carefully considered by the initial architect or builder. Often the doorway is the most eye-catching feature of an older home.

In taking care of an older house, pay special attention to the entrance. Try to retain the original height and width of the door, its framing, and its decorative elements. Altering the dimensions of the door, blocking down a doorway, covering a transom, or removing any embellishments destroys the balanced relationship between the different parts of the house, changing its entire appearance.

DESIGN

The front door may be the original one designed for the house. If so, you have a special treasure. By all means keep it!

How can you tell if the front door is original?

- Take a close look at the door itself. Is the door heavy and thick? Is it made up of solid members? If it is, the door may be old, especially if it has wooden panels. Lightweight, hollow-core, or flush doors are replacements, not originals.

- Examine the area surrounding the door. Are there any additional moldings, decorative parts, or sidelights? Usually these embellishments indicate an older doorway.

- Search the vertical edges of the door for tenons. Visible tenons are found in old doors (Figure 10-1).

- Notice how the panels are constructed. Early doors from about 1700 until the American Revolution ordinarily have raised panels. Recessed or sunken panels appeared after the American Revolution, although you may find raised panels on some late nineteenth century doors, especially in Queen Anne homes.

- Observe the moldings located at the juncture between the panels and the rails and stiles. Until approximately 1835 moldings were cut from the solid wood stiles and rails by hand with molding planes (see Figure 12-5). Doors made before 1776 commonly have plain ovolo moldings with rounded convex profiles about one-quarter of the circumference of a circle. If the house dates from 1776 to 1835, expect to find either an ovolo molding embellished with beads or small channels, called quirks, or an ogee molding which looks like an S with both a convex and a concave curve (see Figure 12-7).

   After 1835 machine-cut strip moldings became increasingly popular, although some carpenters continued to make moldings by hand, particularly in rural areas. These separate molding strips were attached around the edges of the recessed panels to hold them in place (see Figure 12-6). Most often the machine-cut moldings were wider than the handmade ones. Sometimes, too, these later doors had moldings applied in several layers.

- Count the paint layers on a painted door and compare them with the layers on a part of the house you are certain is old. Chapter 13, Paint and Color, describes how to do this.

- Inspect the door for any evidence of earlier hardware. One way to identify very old strap or HL hinges is to see if the nails protrude about ⅜ inch on the back and bend over to the wood, an early technique called peening. In addition, for evidence of missing hardware, look for paint ridges with a raking light.

- Check the following descriptions and illustrations of the doors most often associated with a particular architectural style. Use these as a guide to be certain the door is original or suitable.

A word of caution: Some architectural styles have relatively uniform front door designs. Their distinctive features make these doors quite easy to identify. In other styles doorways vary, especially in Gothic Revival, Mansard, and Queen Anne homes. One reason for these differences is that numerous architectural pattern books were widely used in the eighteenth and nineteenth centuries as sources of design ideas. Also, by the late 1800s millwork shops across the country published catalogs showing types of doors and other special features appropriate for a certain style. Builders and architects simply selected a doorway which appealed to them or the buyer.

SEVENTEENTH CENTURY

The earliest houses in the eastern colonies have plain, practical wooden doors (Figure 10-2). The doors are often formed by two layers of boards—vertical on the outside and horizontal on the inside. Joined together by large-headed, hand-forged nails clinched on the inside, the double surfaces provide extra protection from the weather. For added sturdiness strips of wood, called battens, are sometimes nailed across the back of the door, particularly when the door is a single layer.

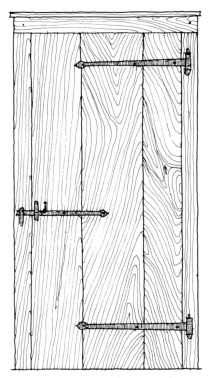

Figure 10-2. Seventeenth Century door.

Occasionally a Seventeenth Century door divides in the center, allowing either the top or the bottom section to open separately. Diagonal battens or battens in an X shape often brace these doors to make them more rugged. Simple strap hinges, sometimes as long as 2 feet, fastened these early doors. A wooden crossbar locked the door. Latches can also be wooden.

The door is set in a narrow wood frame. You will not find any decoration around the door, for these doorways are strictly functional. Few original Seventeenth Century doors survive today, but good reproductions are available because the door's design is quite easy to copy.

EIGHTEENTH CENTURY— GEORGIAN, 1700 TO 1780

Entrance doors are eye-catching prominent features in the overall design of Eighteenth Century houses. The simple doorways of the early part of the century gradually became more elaborate in the later decades, and a great variety of designs emerged (Figures 10-3 and 10-4).

At first builders added a row of four, five, or six small rectangular window panes above the door, called a transom sash, to light the room inside. They also introduced doors with six or eight raised panels (Figure 10-5), the stiles and rails having integral hand-planed moldings (see Figure 12-5), although plank doors persisted in modest homes or in rural areas. Occasionally glass panes were inserted in the

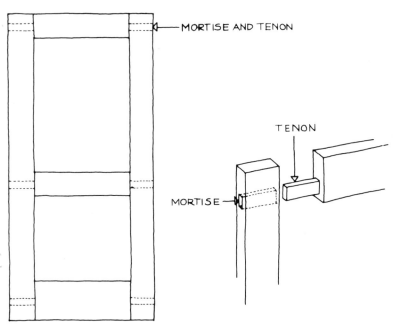

Figure 10-1. Visible tenons.

Figure 10-3. Early Georgian door.

Figure 10-4. Late Georgian door.

upper panels of the door itself. Door frames also became wider.

Some homes have double, or two-leaf, doors. In southeastern Pennsylvania and southern New Jersey pent eaves, or narrow, slightly slanted roofs, often project above the door to protect the entrance.

As the century progressed, the door frame assumed numerous forms. Flat or half-rounded columns, known as pilasters, commonly were attached to the wall on both sides of the door. These pilasters, either plain or with curved grooves called fluting, may extend the full height of the door or rest on small bases known as pedestals. To complete the entrance frame, a cornice, or horizontal board capped with a simple molding, may reach across the top of

the door. In fancier houses this crossband is quite likely wider with more ornate decoration and is called an entablature. Chapter 9, Porches and Porticoes, gives a description of the parts of an entablature.

An elaborate doorway frequently includes a triangular shape, known as a pediment, above the door. In more opulent entrances pediments, instead of being triangular, may have half-oval forms or sloped scrolls, sometimes separated, or "broken," in the center and embellished with ornaments.

Long, narrow windows on either side of the door, called sidelights, appear around the mid-eighteenth century in a few larger houses. At first sidelights remained outside the pilasters or framing. Later they

Figure 10-5. Georgian paneled doors.

Figure 10-6. Federal door.

moved closer to the door, inside the pilasters. Occasionally a glass fan-shaped window or a dummy fan carved in wood extends across the door and sidelights.

FEDERAL, 1780 TO 1830

A Federal doorway seems light and delicate (Figure 10-6). Certain uniform characteristics make it easy to identify. The wooden door usually has six or eight raised panels with hand-cut surrounding moldings (*see* Figure 12-5). Slender sidelights, extending all the way to the threshold or to somewhat above it, frequently flank the door on both sides. A fanlight window, shaped like a wide semicircular or semielliptical fan, nearly always rests above the door on a flat crosspiece, or transom bar. These surrounding windows allow light to surge into the interior.

The panes in the sidelights are simple rectangles, and those in the fanlight resemble a sunburst. If this pattern differs in a Federal house, a later owner may have modernized the glass adding more elaborate tracery, a flowery ornamental design made of metal. Usually a molding encircles the entire door frame. Long, thin pilasters or columns may be attached to the wall at the edges of the sidelights or directly adjacent to the door as delicate decoration. There may also be a graceful triangular pediment with fine-scale ornamentation (Figures 10-7 and 10-8). Around the front door of some brick houses you may find a shallow, recessed brick arch. An elegant iron handrailing occasionally adds another touch of beauty to the entrance.

GREEK REVIVAL, 1820 TO 1860

Doorways in Greek Revival houses are simple and dignified (Figure 10-9). In most cases the wooden door has four to eight panels with the taller ones lo-

Figure 10-7. Federal doorway with pilasters and pediment.

Figure 10-8. Federal doorway.

cated in the upper or middle part. After about 1835 many doors have recessed panels edged with a separate machine-made molding strip (*see* Figure 12-6). Plain, narrow sidelights and a horizontal transom with rectangular panes invariably outline the door. Most often the sidelights are floor length, although they may stop a foot or slightly higher above the threshold. Occasionally square panes called corner lights accent the juncture between the transom lights and the sidelights.

Several types of decorative framing emphasize the front entrance, particularly in northeastern homes. These include flat pilasters tucked into the wall next to the outer edge of the sidelights and a wide, horizontal architrave crowning the entrance. Above the architrave and frieze, a pediment may accent the doorway on an elaborate house.

A recessed entranceway is common with the door and sidelights set back from the front surface. When the entrance steps are steep, iron railings may act as an elegant guard.

GOTHIC REVIVAL, 1820 TO 1860

Verticality is the hallmark of Gothic Revival houses. The entrance doors, often composed of narrow, vertical boards, repeat the upward direction of the vertical clapboard or board and batten siding (Figures 10-10 and 10-11). Two slim, rectangular windows or one elongated window divided into several vertical panes may appear in the upper portion of this type of door. Occasionally a small window is found in an upper corner.

Gothic Revival doors have other attractive designs. Sometimes the door is wood paneled with two long panels extending either the full length of the door or three-quarters of the length with two small panels below. The door itself may have a pointed arch at the top. In more elaborate examples a narrow, horizontal wooden panel crosses the lower portion of the door with two long, slender panes of glass above. Sidelights may extend the full length of the door and have delicate crisscross tracery.

Entrances are accented in different ways. Customarily a molding outlines the doorway to create the appearance of an archway. Sometimes a hood decorated with wooden brackets and other ornamental trim projects above the door, or a gabled second-story balcony or oriel window may extend over the entrance.

ITALIANATE, 1845 TO 1880

Single or paired wooden doors with bold molded panels characterize Italianate entranceways (Figure 10-12). The top panels tend to be long and narrow, and those on the bottom are often smaller squares

Figure 10-9. Greek Revival door.

Figure 10-10. Gothic Revival door.

sometimes with curved corners. The lower panel may also be a raised circle.

A double door with rectangular, round-arched, or semiarched glass panes in the upper section also was used. In some examples the door is round at the top. Occasionally a semicircular or rectangular glass transom exists above the door. Windows with panes shaped like those of the front door may be located near the entry, but sidelights are rare.

Notice the embellishments around Italianate doorways. You may discover a heavy molding surrounding the door to create a simple arch. Engaged, or attached, columns, sometimes with a twisted rope design, may flank the door as part of this archway. A hood supported by ornate brackets may shelter the door, or a small columned porch, often with a low balcony above, may adorn the entrance. Sometimes a long, wide veranda extends across the front of the house obscuring the main entrance.

STICK STYLE, 1855 TO 1900

You may have to search for the entry door of a Stick Style house, for it does not have the starring role in the total design that it has in many other styles. In a seashore cottage the entranceway usually hides behind a small informal front porch or a spacious veranda encircling the house. In urban areas Stick Style houses may have modest, unadorned porticoes.

Frequently the door combines glass panes and plain wooden panels (Figure 10-13). For instance, the upper half of the door may have several small panes of glass or two vertical rows of three rectangular panes. A diagonal lattice pattern may occur in the lower half of the door, or oblong or square wooden panels. In some cases the door is formed of square glass panes set in a sturdy wooden frame. Do not look for elaborate decoration, except for occasional sidelights, around the doorway; look only for the simple structural frame.

MANSARD, 1860 TO 1880

Mansard houses have a pleasing variety of doorway designs, reflecting the extensive number of choices available to architects, builders, and homeowners (Figure 10-14). Although there is great diversity, certain features are usually seen in Mansard doors. Front entrances frequently have paired doors with similar patterns on each side. Often these sturdy doors have prominent moldings or wooden panels arranged in numerous combinations of squares, rectangles, and shapes with curved corners. For instance, an elongated, arched pane of glass may appear in the upper half of the door with a square wooden panel beneath. In some examples the top of the door is rounded. Delicate carved flowers or garlands occasionally decorate the door panels or the frame above the door.

Vestibules, or small halls connecting the outside with the rooms inside, are prevalent, especially in the brownstones abounding in many cities. The two

Figure 10-11. Gothic Revival door.

Figure 10-12. Italianate door.

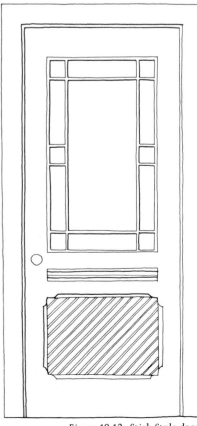

Figure 10-13. Stick Style door.

Figure 10-14. Mansard door.

Figure 10-15. Romanesque doorway.

sets of doors needed for these vestibules generally relate in design to one another. Often the exterior doors have large panes of glass to bring light into the vestibule and allow you to see the double doors beyond, which ordinarily are wood paneled.

Frames surrounding Mansard doors appear in a wide assortment of designs. Sometimes a simple, but conspicuous molding outlines the door, suggesting an archway. Frequently found in stone and brick houses, this arched molding is commonly stone. At times a glass transom, defined by a fine molding, rests above the paired doors.

ROMANESQUE, 1875 TO 1895

You can identify a Romanesque entranceway by its massive, semicircular arch (Figure 10-15). The rounded arch may be flush to the wall with the door recessed in deep shadows. In other examples a porch, perhaps covered with the same tiles as the main roof, conceals the doorway. The arched entrance generally is located on one side of the front of the house, although it also may be in the center.

Romanesque houses are most often built of stone or brick, and so are the entranceways. Coarse stone wedge-shaped pieces called voussoirs may form the

arch, or stone moldings may accent the archway. Now and then squat stone columns with ornate tops decorate the doorway.

The front door is heavy and substantial, in keeping with the robust appearance of this style. Often the door is formed of solid wood panels in combinations of different-sized squares and rectangles. You will also see arched glass panes, at times with a delicate etched design, in the upper half of the door or a narrow rectangular glass pane at eye level. Double doors and paired, or single, arched transoms are common.

QUEEN ANNE, 1876 TO 1900

If you live in a Queen Anne house and there are other homes of a similar style in the neighborhood, chances are you will find that few entrance doors look exactly alike. Builders of this style delighted in putting together the various exterior features so that each house appears unique.

Queen Anne front doors do have one distinct characteristic: large panes of glass inserted in a heavy wooden frame (Figure 10-16). The glass not only adds light to the inside, but also creates a feeling of openness to the outside. The glass panes come in all

Figure 10-16. Queen Anne door.

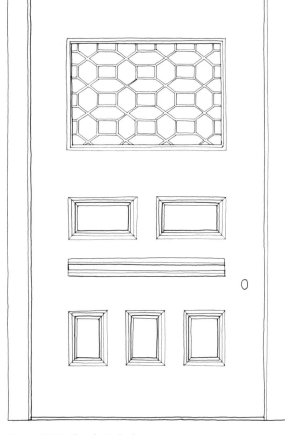

Figure 10-17. Shingle Style door.

sorts of sizes and shapes. A full-length rectangular pane is common, maybe enlivened with fine lattice tracery. Glass ovals or rectangles may reach halfway or three-quarters of the way down the door. Sometimes in the top half of the door builders set bands of square panes to resemble the window panes elsewhere in the house. Glass panes designed as circles were particularly popular in certain cities such as San Francisco. In some examples a carved wreath in the lower portion of the door echoes the circular glass in the upper section. When the glass is confined to the door's top half, stained glass with colorful, delicate patterns may appear. Check the edge of the glass to learn whether it is original. If the edge is slanted, or beveled, the glass may be old.

Decoration on Queen Anne doors is usually fanciful, repeating designs found on the outside of the house. Sunbursts, fans, garlands, scrolls, wreaths, and rosettes animate the wood panels. Even the brass door handles may have floral designs.

Rarely will you see sidelights, transoms, or plain wooden doors in Queen Anne houses. But, as could be expected in this light-hearted style, there are exceptions. Multicolored stained glass transoms, for example, are common in certain localities. The framing around the door may be a simple molding or a more ornate embellishment such as pilasters topped by a small triangular pediment.

SHINGLE STYLE, 1880 TO 1900

Front doors in Shingle Style houses are not easily seen from the street. You will probably discover one tucked behind a wide archway, beneath a veranda with a low, sloping roof, or under a covered entranceway made by extending the main shingled roof or the second story over the doorway area. In a more elaborate house a portico with a low, spreading pediment, adorned with a sunburst design, may mark the entrance.

Wider than most doors, a Shingle Style front door is usually divided into three or more horizontal sections, complementing the overall lines of the house (Figure 10-17). Horizontal rectangular wooden panels generally occur in the lower sections of the door with glass in the upper portion—a single clear pane, many small square panes, or a sunburst design. Occasionally there are solid wood–paneled doors sometimes with a transom above.

A larger Shingle Style house may have rows of square glass panes as sidelights flanking the door or bands of windows near the entrance bringing light into the spacious interior hall.

A word of warning: An old front door may not resemble a typical Shingle Style door even though the house is covered with shingles. In this case the original house was probably built in another architectural style and later "modernized" by shingling.

REVIVALS OF THE GEORGIAN AND FEDERAL STYLES, 1885 TO 1940

Georgian Revival and Federal Revival doorways resemble the earlier styles they are copying although they are not exact duplications (Figures 10-18 and 10-19). In general these entranceways are more elaborate and larger than their earlier counterparts, and the details tend to be heavier and less graceful. Fanlights often span both the door and the sidelights. Columns or pilasters capped by an architrave, a frieze, and a pediment frequently frame the door in a Georgian Revival house.

Figure 10-18. Georgian Revival door.

Figure 10-19. Federal Revival door.

MAINTENANCE AND REPAIR

With effort and know-how you can improve the condition and appearance of your old door and save money and, perhaps, an original door at the same time. Rubbing, warping, decay, and gaps between the door and the frame or between the frame and the wall are all troubles you may encounter at some time. To take care of the door and the entryway, search carefully for problems (Figures 10-20 to 10-22).

- Check the wood for deterioration, especially at the bottom.
- Look around the door and doorway for gaps where air and water might enter, and examine panels for cracks.
- Learn whether the threshold is in good condition.
- Be alert for paint that is blistering or peeling.
- Observe whether the hinge screws are tight.
- Notice whether the door sticks.
- Inspect the glass for cracks and the stops around the glass for looseness.

RUBBING

A small space, at least 1/16 of an inch, should exist between the door and the frame unless weatherstripping is applied. To solve the problem of a door that is sagging and thus sticks, begin by checking the hinge screws. If the wood immediately around the screws has deteriorated or if the holes have become too large, remove the screws and fill the holes with small pieces of wood, such as toothpicks, dipped in glue. Replace the screws when the glue has hardened.

If you have determined that loose hinge screws are not causing the door to sag and rub, notice whether the hinges are too deep or protrude too far beyond the face of the jamb. The hinge leaf should be flush with the jamb. To discover where the door is rubbing, move a piece of heavy paper around the edges of the closed door. The place where the paper does not move easily is the place where the door is rubbing. When the rubbing occurs at the bottom near the outside corner or near the top of the latch edge of the door, the bottom hinge screw may be recessed too far. Remove the screws from the bottom hinge leaf on the jamb and place behind the hinge leaf a piece of cardboard, or shim (or more than one, if needed), slightly smaller than the hinge leaf. Reinsert and tighten the screws in the hinge leaf. If the rubbing is at the top near the outside corner or near the bottom of the latch edge of the door, slip cardboard under the hinge leaf on the jamb (Figure 10-23).

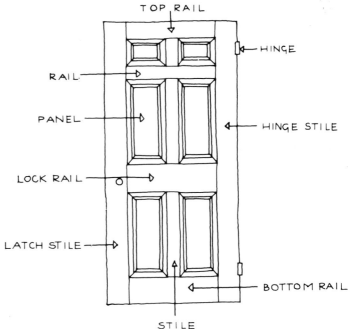

Figure 10-20. Parts of a door.

To fix a hinge leaf that protrudes from the face of the jamb, the door must be taken off. Start this operation with the bottom hinge pin. Hold a screwdriver or wooden wedge at the top of the hinge pin and tap against the wood or screwdriver to push the pin upward. After the door has been taken off, remove the hinge leaf and chisel out enough wood to recess the hinge leaf deeper in the jamb.

If the above techniques do not take care of a door that sticks, you may have to sand or plane the edge where the rubbing occurs, working from the end to the center to prevent split edges. Try sanding first, being careful to remove only the necessary wood. When sanding or planing the top or latch edges, the door can remain in place. Wedge a magazine or

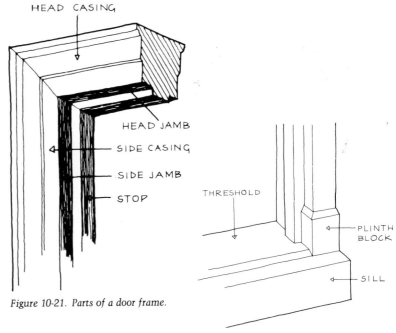

Figure 10-21. Parts of a door frame.

Figure 10-22. Threshold.

newspaper under the door to hold it open while you work. For rubbing over a large part of the latch edge or close to the latch itself, plane or sand the hinge edge because it will be easier to reset the hinges than the lock. Start by removing the door. After taking wood off the hinge edge, you may have to chisel out more wood to set the hinges deeply enough. If possible, protect the exposed wood from dampness by applying a wood preservative before priming and painting or before varnishing. In many neighborhoods, however, removing an exterior door long enough for the preservative to dry is unsafe.

DETERIORATING WOOD

Exposure to the weather causes the door and the decorative framing around it to deteriorate. Try diligently to repair the wood, for the door and framing contribute greatly to the character of the house. Take care of small cracks promptly. Clean out dirt and disintegrating wood. Then apply a sealant designed to fill cracks in wood. Another way to do this job is to brush the crack with linseed oil and wait until it has dried. Fill the crack with linseed oil putty. After the putty has hardened, prime and paint.

Several techniques of repair are appropriate for larger areas of degenerating wood. One method is to fill the holes with plastic wood, although plastic wood has the undesirable characteristic of shrinking after it has been applied and, therefore, it may fall out with vibrations. For holes more than ¼ inch wide or deep, put in an appropriate filler, such as oakum, and caulk over the filler before priming and painting. You can also cut out the deteriorated wood until you reach sound wood. Prepare a patch of the same dimensions from new wood. For maximum protection soak it in a wood preservative before gluing it in place with a durable, waterproof glue. Prime and paint. Another solution is to use an epoxy consolidant or filler in the wood. For more details about these techniques read the Large Cracks and

Rotting Wood section in Chapter 11, Windows. The Decay or Rot section in Chapter 8, Walls, explains more about wood care.

SETTLING

The settling of a house may tilt a door frame out of square. For a minor problem, either place a cardboard shim behind the hinge leaf or sand or plane the door. If the frame slants drastically, the opening will require reframing.

WARPING

If the warping is not excessive, you may be able to straighten the door. When the warping occurs on the hinge stile, installing a third hinge between the existing hinges may correct the warp. If the door bulges, remove it and lay it across supports located at both ends of the door. Set heavy weights on the bulge for at least 24 hours. A badly warped door must be replaced.

RATTLING

A door may rattle when closed because it is too far from the stop molding or because the strike plate needs adjusting. Installing strips of foam or felt weatherstripping on the doorstop will halt the clatter. Another way to stop the noise is to take off the stop molding, if it is a loose molding, and renail it closer to the door.

SQUEAKING

If the door squeaks, the hinge may need oil. Tap out the hinge pin. Wipe oil on the pin and put it back.

THRESHOLDS

Thresholds are particularly vulnerable because of intense use. If you must replace the threshold, make certain the new one fits tightly, for it must bar any water from seeping inside. It is a good idea to use the old threshold as a pattern once it is taken out, or to take careful measurements before its removal.

GLASS

Glass panes in the door and glass sidelights require special care to keep water from running down the glass and deteriorating the wood beneath. One way to protect the wood is to place a piece of molding under the glass to shed water away from the wood. You will have to cut the glass to provide space for the molding. Set both the glass and molding in glazing compound.

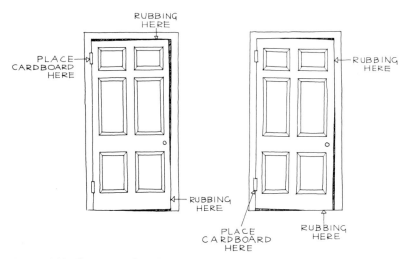

Figure 10-23. Shimming a door that rubs.

PAINTS AND FINISHES

The best gift you can give a valuable old door is to seal it with coatings of paint, stain, or varnish. The door will have less chance of shrinking, warping, sticking, and rotting, and it will endure longer. Include all edges in your work to protect the more porous end grain, giving special attention to the bottom of the door. A wood preservative applied to any bare wood before painting or finishing is an effective safeguard. The door framing and decorative features will benefit, too, from this kind of care.

To display the grain of the wood in a door in good condition, many owners decide to stain or varnish the door. Spar varnish is popular because it will stand up to the weather. If the door is already covered with paint, the first step is to remove the paint. Then smooth the door with an extremely fine sandpaper or steel wool and wipe off all dust with a tack cloth. As with a good paint job, the preparation is the key to pleasing results. See Chapter 13, Paint and Color, for more information about painting.

When varnishing bare wood, thin the first coat with turpentine by as much as 20 percent. Watch for drippings and brush over them immediately. After the coat of varnish has hardened, sand it lightly with fine sandpaper. Dust with the tack cloth. Follow the same procedure for each coat. If possible, take off the door and work on a horizontal surface to ensure an even coating of varnish without runs and sags.

LOCKS

The door may shrink, causing the latch bolt to fit insecurely in the strike plate opening. Place either a cardboard or a metal shim behind the strike plate or place shims behind the door hinges to move the latch bolt into the correct position. Sometimes the opening has become a little too high or too low. Taking off the strike plate and filing the opening slightly in the proper place may be all you need to do. If the latch bolt and the strike plate opening are substantially out of line, try to determine the source of the difficulty and solve this problem. To accommodate the latch bolt, the strike plate may require being moved. Fill the old screw holes with small pieces of wood dipped in glue. You will probably have to chisel out more wood in the opening for the latch bolt.

Locks work better and last longer if they are lubricated now and then. Never use oil, which will only collect dust. Always use a powdered graphite or a lubricant spray manufactured for locks.

WEATHERSTRIPPING

Weatherstripping helps to prevent air from entering and escaping from your home. It is inexpensive and

Figure 10-24. Appropriate and inappropriate storm doors.

effective. Fitted interlocking metal channels are the most efficient type of weatherstripping, but they are hard to install and ought to be left to professionals. Several types of weatherstripping that amateurs can install handily include felt, spring metal, tubular gaskets, adhesive-backed foam, and self-adhesive plastic strips.

Check to make sure the door fits properly. Also, make certain the door frame and the wall meet tightly. Caulk any gaps you find.

When deciding on one weatherstripping material over another, consider its permanence. Felt and adhesive-backed foam, for example, are relatively short-lived. In contrast, spring metal, tubular gaskets, and plastic strips are much more durable. In any case, inspect the weatherstripping annually and replace it when it is worn. Also, purchase weatherstripping with an eye to its appearance. Spring metal, felt, flexible plastic strips, and adhesive-backed foam all have the advantage of being invisible when the door is closed.

Products are available to seal the bottoms of doors. You can easily attach a doorsweep to the door. It is possible, too, to fit a shoe with a gasket to the bottom of the door to secure it effectively, a more difficult procedure because the door must be removed. An alternative is to install a new threshold with a vinyl insert.

STORM AND SCREEN DOORS

In colder climates storm doors help to keep in heat and keep out drafts. They prevent moisture condensation which can cause a door to decay. Unfortunately, a storm and screen door is often shoddy and ugly. It changes the appearance of a home by concealing the front door and alters its design by adding an untoward element (Figure 10-24).

WHAT YOU CAN DO

When storm and screen doors are necessary, the following ideas will help to improve the appearance of the entranceway:

- Choose a simple storm and screen door exposing as much as possible of the door of the house. A storm and screen door is available formed of a single pane of safety glass framed by a narrow strip of anodized aluminum or by white, black, or brown baked enamel.

- Avoid plain aluminum storm and screen doors which contrast too strongly with the natural materials of an older home. Instead, you can paint the aluminum door to match the front door. To ensure that the paint will stick to the aluminum, go over the surface with steel wool or fine sandpaper and a solvent, such as mineral spirits, and then apply a primer manufactured for aluminum. For an older aluminum door, wire brush or sand corroded spots down to bare metal and sand any rough areas before coating with a primer.

- Consider buying an aluminum storm and screen door with either an enamel or anodized finish if these doors are available in colors that will blend with the front door.

- Keep your wooden storm and screen door, if you have one, and paint it the same color as the front door.

- Explore wrecking-company yards for a good wooden storm and screen door to fit your door opening.

- Use a screen door only in the summer in warmer climates and, if practical, remove it in the winter.

- Purchase a wood storm and screen door designed especially for your front door—probably an expensive option.

HARDWARE

If the original hardware is on a door, make every effort to take care of it. Often it is cheaper to repair hardware than to find a new piece, and a manufacturer of quality reproductions may be willing to fix an old latch or hinge. If you must replace it, choose carefully. Hardware is expensive. Remember that hinges, knobs, latches, locks, and knockers must blend with each other in size, design, and materials. They must also suit the house. In the seventeenth and eighteenth centuries the more modest and rural homes had iron hardware. Brass appeared on the fashionable doors in the cities.

The extensive variety of hardware designs is astonishing. If a nearby home of a similar style has its original hardware, use it as a guide for your purchase. To replace hardware, explore the sources listed in the following section on door replacement.

REPLACEMENT

If you have a deteriorated or drastically altered original door or an unsuitable one, try to find a replacement similar in size and material to the original door and appropriate to the style of your home. Remember that many standard doors are not fitting designs or materials for older homes (Figure 10-25). Frequently, they are poorly made of cheap materials, and they will not last. They are often the wrong dimensions for the door frames of older houses. As a substitute, sometimes it is possible to move a door from a little-seen location in the house to a more prominent place.

All exterior doors must be solid-core construction and at least 1¾ inches thick. When searching for a replacement, always carry the measurements of your door with you. Bring along a tape measure, for you may come upon a somewhat larger door which can be cut down a little to fit your door frame.

WHERE YOU CAN FIND DOORS

A number of sources exist where you can search for entrance doors appropriate for an older house.

Wrecking-Company Yards. You may find your perfect door at a wrecking-company yard in a jumble of doors of all sizes, ages, and styles in varying de-

Figure 10-25. Unsuitable front doors for older homes.

grees of repair. Prices range from as low as a few dollars to about one-third of the price of the cheapest new door. There you will also discover a few choice doors that are more expensive. For instance, a carved, 10-foot high, solid cherry door costs about as much as a moderately priced new door.

Antique Dealers. The general-line antique dealer with vast storage space will often stock old doors. For better prices, seek dealers outside the high-rent commercial centers of a city or town. If the dealers do not have what you need in stock, alert them to your requirements, and they will look for the right door (and hardware, too) for you.

Stores Specializing in Architectural Parts. You may be lucky enough to live near a store specializing in architectural parts or a salvage storehouse run by a historical commission. Here amidst a diversity of doors you may encounter the right size and style.

Reproductions. Generally, manufacturers of reproduction doors carry Seventeenth and Eighteenth Century doors with prices comparable to the cost of a new standard door. The catalogs listing products for old houses name several of these firms. Read the manufacturers' catalogs carefully to learn about delivery costs and times and whether the door is stained or finished.

Custom-Made Doors. You can work with a carpenter or a lumber and millwork company to duplicate an original door or to construct one of a different design. This approach is costly, but it will save time. Ask to see some examples of the work to ensure that you will be pleased with the results. Bring along a picture, a photo, or an architect's sketch as a guide for the craftworker.

Auctions. At certain auctions you may find old doors. Learn beforehand which auctions feature architectural parts.

On-Site Salvage. If you come upon a door you can use at the site of a building being torn down, negotiate for it on the spot. Check with the local government agency responsible for demolishing houses to learn which ones are scheduled to be torn down.

Neighbors. In a neighborhood where several buildings have been torn down, someone living nearby may have acquired parts from these structures and stored them in a basement or garage. Inquire whether anyone in the area has such a collection.

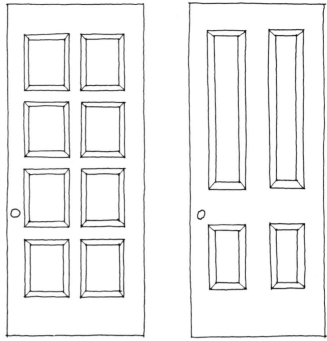

Figure 10-26. Suitable front doors for older homes.

Standard-Stock Doors. When you have thoroughly investigated all other sources without success, a simple wood-paneled stock door could be selected, but only as a last resort. This can be a temporary answer, and your search can still go on. (Figure 10-26).

Even though you may have found it in a wrecking-company yard, the right door may not be cheap. But remember that you, your neighbors, and your visitors will enjoy it for the quality of its materials and craftsmanship and, perhaps, for a design rare in this age of standardization. You can be sure you have made a good investment.

ORNAMENTAL FRAMING

The decorative framing around the door is often in an exposed location, and it may crack, decay, or disintegrate. Repair or replace it, if possible, for it contributes significantly to the house's personality. A home with brick or stone walls may have extra casing, called jamb casing, around the door. Preserve the jamb casing, too, for it often has molding, paneling, or other trim to match the door.

If a decorative piece is missing, you may be able to use a similar piece as a pattern for a craftworker to make a duplicate. Also, stock molding may turn out to be a good substitute for the original molding. Remember that standard stock framing is usually not suitable for the older home. You can order replacement pieces or an entire new framing system from competent firms specializing in accurate reproductions.

CHAPTER ELEVEN

WINDOWS

Windows add sparkle to a house, both to the inside and outside. They let in light and fresh air and offer a view of the surroundings and of events in the neighborhood. Windows can be the most eye-catching feature of an older house. Rarely are they hidden. So many of them exist in a house, they command your attention.

Everything about a window—its size, shape, framing, decoration, number of panes, and location—is important to the appearance of an older house. Within one home there may be an assortment of windows or only one kind. Within each architectural style there may be a variety of windows or only a few different ones.

Window sizes in older homes take many forms from small slits in the wall to large openings. Single windows, pairs, triples, or several windows grouped in a long band occur. Many are double-hung sash windows; others are single-hung sashes, casements, or immovable designs. You can expect to see rectangular shapes regularly, but also look for other configurations. Among these are pointed, square, circular, elliptical, round-headed, transom, bow, bay, lattice, lancet, eyebrow, oriel, Palladian, and tall two-story windows. The window panes, whether squares, upward-turned rectangles, sideways-turned oblongs, or diamonds, vary in number, size, and arrangement. There may also be delicate tracery, stained glass, or glass which is etched, tinted, bent, leaded, beveled, or cut.

The framing around older windows is just as diverse. Sometimes it is plain or outlined with simple moldings; at other times ornate carvings, columns, colonettes, or pilasters are accents. Lintels, cornices, pediments, caps, or hoods may grace the tops of windows. The sills are narrow and unassuming or wide and bold, perhaps supported by brackets. The decoration ranges from none to subtle to exuberant ornamentation. It may be similar throughout all the windows or change from floor to floor or even from window to window. At times some windows are dressed up with fancy grilles across the glass, balconies in front, or balustrades above.

The placement of windows has special significance in older houses. Design handbooks for different architectural styles suggested window locations, which in turn influenced the layout of the inside. In the more formal or classical styles windows tend to be placed evenly. Windows in all stories line up with one another, adding to the symmetry of the house. More informal architectural styles allow greater freedom in the location of windows. There is less precise alignment and more concern for the amount of light needed for a particular room, and there are even some capricious arrangements. A few older houses mix both regular and irregular window placement.

Windows are problem prone, subject to constant abuse by the weather. The key to sound and tight windows is preventive maintenance. Check them regularly for drafts, leaking, sticking, warping, missing ornamentation, broken cords or glass, and any cracks between the various parts of the window and also between the window and the wall. Fortunately, you can solve many of these problems yourself without the added expense of professional help.

Windows contribute significantly to the uniqueness of an older house. Retain, if possible, and carefully preserve all features of an original window—sash, framing, sill, lintel, cap, ornamentation, and the number, size, and type of panes. When replacement is necessary, attempt an accurate duplication of the first window including its materials.

DESIGN

Several considerations led the initial builder or architect of a house to select a certain type of window. The architectural style was a leading factor, and for many styles design handbooks offered guidelines for appropriate choices. Where a house was built, especially the climate, affected decisions about windows. Another element was the purpose of the window—to bring in just a little light or a great splash of sunshine, to serve as a door, or to be purely decorative.

The knowledge of various construction methods and the availability of mass-produced moldings and ornamentation also influenced the outcome. In many instances, local carpenters added their own touches to windows, usually in their embellishments.

Beware! Windows may have been changed over the years to make them more fashionable. It is, therefore, difficult to date a house only by its windows.

How do you know a window is old?

- Examine the number of paint layers and compare them with the paint layers on other parts of your house that you determined are old.
- Look for evidence of tenons where the rails join the stiles.
- Notice any imperfections in the glass panes such as ridges, wavy lines, or amber or violet colors.
- Search in the corners for wooden pegs. These appeared in sash windows made before about 1800.
- Measure the width of the muntins. Muntins, also known as mullions or glazing bars, are the narrow dividers which separate the panes and secure the glass. Early muntins could be as wide as 1⅝ inches; later ones became thinner. By the end of the nineteenth century wider muntins were again used.
- Check the following sections of this chapter for information on the type of sills and framing, the size and number of panes, and the kind of ornamentation likely to be found in older houses.

SEVENTEENTH CENTURY

Windows in Seventeenth Century homes probably are not original. Houses built before 1650 hardly ever had glass window panes. Instead their window openings were covered with oiled paper or closed with simple batten or sliding board shutters. Although glass panes were more common after 1650, they were still a luxury. Because all glass was imported, it was expensive and highly valued. Individuals even bequeathed glass in their wills.

Original windows also disappeared during the Revolutionary War when the lead securing the glass panes was used to make bullets. Most of the remaining Seventeenth Century windows were replaced with "modern" double-hung sash windows in the eighteenth and nineteenth centuries. Because early houses often had only one window for each room, later owners may have added windows to brighten the interiors of their homes. For these reasons it is probable that a Seventeenth Century home has newer windows, which may or may not resemble the originals.

What should you look for to find out if the original windows survived or if the reproductions are satisfactory? A typical Seventeenth Century window is a casement with long corner hinges attached to the structural frame along one side and with the sash swinging outward at the opposite edge (Figure 11-1). Small diamond-shaped panes, known as quarries or quarrels, are set in slotted lead strips called cames. The casement frame is made of wrought iron or thin wooden bars. A simple wooden frame, flush with the window or set back approximately 1 inch, surrounds the window. The wall studs may serve as the side jambs with the sill and top mortised into the studs. Brick houses, especially in Virginia, may have windows crowned by low arches and framed by a pattern of the smaller ends of bricks, called headers.

Glass panes vary in size. The two most common types are the long diamond-shaped quarrel measuring about 4 by 6 inches and the somewhat larger rectangular quarrel, 4⅝ by 6 inches. Occasionally oblong shapes (horizontal rectangles) or square panes appear. Early glass may be only about 1/16 inch thick, although some is thicker. Look for a wavy surface and a slight violet or amber tinge to the glass.

Some windows are fixed and do not open. In this case there is no sash, and the leaded glass fits directly into the surrounding frame. Cross bars (saddle bars) or vertical pieces of wood (guard bars) set into holes in the window sill and the top of the frame are sometimes included to add stability.

Windows appear in different types, sizes, and combinations, often in the same house. Casements are vertical or square and are usually about 2 feet high. They may be grouped together in twos, threes, or fours. Frequently, fixed windows adjoin each side

Figure 11-1. Seventeenth Century casement windows.

of a central movable casement, creating a wide horizontal band. Single windows are common in third-story gables; less often, these may be the only type of window in the house. Sometimes a window is divided by a horizontal bar into two sections either similar in size or larger on the bottom. When two windows of this type are placed together, the horizontal and vertical bars form a cross, an effect described as cross mullioned. The upper panes are generally fixed, with hinged casements below.

In the seventeenth century window placement was haphazard because no design rules existed prescribing where windows should be located in the house. Instead, a few windows were positioned wherever needed to provide light inside. Only in some larger houses did builders attempt to put second-story windows directly over those on the first floor.

EIGHTEENTH CENTURY—
GEORGIAN, 1700 TO 1780

Windows changed dramatically in the eighteenth century. Small casements persisted during the early 1700s, but improvements in glassmaking and construction techniques made possible an entirely new type of window: the double-hung sash. The sash is opened and closed by moving it vertically, providing easy ventilation. Both the glass panes and the win-

dows became larger, permitting more light to enter houses.

Sliding sash windows, an idea borrowed from England, first appeared in Massachusetts homes around 1714, although some were installed in government buildings in Virginia several years before this date. By 1725 this style of window was in general use in rural as well as urban homes.

Single-hung sash windows came first, with the top portion usually fixed and the lower sash movable. This type of window, called a guillotine, did not have counterweights to prevent the window from falling. Either sticks or a peg, inserted through a hole in the frame, held the sliding sash open. Three other types of pegs—a spring-operated peg, a stepped plunger, and a curved lever—were sometimes attached to one side of the sash to secure it in place. The lower sash frequently was smaller than the upper one, making it easier to lift.

Popular after the middle of the century, the double-hung window has an inside sash which moves up and an outside sash which slides down, both balanced by lead counterweights at the end of cords or chains. A box frame fits around the window sashes to accommodate the pulleys and weights. The sash frame itself is fairly light, often about 1 to 1¼ inches thick. Before the American Revolution muntins were relatively heavy, 1¼ to 1⅜ inches wide (Figure 11-2).

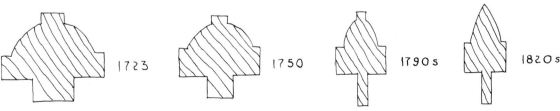

Figure 11-2. Muntins.

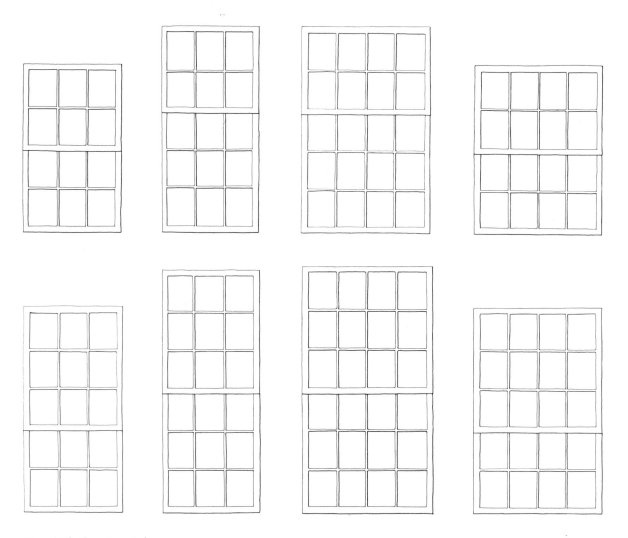

Figure 11-3. Georgian windows.

Prior to 1776 the size of the window panes varied considerably. The prevailing sizes were 6 by 8 inches, 7 by 9 inches, 8 by 10 inches, 9 by 11 inches, and 10 by 12 inches. Early Georgian homes and less pretentious houses usually had very small panes, and homes built later in the century, or more elaborate houses, often had larger panes.

The number of panes and their arrangement in the sash also differ markedly (Figure 11-3). Eighteen or twenty-four panes per window were common in earlier homes. Windows with twelve panes first appeared about 1730 and gained in popularity as the century progressed. You will also find windows with eight panes in the upper sash over eight in the lower section, nine over six, eight over twelve, twelve over eight, or twelve over twelve. Occasionally, especially in rural New England, the number of panes in first-floor windows differed from those on the second story in a single house. Gradually six over six became the most favored and most consistent combination.

Figure 11-4. Early Georgian window.

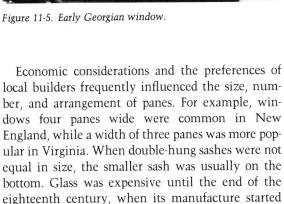

Figure 11-5. Early Georgian window.

Figure 11-6. Georgian window pediments.

Economic considerations and the preferences of local builders frequently influenced the size, number, and arrangement of panes. For example, windows four panes wide were common in New England, while a width of three panes was more popular in Virginia. When double-hung sashes were not equal in size, the smaller sash was usually on the bottom. Glass was expensive until the end of the eighteenth century, when its manufacture started on a large scale in this country.

Windows in early Georgian houses are usually surrounded by plank-front framing consisting of simple boards set almost flush with the exterior wall and mortised and pegged at the corners (Figure 11-4). Plank-front framing appears heavy and boxlike. Later a simple molded frame, or casing, was used on the face of the wall.

Sometimes a small decorative band called a cornice caps the window (Figure 11-5). The cornice may be plain and narrow or embellished with fluting and moldings. On a larger Georgian house built after 1750 a small-scale triangular pediment occasionally graces the top of the window (Figure 11-6). Separated, or "broken," and scroll pediments are more rare. Cornices and pediments generally appear only on first-story windows because second-floor windows are often flush against the frieze, a flat band of decoration under the eaves at the top of the exterior wall.

In a masonry home the window framing is usually flush with the outside wall, but occasionally it projects beyond. Once in a while you will see a recessed window with the masonry side jambs revealed. At times adding emphasis to the window is a stone or brick lintel, a cross-member at the top of the window which supports the weight above the opening. A lintel usually extends slightly beyond the window frame. A flat arch accented by a wedge-shaped keystone in the center and a low segmental arch may also top the window. In some cases windows are outlined in a brick pattern or by heavy stones. Wood cut to resemble stone also may surround the windows.

Most Georgian windows are rectangular, but you will find at least two other shapes. A long, round-arched window often marks the stair landing. Around 1750 the Palladian window became prevalent above the main, centrally located entrance. The Palladian window is comprised of three windows usually divided by columns or pilasters: two rectangular windows flank a taller, round-arched window (Figure 11-7). Less frequently, the side windows are also arched. Until about 1800 builders continued to place Palladian windows in houses, especiallly in New England and the South.

In a Georgian house, look for regular, evenly placed windows of equal size and for a consistent number and arrangement of panes. The first- and

Figure 11-7. Georgian Palladian window.

second-story windows line up exactly with one another. Usually there are four windows and a central door on the first floor and five windows above. In more elaborate late-Georgian houses window proportions may differ, however, with those on the first story having taller dimensions and larger panes than those above.

FEDERAL, 1790 TO 1830

Federal windows are formal and subdued. They reflect the builder's interpretation of the classical influence (Figure 11-8).

As soon as glassmaking began in America around 1792, larger panes became available at much lower costs. Because of their increased size, fewer panes were needed for an individual window. The most common arrangement was six panes in the upper sash and six panes in the lower section of a double-hung window. Do not be surprised to find twelve over twelve panes in a Federal house, however, as this earlier style continued in use, especially in rural New England and other remote areas.

More refined details in Federal windows became possible after the American Revolution because craftworkers had better tools and developed greater woodworking skills. Muntins, which had been at least 1 inch wide, narrowed to ⅝ inch or only ½ inch

in width. These slender bars made Federal windows appear light and delicate (*see* Figure 11-2).

Window proportions are taller and narrower than those in the Georgian style. The panes are longer— 10 by 14 inches, 11 by 15 inches, and 11 by 16 inches—and the windows are customarily only three panes wide. Sometimes the second story of Federal townhouses will have elongated windows three panes wide and six panes in length instead of the usual six over six panes.

The heavy plank-front framing prevalent in the beginning of the century disappeared in Federal houses, replaced by a narrower frame, known as a reveal, which is recessed in the wall. The simple molded framing around a window in a wood house may include a cornice or a frieze across the top. Look for carving and fluting more delicate than Georgian decorations.

In masonry homes of the early Federal period, window frames are flush with the walls. Later brick houses have thin frames set back slightly from the wall's surface. A narrow lintel, extending a few inches beyond the frame, usually tops the window. A variation to the lintel is a flat arch having a wedge-shaped keystone and slanting edges. In brick houses stone lintels are common, sometimes with ends jutting upward. Windows may also be decorated by low brick arches formed by the long, or stretcher, sides of the bricks in wide fanlike shapes or by the heads of the bricks in single or double rows. Occasionally semicircular brick arches appear.

Figure 11-8. Federal window.

Once in a while you may discover the rectangular window recessed slightly behind a tall round arch. Flat pilasters or wider piers attached to the wall may support the arches. This arrangement is usually found on the first-floor windows, sometimes only on windows adjacent to the main entrance.

One type of decorative window appearing in Federal homes built before 1800 is the Palladian window, which often accents the center of the second story in the front. A later version, especially after 1810, may have triple windows without the taller arched window in the center. Sometimes you will see a semicircular or an elliptical window shaped like a fan in the center of the third story above a Palladian window.

Federal windows are evenly spaced and carefully aligned. Subtle differences in window size and framing frequently distinguish each floor. Usually first-floor windows are tall with narrow frames. The second-story windows may have the same number of panes (six over six), but their dimensions may be somewhat smaller and the framing may be wider, particularly in earlier Federal homes. Third-story windows are even smaller and may have three over six, six over three, or three over three panes. Graceful wrought-iron balconies adorn the windows of some townhouses.

Figure 11-9. Greek Revival window.

GREEK REVIVAL, 1820 TO 1860

Windows in Greek Revival homes are dignified and uniform. Consistency in size, proportions, and details occurs because builders generally followed design guidelines from books and because glass sizes had become standardized. There are differences, but these are not glaring or frequent (Figures 11-9 to 11-11).

Usually the window has large rectangular panes arranged as six over six in a double-hung sash. Less often, nine over six panes appear. Sometimes two window types are combined with six over nine panes on the first floor and six over six on the second story.

Frequently a Greek Revival home has large, tall windows on the first floor reflecting the high ceilings inside. A brick townhouse or a home with a spacious columned portico may have first-story windows extending to the floor level. In these examples you will usually find six to eight very large vertical panes arranged in rows two panes wide. Many times such a window is without a movable sash.

Two window types are unique to the Greek Revival style: frieze windows and attic windows on the third floor. A home designed with a pediment-shaped gable facing the front occasionally has an attic window in the center of the gable (Figure 11-12). Usually an attic window is a long, narrow rec-

Figure 11-10. Greek Revival window.

tangle with a single row of three panes or a double row five panes wide. In a more elaborate house small, fluted engaged columns may flank the attic window.

A Greek Revival home sometimes has a frieze, a wide horizontal band located under the eaves where the roof joins the wall, which may include frieze windows (Figure 11-13). These are also called eyebrow windows because they are near the top of the

Figure 11-11. Greek Revival window.

Architects and builders handled the window framing in several ways. Sometimes only a simple flat or molded frame outlines the window. In a clapboard house the framing often extends slightly out from the wall, but in a brick house it is usually flush with the wall's surface.

Lintels with either straight or slanted ends are prevalent. These may be flat or paneled with raised centers or with upward-turned end blocks. In masonry houses lintels are customarily stone, sometimes enriched with moldings which cap the edges. Do not expect to find lintels in the shape of segmental or semicircular arches in Greek Revival homes.

In other examples a plain, narrow cornice crowns the window, or a small pediment accents a townhouse window. The trim on the top may also take the form of a shouldered architrave, a horizontal molded band which protrudes slightly beyond the sides of the framing and gives the appearance of shoulders. Wider framing with more pronounced shouldered architraves may accent first-floor windows. Where these windows are six over six, the framing frequently extends to floor level with a decorative wooden panel filling the space below the window. A taller first-story window may be bordered by flat or molded full-length pilasters and topped with a molded architrave or a more elaborate cornice.

Windows on different floors line up exactly with one another in Greek Revival homes even though their sizes may differ.

wall in the place where eyebrows appear on a face. Less frequently, in fancy columned porticoes, false frieze windows, which are merely decorative, may be part of the entablature, the entire crosspiece between the top of the columns and the eaves. Most of those openings are low rectangles covered with pierced grilles made of wood or cast iron. The grilles generally have delicate scroll patterns copied from builders' guidebooks.

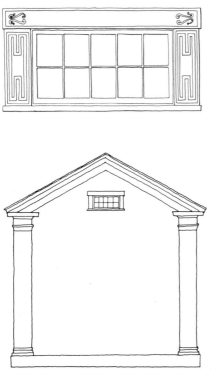

Figure 11-12. Greek Revival attic window.

Figure 11-13. Greek Revival frieze window.

Figure 11-14. Gothic Revival window.

Gothic Revival windows have fanciful shapes and surprising locations. Architects and builders not only copied pattern books, but they also created imaginative designs of their own. Expect the unexpected!

One characteristic of Gothic Revival windows is their vertical emphasis (Figures 11-14 and 11-15). Most are tall and narrow, frequently shaped in sharply pointed arches. These are called lancet windows. Also look for windows with gently curved arches or flat tops on elongated rectangular windows (Figures 11-16 and 11-17). Long windows with elliptical tops appear more rarely.

Glass panes are arranged in numerous ways. Windows, known as lattice windows, have leaded diamond-shaped panes. Occasionally a window with small diamond panes has a large, single pane in the lower section. Tall, rectangular panes may be combined as four over four, two over two, two over six, or even one over one. Windows that are two panes wide and four panes high are sometimes seen.

In Gothic Revival windows slender tracery with intricate curved or geometrical patterns is not unusual. The tracery may form twin pointed arches within a flat-headed or arched window, or it may branch outward in the upper section to create several interlocking arches. You will find many inventive designs.

Figure 11-15. Gothic Revival window.

Figure 11-16. Gothic Revival window.

Figure 11-17. Gothic Revival window.

Figure 11-21. Gothic Revival window with hood molding.

Figure 11-18. Gothic Revival oriel window.

Unusual decorative windows often enliven Gothic Revival houses. First-story bay windows are common. Oriel or bow windows with three or more tall windows may project from the second story (Figure 11-18). Graceful, slanting roofs or simple flat covers top oriel windows. Usually an oriel window is supported by a bracketed corbel which tapers inward toward the wall. Delicate ornamentation may be applied above or below the windows.

Windows with ingenious shapes were also popular, especially in gabled dormers. Among these designs are round windows, three-lobed "trefoils," (Figure 11-19) and four-lobed "quatrefoils" (Figure 11-20).

Bold trim, either flat or molded, accents Gothic Revival windows (Figure 11-21). In some examples the side framing curves gently. A window is often capped with heavy hood moldings which project over the window, around the corners, and partway down the sides to resemble a hood. The ends of hood moldings may protrude perpendicularly to the frame, curve upward, or terminate with rounded pendants.

There is no standard window placement in Gothic Revival houses. First- and second-story windows may align, or variations may occur, particularly on the side walls. Oriel windows or tall double windows sometimes appear over the main entrance. Small balconies occasionally grace second- or third-story windows. It is also common to see windows grouped in twos or threes or paired as twins under a single hood. Diversity abounds.

Figure 11-19. Gothic Revival trefoil window.

Figure 11-20. Gothic Revival quatrefoil window.

Windows in Italianate homes are prominent and most often richly embellished. In their regular placement, size, and detailing they add to the overall formality of this style (Figure 11-22).

You will find tall windows with large vertical panes. Arched or round-headed windows are common, sometimes with a gentle curve, at other times with a semicircular or elliptical shape (Figure 11-23).

The number and arrangement of panes varies. In urban brownstones one over one and two over two are favored. Larger first-story windows may have four over six panes or two over eight. You can also expect to see four over four and six over six, particularly in small towns. Frequently Italianate windows are grouped together in twos (especially in earlier houses) and threes, perhaps joined by a single sill or enclosed within the same frame.

Eye-catching bay and oriel windows adorned with decorative brackets may appear on more elaborate houses (Figure 11-24). Sometimes small balconies embrace second-story windows. If an Italianate home has a tower, look for combinations of windows there unlike those elsewhere in the house: a single, round-headed window; two large rectangular windows; three narrow, arched windows; or even a round window.

The framing around Italianate windows is generally ornate and bold. Wide, heavy moldings around the windows give them a sturdy appearance. The window is usually topped by a substantial cornice, a rounded hood, or a decorative window cap projecting from the wall and supported by ornamental brackets.

Cornices appear in imaginative versions. Some are simple, flat crosspieces occasionally with small triangular extensions in their centers. Others undulate gently; several layers of decorative moldings embellish still others. Shallow or more sharply pointed triangular pediments may also adorn Italianate windows. Simple lintels without fancier decoration are rare, but you will see them.

Decorative brackets are common for windows in all sizes of Italianate houses. Most cornices are supported by carved brackets, which also frequently appear under window sills. Larger Italianate houses may have even more elaborate window ornamentation. Pilasters or engaged columns may flank both sides, and a rounded arch may spring from their capitals to encircle the top.

Although windows tend to line up vertically, their designs do not always match each other. First-story windows are usually taller and have more elaborate embellishments than those on upper floors. Hoods and cornices also may differ in design in a house or within a single story.

Figure 11-22. Italianate windows. (Based on drawings from To Grandfather's House We Go by Harry Devlin, by permission of Four Winds Press, division of Scholastic Inc., copyright © 1967 by Harry Devlin.)

Figure 11-23. Italianate round-headed window. (Based on a drawing from To Grandfather's House We Go *by Harry Devlin, by permission of Four Winds Press, division of Scholastic Inc., copyright © 1967 by Harry Devlin.)*

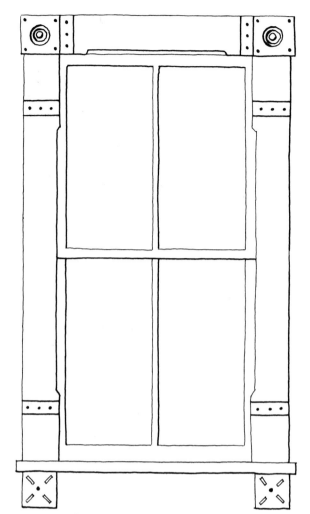

Figure 11-25. Stick Style window.

Figure 11-24. Italianate bay window.

STICK STYLE, 1855 TO 1900

Stick Style windows are what their name implies—sticklike. There is nothing fancy, pretentious, or bold about these windows. Instead they fit into the overall surface patterns of the clapboard siding and skeleton framing like pieces in a jigsaw puzzle (Figures 11-25 to 11-27).

Most Stick Style windows are tall rectangles set close to the surface of the exterior wall. Except for rare examples, all windows are surrounded by plain wood frames which usually tie into the framing exposed on the wall's surface. The top of the window frame, for instance, may join a wooden horizontal strip circling the house several inches under the eaves. Or the sills may line up with another cross-piece of the exposed skeleton. The side window framing may reach above the window to touch the eaves or to link with still another horizontal band overhead.

Seen frequently on Stick Style houses, decorative wooden braces are sometimes put near the windows,

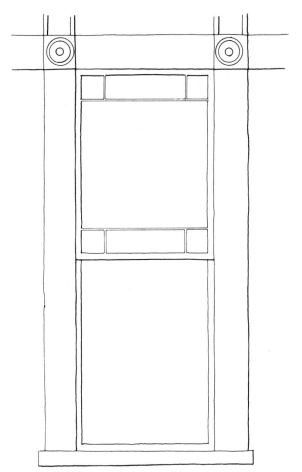

Figure 11-26. Stick Style window.

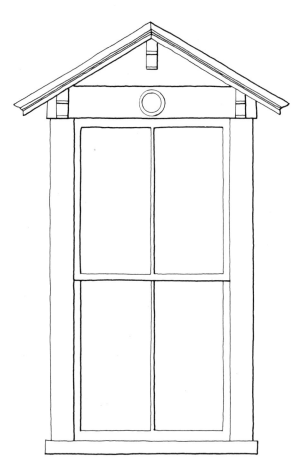

Figure 11-27. Stick Style window.

extending diagonally from the side framing to the horizontal band above. Braces shaped as Xs may also accent a panel over the window (Figure 11-28).

Occasionally you will find lintels, narrow cornices, subtle decoration on the framing, or even simple bracketed pediments. Enlivening the upper corner blocks and the side framing may be a unique ornamentation: shallow holes, tiny circles, and finely grooved lines. The delicate appearance of this decoration seems almost like the tracks of a small bird on the sand.

Double-hung sash windows with large panes are prevalent, although you may sometimes see casements. One over one and two over two panes appear most often; nine over nine, twelve over sixteen, and sixteen over one occur less frequently. Other window designs have small square and oblong panes in various combinations in the upper section with a single pane or two vertical panes in the lower sash. Bay windows and paired twins under a single cap may also be seen.

Figure 11-28. Stick Style window.

In most Stick Style homes the windows on the second and third floors are in line with those on the first story, but some variations do occur.

MANSARD, 1860 TO 1880

There is nothing bashful about Mansard windows. They are conspicuous, elaborate features of these houses. Enjoy them!

Rich embellishments surrounding these windows largely account for their prominence. The framing, which may be several layers of molding, is usually wide and protrudes beyond the wall's surface. Pilasters or engaged columns may border the windows, or the framing may undulate along the sides ending with curves or scrolls. Even the simpler Mansard houses may have windows with molded frames decorated with garlands or central keystones at the tops (Figures 11-29 to 11-31).

Window hoods, bracketed cornices, caps, and pediments are the most noticeable parts of the framing (Figure 11-32). These are imaginatively designed. Dripstone hood moldings may curve around the top and drip about one-third to one-half of the way down the sides, often ending with pendants which look like tassles. Hoods or caps shaped like eyebrows are common and appear above eyebrow-headed, rectangular, or round windows. Deep pediments and robust cornices resemble pieces of sculpture. Even a comparatively simple lintel will be highly visible. Central accents are also popular, including keystones and scroll-like decorations.

Ornamental windows may appear above the front door on the second or third floors. These decorative windows may be more ornate when the central portion of the house projects forward or when the roof line surges upward on the central axis. Paired arched windows under a large single hood, for example, may rise over the entrance, and they may have a round-headed single window covered by a curving hood overhead on the third floor. Possibly you will even find a round-arched window flanked by engaged columns sitting on a richly carved bracketed sill with a round window, encircled by elaborate ornaments and topped by a keystone, nestling on its shoulders above.

Bay windows abound. Some protrude sharply; others are more shallow. Some are round; others are rectangular. Some are only on the first floor, crowned with balustrades or low-pitched roofs adorned with delicate iron cresting; others are two stories high. Often the bay window includes three windows, possibly three tall one over one windows or a large two over two central window bordered by narrower one over one windows. Among the decorations may be wooden panels below the windows, ornamental carving along the sides, and brackets supporting the roof.

Figure 11-29. Mansard window.

The number of panes per window in Mansard homes is not consistent, but one over one and two over two double-hung sashes are common. One over two, four over two, and four over four, which may be grouped as twins, also are seen. Occasionally you will find six over six and, less often, colored glass.

Window size, shape, and decoration may be the same throughout a Mansard house, or variations may occur. Often first-story windows are taller, sometimes extending to floor level. Hoods or cornices on the first story may differ from those on the second floor. You may even discover mismatched windows next to each other. The same delight in variation is found in window shapes: An eyebrow-headed window may be next to a rectangular one. All windows, however, usually align precisely with one another. If the house has narrow, molded horizontal bands, called stringcourses, defining the floor levels, the windows will usually rest on them.

Figure 11-30. Mansard window.

Figure 11-31. Mansard window.

Figure 11-32. Mansard windows.

Heavy framing and relatively wide dimensions give Romanesque windows a robust and substantial appearance. Most Romanesque homes are masonry, and window designs reflect this sturdy construction (Figure 11-33).

Round-headed and semicircular arched windows are common. Arches tend to be squat, emphasized usually by bricks with their longer, stretcher, sides exposed, or by colored stones. Occasionally there is a Moorish window with gently curving top corners rising to a peaked center.

You may also see rectangular windows, possibly with heavy stone lintels on top. Sometimes the lintels will be part of a belt course, a flat-edged, slightly projecting band of stone running horizontally across the outside of the building like a belt, creating a continuous lintel. Belt courses may also link with other sections of the window such as the sills or horizontal stone muntins.

There is little consistency in the number of panes seen in Romanesque windows. You will find one over one, two over one, four over four, six over six, nine over nine, and large single panes. The upper half may have diamond-shaped panes with a single pane below. In a more elaborate home the lower portion may be covered with small squares. On rare occasions you will discover etched glass or tracery in simple geometrical patterns or fancy foliage designs.

Transom windows are another common feature. To add height and to give more light inside, tall rec-

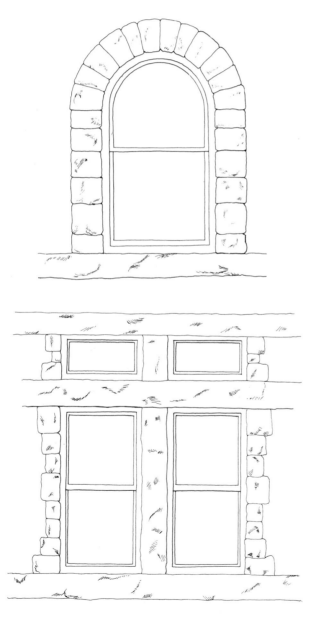

Figure 11-33. Romanesque windows.

Figure 11-34. Queen Anne window.

tangular windows may have oblong transoms. In other examples the upper portion of a round-arched window becomes a transom often enlivened with tracery or circular patterns resembling bubbles.

Romanesque windows have other embellishments. Above the window look for wide or narrow terra-cotta panels with garlands or floral motifs. A decorative terra-cotta band may edge the windows, or squat columns may flank them. A deeply recessed window may be accented by rows of short colonettes, or tiny columns.

You will notice various combinations of windows in Romanesque houses. Three or four windows grouped together in a horizontal band are common as well as paired windows under a single arch or lintel. Deep bay windows may appear, or oriel windows may project from the second story or rise to the third story.

Determining the original window style or styles in a Romanesque house is difficult, for there are no standard design guidelines. Window placement is unpredictable, and one home may have several different types of windows. If the first-story windows are alike, diversity in size and design will probably occur on the second or third stories.

QUEEN ANNE, 1876 to 1900

Anticipate almost anything in fanciful Queen Anne windows: rectangular, arched, square, circular, elliptical, and eyebrow-headed shapes; single, twin, triple, bow, bay, oriel, and Palladian windows; cut, bent, leaded, beveled, tinted, etched, and stained glass windows—and more. The original builders and owners relished this exuberance, and so can you (Figures 11-34 to 11-37).

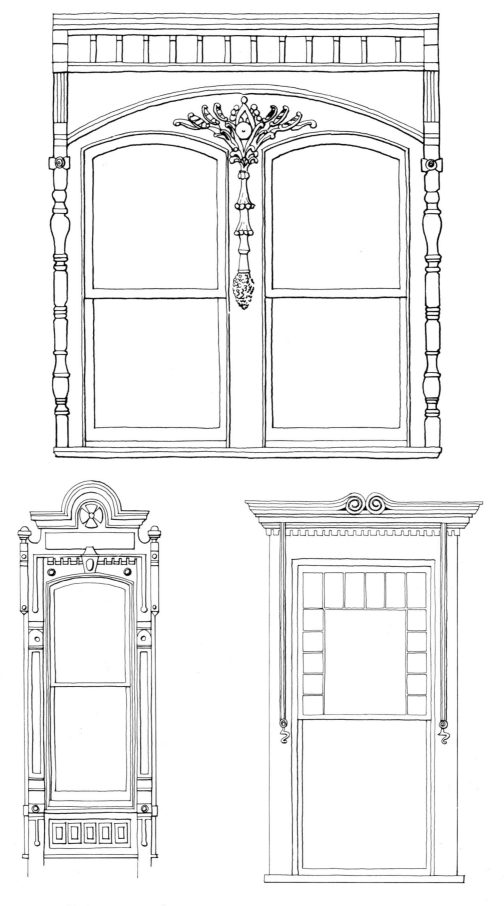

Figure 11-35. Queen Anne windows.

Several types of windows do appear more frequently than others in Queen Anne homes. One over one and two over two double-hung sash windows are common in both lavish and more subdued houses. Windows that are subdivided into intricate combinations of small square, oblong, or rectangular panes in the upper section with large single panes below are a hallmark of Queen Anne houses. Simpler designs have two, three, four, five, six, or seven panes over one or two panes; and more complex patterns include nine, sixteen, eighteen, thirty, or even forty-two panes in the top portion. A border of small panes arranged around a large square pane often appears, and occasionally small panes of various kinds fill the entire window. You will also observe diamond-shaped panes, arched tracery, elliptical motifs, interlocking circular patterns, and geometrical designs in the upper sash.

Transoms of small, square panes, etched glass, or stained glass may rest above the windows. Look for richly colored stained glass windows in other locations, too, especially near interior staircases or entrance halls. Stained glass windows come in a wealth of lovely patterns and are particularly common in certain localities such as San Francisco.

Large-paned bent, or curved, windows may be used in corner towers, turrets, or rounded bay windows. Tall rectangles, however, are more typical in these locations. Sometimes a window extends beyond one story. It may connect two stories near the interior staircase or become two full stories high by reaching from the second floor into a third-story gable.

The framing around a Queen Anne window may be no more than a plain wooden frame, perhaps enlivened with fluting. Or it may be elaborately embellished with engaged columns and ornate carvings. Simple lintels, decorative wooden panels, flat or scrolled cornices, and richly adorned pediments may garnish the windows. The ornamental carving is small in scale, usually in graceful garland, sunburst, scroll, flower, and foliage designs. Occasionally a large sunburst animates a panel just above a window or along each side. Showy brackets may support the sills, and decorative panels sometimes appear beneath the windows.

Figure 11-36. Queen Anne window.

Windows are often placed in irregular and what may seem like illogical locations. Even in the most restrained Queen Anne homes you will find more than one type of window and unevenly positioned windows. In the most imaginative versions of this style almost every window is unique. Remember, Queen Anne builders had fun!

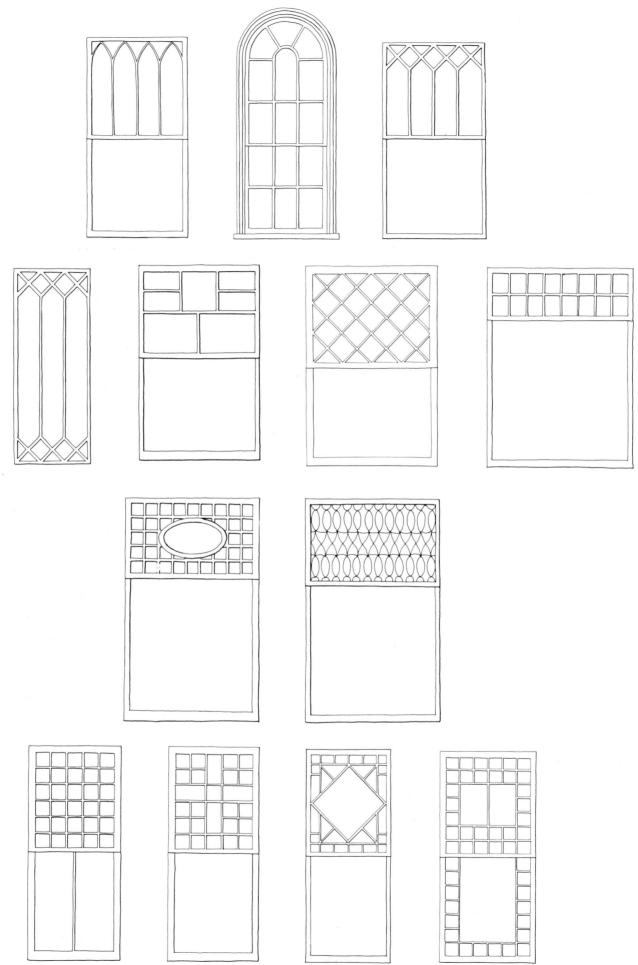

Figure 11-37. *Queen Anne windows.*

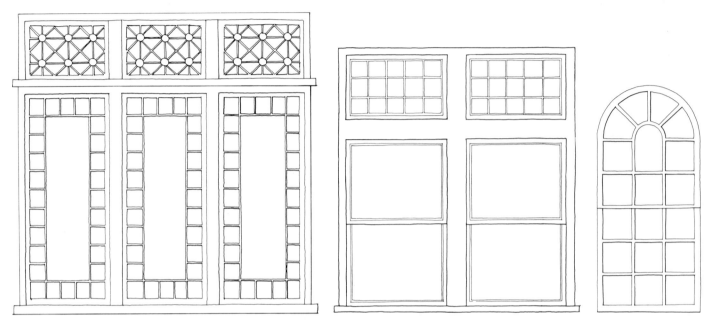

Figure 11-38. Shingle Style windows.

SHINGLE STYLE, 1880 TO 1900

Windows in Shingle Style homes are subtle and restrained. Sometimes they resemble the most simple of the Queen Anne windows without any of their flamboyant decorations such as pediments, pilasters, engaged columns, and elaborate cornices (Figure 11-38).

Shingle Style windows have two identifying characteristics. They are usually grouped in twos and threes to form horizontal bands which echo the overall lines of the house. Often, too, you will find shingles curving around the edges and side jambs of recessed windows.

Both casements and double-hung sash windows appear in Shingle Style homes. Small panes of equal size are common or the upper portion may have more panes. Look for various combinations: one over one, two over two, six over one, six over six, eight over eight, nine over nine, ten over one, twelve over one, twenty over three, or diamond-shaped panes in a single window or possibly, in the top half above a large pane below. Occasionally transoms with as many as fifteen small square panes or bubblelike patterns are seen.

Bay windows are everywhere. Accent windows also include a simplified Palladian window designed with a low, central arched window and without any fancy decoration, a tall round-arched window, and a fan-shaped or shingled eyebrow-shaped window placed in a gable. Sometimes you will discover a colored or stained glass window.

Every once in a while the window framing has unpretentious decorations such as a plain cornice, a small, narrow pediment, lintels, or a central keystone. These, however, are so quiet you may not even be aware of them.

Windows tend to be evenly placed in Shingle Style homes. First-floor designs usually differ from those above, and often a single house has a mixture of as many as ten different window types.

Georgian Revival windows and Federal Revival ones, to a lesser extent, look like overgrown cousins of the earlier Georgian and Federal styles. The dimensions are wider and more squat, panes are generally larger, and the decoration is more elaborate. You will also find imaginative interpretations of the earlier eighteenth century characteristics (Figure 11-39).

Rectangular double-hung sash windows are the most popular type, usually with six over six square panes. Sometimes six over nine or one over one panes appear. A Georgian Revival window occasionally has a rectangular or curved pattern placed in the upper half with a single, large pane below.

Simple wooden framing usually surrounds the windows. Sometimes Georgian Revival windows are capped with lintels, plain cornices, or small pediments. Delicate garlands or floral designs may garnish the cornices.

In a Georgian Revival home a Palladian window often accents the second story above the main central entrance, or it may occur in a pediment which breaks the roof line (Figure 11-40). Although these windows may be called "Palladian" because they are triple windows with a taller, arched central window and classically inspired ornamentation, their proportions and details differ from the earlier eighteenth century versions, which are more properly classical. In a Georgian Revival Palladian window, the round-arched window may be very tall with squat flanking windows, or all three windows may be narrow and tall, encircled by another arch above. A fan-shaped louvered decoration is put across the top portion of the arched window.

Other types of decorative windows seen in Georgian Revival homes include bay windows, which may be semicircular and many-storied, and an oculus, or round window, which is sometimes put in a gabled pediment.

Second-story windows almost always are placed directly above those on the first floor. Differences in the number of panes per window do occur. The most frequent variation is six over nine panes on the first story with six over six in second-story windows.

MAINTENANCE AND REPAIR

Windows rot, stick, warp, shrink with age, and pull away from the wall. Glass breaks and paint peels. As a result cold air and water may enter a house. Check the windows frequently. Discover the cause of any problems and find out what to do about it. Trouble with one part of the window does not necessarily mean replacing the entire window. For instance, you can exchange a new sash for a rotted one without having to put in a new window frame.

Where should you look for trouble (Figure 11-41)?

- Examine the glass for cracks and holes.
- Inspect the putty around the window for cracking and looseness.
- Find out whether the sash cords are either worn or broken.

Figure 11-39. Georgian Revival window.

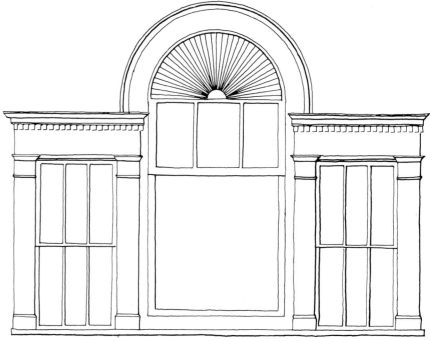

Figure 11-40. Georgian Revival Palladian window.

- Search for gaps between the window and the wall and for loose joints in the sash.
- Look for large and small cracks in the wood and for decayed wood.
- Check the condition of the paint.
- Be certain the sill slants away from the window.

It is almost always easier to take care of windows at once rather than to spend more time and money later to find a replacement. Acting now will safeguard a window meant for your home.

BROKEN GLASS PANES

One repair that homeowners can learn to do themselves is replacing broken glass. The procedures are simple and can save the expense of hiring a carpenter or other worker.

If the window cannot be reached easily from the outside, you will have to take out the sash to put in new glass. Look at the section on Sticking in this chapter to find out how to do this.

To begin, put on a pair of heavy gloves and carefully remove the broken glass. It is most important to scrape out all of the old putty. You may have to soften it first using a soldering iron or paint remover or allowing linseed oil to work on the putty for a half hour. Take out the glazier's points (pointed pieces of metal concealed in the putty that hold the glass to the wood sash members). Next, scrape the groove clean with a chisel or putty knife and dust it out.

The new glass should be ⅛ to 3/16 of an inch smaller than both the width and the height of the opening. You may be able to obtain the correct dimensions by measuring the old glass. Hardware stores will cut the glass in the proper size.

To seal the wood, use either linseed-oil putty or glazing compound. Place a thin strip of glazing compound or putty in the grooves on all sides of the window. For glazing compound, apply a coat of boiled linseed oil and prime with an oil-based primer or paint. Proceed after the primer or paint has dried. Gently press the glass against the compound or putty, checking to be certain the glass fits tightly everywhere.

Tap in the glazier's points to hold the glass in place — one to about every 6 inches of glass or at least two on each side of the glass. The flat side of the glazier's point touches the glass. The next step is to put glazing compound or putty around the sash on the outside. Smooth the material into a triangle with a putty knife, making sure there are no cracks or openings. The directions for the product will state how long it will take to cure. Once a "skin" has formed, paint to protect the glazing compound or putty from moisture, brushing the paint slightly onto the glass.

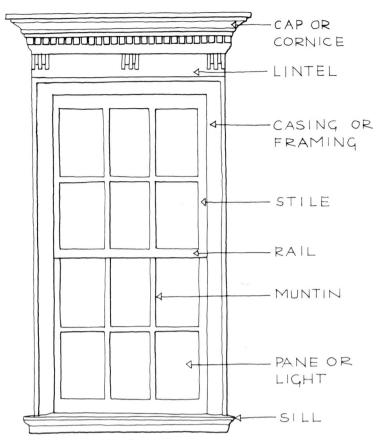

Figure 11-41. Parts of a window.

LOOSE AND CRACKED PUTTY AROUND THE WINDOW GLASS

Old putty around the glass may present problems. Throughly remove all the loose or cracked putty and replace it with new glazing compound or linseed-oil putty. Because it is more flexible and will not dry out and crack, glazing compound is said to last longer than putty. For metal windows, use only glazing compound. Follow the directions for the product you choose. Remember to apply glazing compound only to wood that has been brushed with boiled linseed oil and an oil-based primer or paint.

STICKING

When wood swells or paint seals the windows, they are likely to stick. Paint buildup is the most common cause of sticking. If excess paint is the problem, carefully break the paint seal, with a putty knife or other similar sharp tool, between the sash and the stop molding or between the sash and the parting strip or both (Figure 11-42). Tapping on the putty knife with a hammer may be necessary. When the sash moves, scrape away all excess paint wherever you find it and smooth these areas with a wood scraper and sandpaper. Clean out any dirt.

To help prevent sticking, do not paint the channel for the lower sash. When painting windows, move

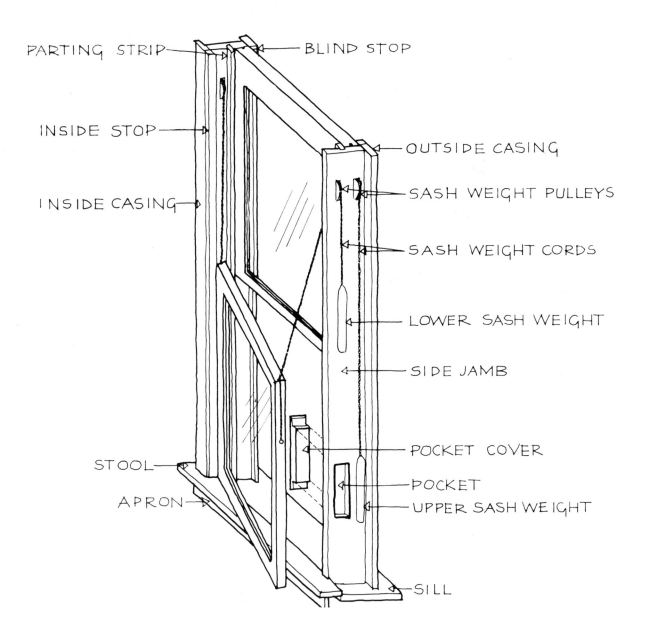

PARTING STRIP — BLIND STOP

INSIDE STOP

INSIDE CASING

OUTSIDE CASING

SASH WEIGHT PULLEYS

SASH WEIGHT CORDS

LOWER SASH WEIGHT

SIDE JAMB

POCKET COVER

POCKET

UPPER SASH WEIGHT

STOOL

APRON

SILL

Figure 11-42. Double-hung window.

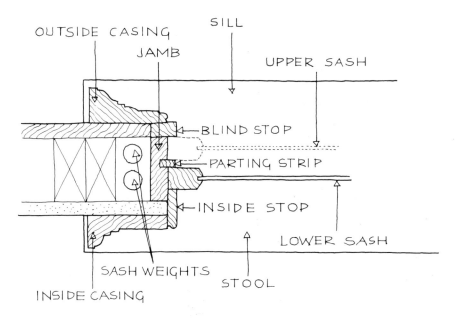

OUTSIDE CASING

JAMB

SILL

UPPER SASH

BLIND STOP

PARTING STRIP

INSIDE STOP

LOWER SASH

SASH WEIGHTS

STOOL

INSIDE CASING

the sash up and down after the paint has dried overnight.

If swollen wood causes the sash to stick, place a block of wood along the window stops where the binding occurs and gently tap the block with a hammer to push the stops away from the sash.

The window may still not move easily after you have taken these steps. Try cleaning out the sash channels or the metal weatherstripping if you have it. Apply a hard soap, paraffin, or silicone lubricant to the sash channel. The silicone lubricant will work well on metal weatherstripping.

You may have to remove the sash if none of these methods have loosened the window. Begin by cutting the paint film. Then take out any nails or screws found on the lower inside stop on one side of the window. Carefully pry out the stop. The lower sash may then move easily. If so, you can probably solve the problem by cleaning out any dirt and lightly planing and sanding the parting strips and stops touching the lower sash. You may find that sanding alone is enough.

When the sticking occurs on the upper sash, take out the parting strip on the same side from which you removed the lower inside stop. If the upper sash slides freely, clean out any dirt you find and sand, or gently plane and sand.

If the preceding steps do not help, you will have to remove the sash. In this case, move the lower sash out far enough to unfasten the sash cord from both sides of the sash. Inserting a nail in the knotted end will prevent the cord from slipping inside the jamb. Then plane the window only the small amount needed to allow it to move freely. To take out the upper sash, remove the lower sash first and the parting strip from the upper sash. Then unfasten the sash cords on the upper sash before removing the upper sash.

Check the condition of the sash cords. If they are worn, replace them while the sash is out of the frame.

WORN OR BROKEN SASH CORDS

To replace worn or broken sash cords, remove the lower sash. You may find a pocket cover in the frame. To help locate the outline of the pocket cover, tap the frame with a hammer. Remove any screws and then lift out the cover. If there is no pocket cover, remove the casing.

Measure the old cord and replace it with chain the same length. Use chain because it is more durable than cord. While the window is out, it is a good idea to exchange the cord on the other side for chain as well.

For the sash cord on the upper sash it will be necessary to remove the lower window and the parting strip before removing the upper sash. The weight and cord can be reached through the same opening used for the lower sash or sometimes through a separate pocket cover.

Before putting back the parting strip or the inside stop molding, test to be certain the window moves up and down all the way. Be sure the sash weight does not touch the sill. Then you know the new chain is the right length.

Be careful when propping a window that does not stay open. This practice is dangerous and may damage the window.

GAPS BETWEEN THE WINDOW AND THE WALL

Look for gaps where the window frame, the trim, or the drip cap meets the wall. Check the joints between the window sill and the frame. Scrape out all the loose caulk and dirt from any cracks discovered. In this step you will benefit by being a perfectionist. Clean the area with a solvent. If the surface is porous, use a primer. Then caulk the joints. Remember that any caulking that cannot be painted, such as silicone caulking, is not a good choice in areas where it can be readily seen. It may be possible, however, to locate a caulking color to match or closely resemble the paint color.

When there is an opening between the window framing and the wall, apply caulking on the inside over the crack as well as on the outside of the house. If this opening is large, fill it with oakum before you caulk. For an exceptionally large gap you may have to hire a carpenter to reset the window or to build a new frame.

SMALL CRACKS IN WOODWORK

Small cracks may appear harmless, but they can cause much damage by allowing water to seep into and rot the wood. Regular inspection and simple repairs can prevent further deterioration. For repairing small cracks within the window frames and sills, begin by cleaning out the old material and dirt. Be certain the wood is dry. Then apply a sealant designed for this purpose. Another technique is to brush two or three applications of linseed oil over the crack, waiting 24 hours between each one. When the linseed oil has dried, fill the crack with putty. Allow the putty time to form a "skin" and then paint the surface.

LARGE CRACKS AND ROTTING WOOD

Although the problem of badly deteriorated wood may seem hopeless, you may be able to rescue a window sill or other wooden part of the house by knowing what to do. Several approaches can be taken. But before beginning any work, track down the cause of the decay and correct the source of the trouble. Was it because of paint failure? Did moisture condense on the storm window and run down to the sill? In this case, vents at the juncture of the storm window and sill may prevent new rot. The Decay or Rot section in Chapter 8, Walls, gives more information on wood rot and what to do about it.

One way to repair small sections of rotted wood is to cut out carefully all the bad wood and thoroughly clean the surface. Use a wood preservative according to the directions. Fill the holes with plastic wood, wood putty, or a mixture such as sawdust and resorcinol glue, following the instructions on the container. Plastic wood, however, has the disadvantage of shrinking once in place. For large holes you can use wood strips, oakum (good for irregular openings), or ethafoam backing rods (better for a relatively uniform opening) as a filler. Caulk over the filler and then paint.

If it is necessary to cut out a large section of damaged wood, you can still salvage the larger wooden part. Remove the rotted wood. Saturate the hole with preservative and let it dry. Substitute a new piece of wood, called a Dutchman, in the shape of the original piece, with the grain running the same way. Treat the wood with a preservative and use a long-lasting, waterproof glue to hold the new wood in place. You may need the help of a professional with this method to duplicate the original shape or to set the replacement carefully within the remaining wood.

A technique for saving generally deteriorated wood is to impregnate the wood with an epoxy consolidant made especially for this purpose. With an epoxy consolidant you will not have to remove any deteriorated pieces of wood. As long as the wood is not too dense to absorb the liquid, this method will work well. End grain absorbs better than cross grain. Fill small holes or cracks, or drill small holes in a close pattern to encourage absorption.

Holes or cracks with two of their three dimensions measuring no more than 1 inch can be filled with an epoxy filler similar to automobile body filler. It is best to consolidate the wood around the hole to be filled prior to applying the filler. A marine supply store is one place to locate the consolidant and filler products. When working with these materials, follow the manufacturer's directions to avoid harming yourself.

One cause of a window's deteriorating wood may be a roof with no overhang, or an overhang of insufficient depth. An opportunity to correct this inadequacy arises when a house is getting a new roof. Because adding or enlarging an overhang changes the house's appearance, you may decide to consult an architect before going ahead with the work. A proper overhang not only protects the windows and doors but also the walls.

When the roof overhang provides good protection from rain and weather, flashing over a drip cap is not necessary. In wet climates if the roof overhang is not adequate, flashing will help to safeguard both the drip cap and the window or door beneath. The flashing should extend out over the drip cap and up behind the exterior wall material. Adding flashing to a window already in place may be difficult; installing it at the time a new window is put in is a good practice.

LOOSE JOINTS IN THE SASH

When there is a loose joint in the sash, take out the sash and gently push the rail and stile back together. If this method fails, you may have to hold them together with wood screws or with dowels soaked in a waterproof glue. Before putting in the screws or dowels, predrill holes through both pieces of the joint. You can also screw on corner braces to keep the rail and stile firmly in place. To avoid splitting the wood, predrill the holes first. Paint the braces to make them less conspicuous.

BADLY PEELING PAINT

If the paint on the window or framing is badly peeling, the first step is to scrape off the old paint. To make the surface as smooth as possible, sand the wood. Clean the wood thoroughly. Next, apply a wood preservative, following directions for the length of drying time and for the number of coats required. Brush linseed oil on any cracks and fill them with putty. Paint after the putty is dry. Touching up the paint as soon as you notice peeling or cracking on the sill or on any part of the window will help to keep the wood in good shape.

IMPROPERLY PITCHED SILLS

Look at the pitch of each window sill. Sills should slant away from the window. If they do not, water, instead of running off harmlessly, will flow into the sill and the window frame and cause serious deterioration. A new sill is the solution.

Remember to check the window frame and the subsill to be sure water has not damaged them. Sometimes the frame or subsill must be replaced at the same time that you or the carpenter you have hired puts in a new sill. Before installation, treat the new wood with a preservative. Prime the wood before painting.

WEATHERSTRIPPING

Making the windows nearly airtight will lower the heating bill and reduce drafts in a home. A good way to start is to install weatherstripping. Even though the windows have storm windows, weatherstripping may be necessary to seal out cold air.

Before choosing the type of weatherstripping to use, think about its appearance. Weatherstripping should not be conspicuous. Spring metal is excellent for windows because it can be hidden from sight in the window channels and on the bottom of the lower sash and the top of the upper sash. It is also the most durable type of weatherstripping you can install yourself. To keep air from flowing into any gaps where the upper and lower sashes meet, attach the spring metal to the inside of the bottom rail of the upper sash.

Manufacturers are now marketing flexible plastic strips which also form an effective, almost invisible seal against cold air. Another possibility is to place felt strips on the bottom of the lower sash and the top of the upper sash. You can tack felt to the back of the top rail of the lower sash. Be aware that felt has the undesirable characteristic of absorbing and holding moisture.

Avoid weatherstripping products that are formed by a flexible material attached to a rigid strip. This type of weatherstripping is unsightly.

Another way to help keep the windows airtight is to caulk the ones you do not open—either the entire window or just the top sash if you plan to use the lower sash. A convenient product for this task is rolled caulking placed around the inside edges of the window. In the spring you can remove the caulking from the windows you plan to open in warmer weather.

STORM WINDOWS

Storm windows keep out cold air, noise, and dirt. They also cut down on the loss of heat through the window glass and reduce the amount of condensation on the windows.

The buyer of storm windows has many choices. But the owner of the older home, before making a purchase, must think seriously about the appearance of each kind of storm window. How well will the style, color, and material of the storm window blend with the window of the home?

WHAT YOU CAN DO

When deciding on storm windows, there are several things you can do:

- Choose a storm window that reveals as much as possible of the window of the house. A one over one storm window is acceptable. A single sheet of clear, rigid plastic set in a frame is satisfactory if the color, size, and material of the frame are inconspicuous.

- Avoid a storm window with a natural aluminum finish. If no other alternative can be found, paint the aluminum the same color as the sash. Carefully prepare the surface by wire brushing corroded spots or, for a new aluminum surface, by applying mineral spirits. Before painting, use an appropriate primer.

- Take care of old wooden storm sashes and paint them the same color as your window sash.

- Try to match the color of the window sash with new storm windows. A baked-enamel finish, for example, is common in white or brown, and you may be able to find it in other colors as well. You can paint over baked enamel if you use fine sandpaper before applying exterior enamel.

- Use interior storm windows. A serious disadvantage of interior storm windows is that they frequently cause moisture condensation on the sash or sill of the window, a condition which may lead to deteriorated wood. The chance of damage will be less if the interior storm window is raised or removed in warmer weather to dry out the wood. Before purchase, check these storm windows to be certain their method of installation will not harm the window sash. Interior storm windows do offer excellent protection, and they are easy to install in places difficult to reach from the outside such as the third floor or attic.

- Order custom storm windows either from a craftworker in your area or from a company specializing in good reproductions. Arched windows or one-of-a-kind decorative windows will require custom storm windows.

- Keep these hints in mind even if you are purchasing screens only. The screen, like the storm window, should not detract from the window's design.

MOVABLE INSULATION

Movable insulation, such as thermal draperies, shutters, or thermal shades, offers excellent protection against heat loss and infiltration of cold air. In hot weather these insulating devices also will keep a room cooler. A number of products are manufactured for this purpose. In addition, an ingenious individual can improvise to solve specific problems.

Figure 11-43. Queen Anne window.

SPECIAL CONSIDERATIONS

Knowing what to do about problems special to windows in older homes will help to retain the appeal and the value of your home. A list of possible solutions follows.

WINDOW GUARDS

A few simple bars to protect a window may be necessary for urban homes. Paint window guards black or a color to blend with the window. Do not choose complicated grilles and screens which will conflict with the window's design. For increased security and added insulation you may decide, instead, to attach a sheet of unbreakable plastic to the inside of vulnerable windows. Use oval-headed screws for a better-looking job. Check to be certain the plastic does not cause condensation and subsequent deterioration on the inside of the window.

ORNAMENTAL GLASS

As their value increases, stained glass and other fancy windows have become targets for thieves (Figure 11-43). One way to make these windows less accessible is to use window guards. Another solution is break-resistant plastic attached tightly to the out-

side of the window; this also protects the glass from rock-throwing vandals. Unfortunately, the plastic partly obscures the window from the outside. As another deterrent, consider securely nailing the window to the frame.

LOOSE LEADED WINDOWS

Glass held together by lead can become loose because of age or exposure to the weather. With some searching you may be able to locate a craftworker to repair a leaded window. Storm windows or rigid plastic attached to the outside of the window will keep the wind from separating the glass farther from the metal. If a standard-stock storm window does not fit the shape of a leaded window, have one custom made.

AIR CONDITIONERS

Sometimes the walls of an older house are thick enough to keep the inside quite cool in summer, but if an air conditioner becomes necessary, try to make it inconspicuous. Place air conditioners in a little-seen location such as the side or back of the house. An alternative to letting your air conditioner overpower a window on the outside is to install it nearly flush with the window on the exterior, letting the bulk of it protrude inside.

AWNINGS

Canvas awnings were popular in the late nineteenth century, especially for houses at seaside resorts. Awnings are rarely appropriate in other circumstances because they detract from the appearance of older homes and hide the decorative details which were meant to be enjoyed. Do not use metal or plastic awnings, for these materials clash garishly with the wood, brick, or stone in older homes.

ATTIC WINDOWS

See Chapters 6 and 7, Gables and Dormers, for suggestions on maintaining attic windows.

REPLACEMENT

Try everything to preserve all parts of any original windows and trim. Consider replacement only if the windows are in such poor condition that none of the suggestions in the Maintenance and Repair section of this chapter will work.

Newer windows may already have been installed in your home. If these do not resemble any of the original windows or if they are unlike any windows described for the architectural style of your house, attempt to find more suitable windows.

When it is necessary to replace one or more windows, there are several guidelines to follow so that any changes will agree with the initial appearance of the house.

- Give particular attention to windows on the front of the house or on the sides clearly visible from the street. Windows can be changed or added in the back of the house or in an area not seen from the street, if necessary, but be cautious so that the house will not be disfigured. An architect will be able to advise you in these circumstances. When a front window needs replacing, consider as a last resort making the replacement in a little-seen section of your home and moving a matching window with the same dimensions from that location to the front. This prodecure is risky, however, and may damage an old window.

- Retain the dimensions of the original window including its width and height, the width of the muntins, and the number and arrangement of panes. For example, if six over six panes are suitable for the style of the house, do not change to four over four panes.

- Make certain the window panes are vertical. Most older homes have rectangular panes with the length of the rectangle upright, making the window appear vertical. Although there are a few exceptions which are identified in the Design section of this chapter, horizontal window panes are not appropriate.

- Select windows with slender muntins and steer away from heavy muntins unless you live in a very early house or one built in the late nineteenth or early twentieth century.

- Choose a material similar to the original material. Replace a wooden window with another wooden window. Wood has the advantage of being an excellent insulator. Cheap aluminum sash windows tend to jam, corrode, and bend easily. They are also difficult to repair.

- Keep the same size window opening. Do not change the shape by enlarging or reducing it just to accommodate a standard-stock window. If you find evidence that the original dimensions have been altered, remove the alterations and use a window of the correct size for any replacement. You may have to consult an architect or builder for this procedure, especially if there are major structural changes involved.

- Retain any trim and decorative details surviving from the house when it was first built.

- Preserve the initial locations of the windows in the house.

- Avoid purchasing certain "modern" stock windows which are totally unsuitable for an older house. Manufacturers offer numerous kinds of comtemporary windows which they claim are easy to install, simple to maintain, effortless to operate, and long-lasting. Do not fall for these sales pitches, especially if they come from a door-to-door salesperson. In particular avoid (Figure 11-44):

  Awning windows with movable, wide, horizontal panes
  Sliding windows which move on tracks
  Picture windows with large single panes of glass
  Jalousie windows with many movable glass slats which look like Venetian blinds

- Use only as a last resort the clip-on metal grilles which look like muntins when placed over a large pane of glass. Clip-on grilles are often too thin and flimsy and are easy to identify as fakes.

- Try to keep the original window framing when residing a house. Do not cover or replace a handsome wood frame with a narrower metal substitute.

WHERE TO FIND WINDOWS

A number of sources for replacement windows are worth exploring.

Reproductions. There are several manufacturers from whom you can order excellent handmade sashes. Some of them carry only stock designs; others will duplicate any style. The catalogs specializing in products for old houses list these firms.

Custom-Made Windows. An expensive, but time-saving approach is to hire an expert carpenter to construct a window in an appropriate design or to have it made in a millwork shop. Before proceeding, look at examples of the work to check the quality of the craftsmanship.

Wrecking-Company Yards. If you have time, it is worth checking wrecking-company yards for windows. Before journeying forth, measure the windows and the panes. Even though you will find a welter of inexpensive windows, you probably will not discover the style you need in the right dimensions. This task becomes even harder when looking for a window to match exactly others already in place in your home. Wrecking companies also sell stained glass and other fancy windows, but at higher prices.

Salvage Storehouses. Historical commissions in cities, such as Baltimore and New York, are retrieving parts from old houses, storing them, and selling them at reasonable prices. Like wrecking-company yards this source is also a long shot for old windows.

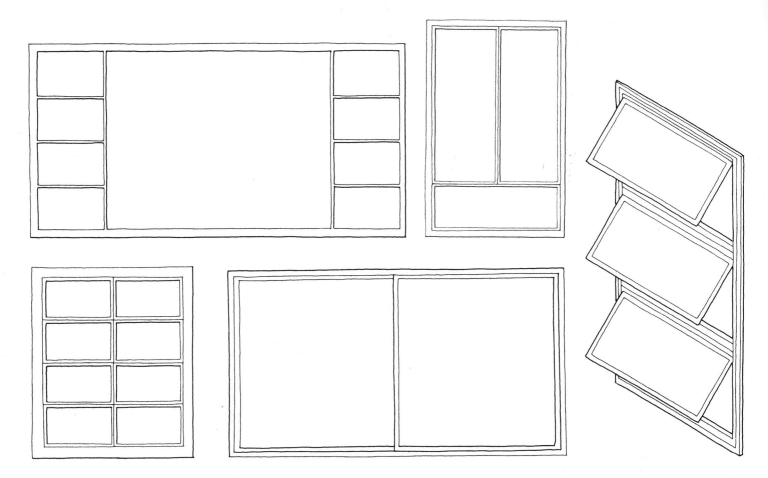

Figure 11-44. Inappropriate replacement windows.

Antique Dealers. If you are trying to find something special, such as a stained glass or a leaded window, an antique dealer may be willing to search for one for you. Otherwise, the antique shop is not a likely place to find old windows.

Stores Specializing in Architectural Parts. Generally, unless you are looking for an unusual window with fancy glass, this type of store is not the one to investigate.

Stock Windows. Suppliers of stock windows are usually not a satisfactory source of windows for the older home. Do not be taken in by advertisers' claims about the benefits of turning in an "unsightly" rotting wood window for a "modern" aluminum window. It is easy to buy an aluminum window in the correct size, but more difficult to find a suitable style and color. A natural aluminum finish is never appropriate because of its glaring appearance and susceptibility to corrosion. Painting an aluminum window and other synthetic finishes is possible. Find out about the practicality of painting and

the best method before purchasing the window. Although you may be able to obtain the color you desire, locating an acceptable style in any kind of stock window is more troublesome.

Glass. Old glass is almost impossible to find. If you are fortunate enough to locate a supply, purchase more than you need because it breaks easily during cutting. Reproductions of old glass are available, and they may be an acceptable answer for replacing old glass.

Ornamentation and Trim. Surprisingly, you may easily match your original moldings with stock wood moldings, which come in a multitude of shapes and sizes. If none of the stock moldings are like the ones around your window, a craftworker can duplicate these and other decorative details. Also, there are a few firms specializing in good-quality polyurethane ornamental details. From them you can order everything from a sunburst to a peaked pediment.

CHAPTER TWELVE

SHUTTERS AND BLINDS

Shutters and blinds on older houses once served useful functions. The earliest solid wood shutters, when closed, protected the glass from breaking and the house from intruders and cold weather. Later, louvered blinds with movable slats were designed to shade rooms from the summer sun and to improve ventilation. Today, shutters and blinds are primarily decorative. If exterior shutters do work, however, closing them at night in the winter to keep out cold air and during the day in the summer to cover windows exposed to the sun can help to conserve energy.

DESIGN

Retain shutters if they are original and if they add to the overall appearance of the house. The following clues may help you decide whether you have old shutters:

- thick and heavy wooden parts
- wide rails and stiles with the bottom rail having the widest dimension
- panels that match the front door panels
- tenons poking through the shutter stiles
- paint layers similar to the number of layers on a part of the house already identified as old
- marks showing the existence of earlier hardware
- dimensions that duplicate exactly the height and one-half the width of the window opening
- nails on old hinges which protrude about ⅝ inch on the back of the shutter and bend over to the wood, a method known as peening
- half-round moldings, known as astragals, on the inner vertical edge of the shutters, used to create a tighter closing
- workable shutter fasteners or evidence that former fasteners have been removed
- shutters similar to those described below for a house of the same style as your home

Being familiar with the architectural style of a house can help you determine whether shutters are appropriate. The style will also indicate what kind of shutters an older home requires.

Simple, heavy, board and batten wood shutters are often seen on Seventeenth Century houses and on some rural homes built in the eighteenth century (Figure 12-1). A single shutter usually covers the entire width and height of the window opening, although there may be two shutters for each window.

Solid wood–paneled shutters, first used about 1720, are common features in the Georgian and Federal styles. Sometimes for cost-saving or security reasons, they were placed only on the first floor.

There is no such thing as a standardized paneled shutter. Not only do the heights and widths of these early shutters match the dimensions of each window, which varied considerably at that time, but also the number, size, type, and placement of the panels differ. Square and rectangular panels combine

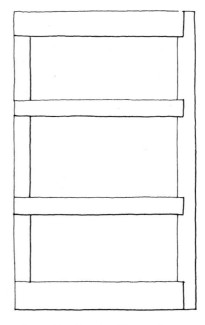

Figure 12-1. Board and batten shutter.

Figure 12-2. Paneled shutters.

Figure 12-3. Six over six pane window with shutters.

Figure 12-4. Six over nine pane window with shutters.

in a number of ways (Figure 12-2). The simplest design is two long, rectangular panels. At times the panels' proportions resemble the panels on the front door. The size of the early panels also relates to the number of window panes and their arrangement because the shutter fasteners are placed on the middle rail of the shutter and must be located below the bottom rail of the upper window sash. For this reason, a window with six over six panes has shutters with the rectangular top panel slightly longer than the bottom one (Figure 12-3), while a window having six over nine panes has a shorter top panel and longer bottom one (Figure 12-4). Shutters with two panels of similar size are usually later, nonoperable ones. Where there are three panels, a common occurrence in the eighteenth century, each may be a different size, two of the three may have the same dimension, or all three may possess similar proportions. Larger windows have correspondingly longer shutters frequently with four wood panels.

Up to the Federal period, most panels are raised and flush with the rails and stiles (Figure 12-5). After this time, recessed panels were generally used, although raised panels reappeared in the late nineteenth century (Figure 12-6).

The moldings on early paneled shutters may offer hints to dating a house. Shutters made before 1776 have either plain quarter-round or ovolo moldings with a convex outline edging the panels (Figure 12-7). After 1776 to about 1835, you will find ovolo moldings scored with one or two small channels called quirks or with beads. Ogee, or reverse curve moldings with a concave contour above and a convex profile below, also appear at this time. All moldings before 1835 were handmade, planed with special molding tools from the solid wood panels.

Machine-made moldings were introduced around 1835. First used on the more fashionable houses, these moldings slowly became widespread, although handmade moldings continued for many years, especially in rural areas. The machine-made moldings, generally wider than the earlier handmade moldings, are separate strips which are attached around

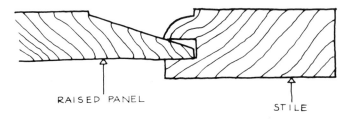

Figure 12-5. Raised shutter panel with handmade moldings.

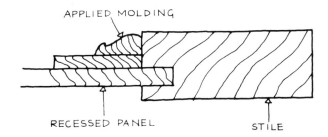

Figure 12-6. Recessed shutter panel with applied moldings.

the edges of the panels, often applied in several layers.

In the eighteenth century solid pieces of wood generally were used to back the shutters for added strength. The rails and stiles are joined by mortise and tenon joints. The shutters are attached directly to the window frame. When the shutters are open, large-headed nails are visible. These nails hold long, wrought-iron hinges across the top and bottom which are seen only when the shutters are closed. Wrought-iron crossbars are typical fasteners used to close shutters from the inside.

Appearing at the end of the eighteenth century was a new kind of window covering called a blind.

OVOLO WITH BEAD

OGEE

QUIRKED OGEE

QUARTER ROUND

Figure 12-7. Molding types.

Early blinds are a series of fixed, horizontal slats, or louvers, placed within the rails and stiles (Figure 12-8). Cross rails may divide the louvers into two or three sections although blinds occur without cross rails. Often, these blinds were placed only on the second-floor windows with paneled shutters persisting on the first story.

Although adjustable louvers were introduced around 1800, they did not become common until the late nineteenth century (Figure 12-9). A vertical bar adjusts the slats at different angles allowing either a little or a lot of air circulation from the outside. A cross rail separates the blind into two sections of movable louvers though the top portion occasionally has fixed slats. Later blinds sometimes have three divisions with either one or three sets of adjustable louvers.

Most Greek Revival homes have louvered blinds of the two-section type. When the first-story windows extend to the floor, the blinds are the same length. These often include four sections of louvers or louvers on top with a panel on the bottom (Figure 12-10).

In general, shutters or blinds are appropriate for most homes built before 1860, but there are exceptions. You will rarely find them, for example, on early eighteenth century brick buildings in Williamsburg or on Gothic Revival houses. Only occasionally do they appear on Italianate or Stick Style homes.

A few of the later Mansard houses have shutters, but Romanesque, Queen Anne, and Shingle Style homes seldom have shutters of any type. Shutters, which are purely decorative, reappear on Georgian Revival homes. At times louvered blinds were employed on these Georgian Revival houses, but more frequently paneled shutters were used on the first floor and louvered blinds on the second story.

Warning: Dating a house only by whether or not it has shutters is risky. Some early houses never had shutters or blinds, and shutters unexpectedly adorn a few of the later styles. In other cases shutters were added years after the house was built to make it look "Colonial."

WHEN ARE SHUTTERS SUITABLE?

It is not enough to know the architectural style of an older home to determine whether shutters are suitable. No set guidelines apply even within one style. If your home does not have shutters or has flimsy modern replacements, explore further.

Look carefully at the face of the window frame. Are any holes visible near the top or bottom? If so, these may be the holes for the pintles, or upright pivot pins, which hold the hinges. Early pintles are called drive pintles because they are attached to a spike which is driven into the solid wood frame. The supports for pintles on later houses are either

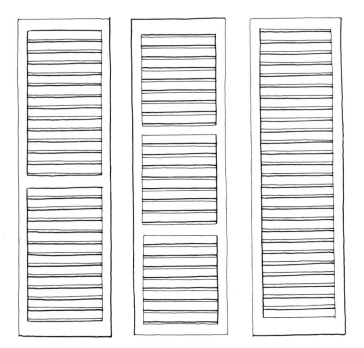

Figure 12-8. Fixed louvers.

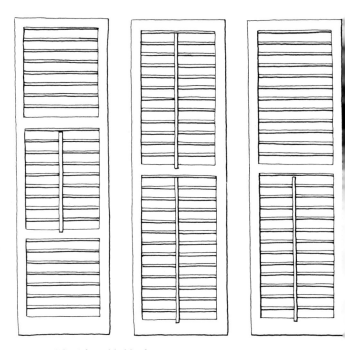

Figure 12-9. Adjustable blinds.

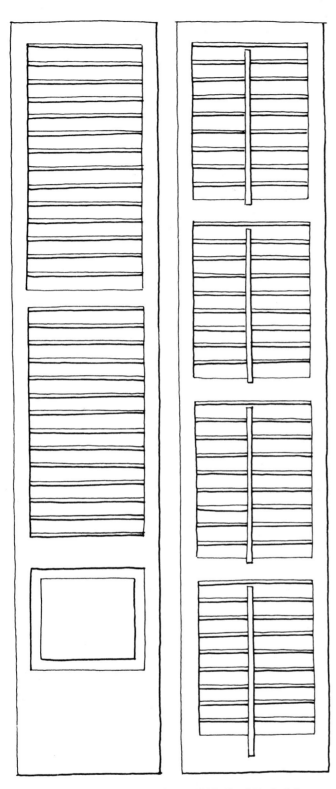

Figure 12-10. Greek Revival shutters.

screwed to the frame or wedged between the wall and the window frame. Search, also, on the exterior walls near the windows for areas of faded paint having the silhouettes of shutters. These are clues that shutters probably had been installed. It may be desirable, though, if the window trim is handsome, to let the windows remain unadorned.

When removing old shutters, store them in a dry place. Do not throw them away because a future owner may want to put them back.

Some older houses have paired blinds at the front entrance or beside other outside doors. Door blinds are especially common in the South where they help ventilate the house. If your home has useful and suitably designed door blinds, retain them.

WHEN ARE SHUTTERS NEVER APPROPRIATE?

In what circumstances are shutters never appropriate? They should not be used when they overlap, if opened, or when there is not adequate space for them to lie flat against the wall (Figure 12-11); when they are adjacent to long bands of windows (Figure 12-12); or when they surround ornamental windows such as oriel or rose windows—the decorative details around these windows are meant to be seen and enjoyed. Never put shutters on dormer windows or windows in mansard roofs. Shutters are meant to look as though they work. They will not seem func-

Figure 12-11. Overlapping shutters.

Figure 12-12. Shutters on long bands of windows.

Figure 12-13. Right and wrong shutters for arched windows.

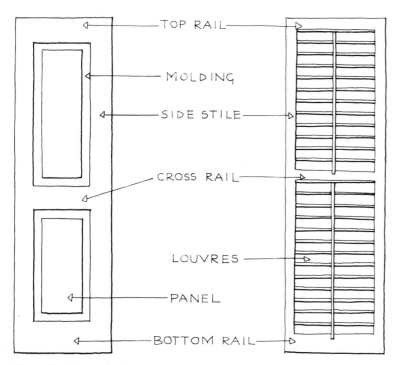

Figure 12-14. Parts of a shutter and blind.

TOP RAIL

MOLDING

SIDE STILE

CROSS RAIL

LOUVRES

PANEL

BOTTOM RAIL

tional in any of these situations. Covering arched windows with shutters or blinds is acceptable if they are cut in the shape of the arch (Figure 12-13).

MAINTENANCE AND REPAIR

Often a homeowner can repair old shutters without the added expense of professional help (Figure 12-14). A few of the common problems are described below.

SAGGING SHUTTERS

When a shutter sags, there could be several causes. It may be out of plumb because the connections need tightening. Early shutters have nails as connections; screws came into use later. In cases where the holes have become somewhat too large but the wood is basically sound, try substituting larger connections for the ones already in place. As an alternative, take out the nails or screws and fill the holes with plastic wood or with matchsticks or other small pieces of wood dipped in glue before putting back the nails or screws. If the connections have rusted, replace them.

When the wood is decayed around the holes, the shutter will have to be removed and the wood repaired. Making a patch called a Dutchman is one way to repair small deteriorated areas. Cut out the section of rotted wood. Cut a piece of the identical size from a new piece of wood. If the shutter is finished to reveal the grain of the wood, use the same type of wood as found in the shutter. Insert the patch into the shutter and secure it with waterproof glue. Make new holes in this patch for the connections.

Shutters may also sag because the mortise and tenon joints are separating. Check the joints carefully to be certain they are not causing the sagging. To repair loose joints, gently push the rail and stile back together. When this technique does not work, either wood screws or dowels soaked in a waterproof glue may hold them together. A corner brace is another way to keep the rail and stile in place. Predrill the holes before screwing in the brace.

CRACKS, LOOSE JOINTS, ROTTING WOOD, AND BADLY PEELING PAINT

To help protect wooden shutters or blinds from rot, mildew, and warping, put a narrow strip of metal across the upper edge of the top rail. All the edges of the metal should be turned down approximately ½ inch and tacked to the sides with small brass nails. This metal cap flashing will prevent rain and moisture from seeping into the shutters. The Decay or Rot section in Chapter 8, Walls, gives more information about taking care of the wood in shutters or blinds.

PAINTING AND STRIPPING

Shutters and blinds should be painted whenever the house is painted, although shutters under the eaves will not need repainting as often because they are more protected. Chapter 13, Paint and Color, suggests colors suitable for a particular architectural style.

When too many layers of paint cover the shutters or if a clear finish is desirable, consider stripping the shutters. See Chapter 13, Paint and Color, for the best way to proceed. Be sure the shutters are in sound condition before going ahead with a finish that will expose the wood. Remember to put a metal cap along the top for protecting the open grain and to treat the shutters with a wood preservative.

REPLACEMENT

If you must replace a shutter, first measure the sash opening. Each member of a pair of shutters or blinds should cover one-half the width and the full height of the sash opening (Figure 12-15). Some early shutters have half-round moldings called astragals, either cut into the wood or attached as strips along the inner edges where the shutters join together, to create a tighter fit. Make an allowance for these astragals in the measurements. Next, study the Design section in this chapter for help in selecting a style appropriate for your house. Certain contemporary designs are never suitable (Figure 12-16). Look for sturdy wood shutters and blinds and avoid flimsy wood shutters or aluminum, vinyl, and foam imitations. Aluminum, for instance, dents easily and clashes with the older materials in your house.

Figure 12-15. Shutters with the wrong dimensions.

Figure 12-16. Unsuitable shutters for an older house.

Mount the hinges on the face of the window frame, allowing the shutters to cover the window when they swing inward. When the shutters or blinds are open, latch them with holdbacks or shutter dogs. Some manufacturers sell clips to hold the shutters open, claiming these are easy to install. Clips are inadequate because shutters frequently break free from them in storms or high winds.

WHERE TO FIND SHUTTERS AND BLINDS

Check wrecking-company yards and dealers in architectural parts for old shutters and blinds. With luck, you will find a mass of shutters at low prices. But you will need even more good fortune to discover the right size and style. When searching, be certain to take along accurate measurements of the window openings.

You can locate shutters quicker from a company that manufactures millwork, usually identified as a "lumber and millwork company." Some manufacturers also specialize in making fine shutter reproductions, but these are more expensive. An experienced carpenter can produce the correct shutters for an older home, but again this work will be costly. Remember to look at samples of a carpenter's work to evaluate its quality before proceeding.

WHERE TO FIND HARDWARE

For hardware replacements for shutters and blinds, try antique dealers and stores selling architectural parts. Hardware stores sell reproductions, too, but make certain these are good-quality products, not shoddy imitations. There are manufacturers who specialize in excellent hardware reproductions, and they may be able to make copies of the original hardware as well. These firms repair old hardware, too — a process often cheaper than purchasing a new piece. A metalsmith or other craftworker can create custom-designed hardware, but this process will most likely be expensive.

CHAPTER THIRTEEN

PAINT AND COLOR

Paint is one of the first things noticed about the outside of a house. A fresh coat of paint can transform an older home, enhancing its attractiveness and individuality as well as protecting and preserving the wood siding and trim. Thoughtfully selected colors will bring out the unique character of a house by complementing its architectural style, defining its shape and lines, and accenting special decorative features. No matter how carefully an older house has been renovated, if the paint is peeling it looks shabby and unloved. When the exterior colors are garish, the renovation seems misguided rather than sympathetic. A diligent, caring homeowner will make certain an older home is regularly and sensitively painted to let its full brilliance shine forth.

When choosing exterior colors, a homeowner has at least four alternatives:

1. To attempt an authentic restoration by exactly matching the original colors. This approach requires systematic research which can be undertaken by the homeowner or with the expert help of an architect or a professional paint-research consultant.

2. To use a color scheme suggested by the color guidelines for each style outlined in the Design section of this chapter. Also, consult a local historic district organization, a historical society, or a knowledgeable architect about suitable colors.

3. To copy colors chosen by neighbors. Unless these colors are indeed harmonious with the style of the house, this method is not recommended. Be willing to take the time to analyze precisely what colors would be most fitting for your particular house.

4. To pick colors based entirely on your personal taste. This route is risky because you may develop a color scheme that deforms the historical and architectural character of your home. If the house is located in a historic district, it is sometimes necessary, before you begin work, to con-

sult the organization supervising the historic district, which may have imposed certain restrictions on exterior colors.

WHAT TO CONSIDER BEFORE SELECTING EXTERIOR COLORS

Consider several factors before selecting exterior paint colors.

YOUR OBJECTIVES IN RENOVATING A HOUSE

Are you aiming for an accurate restoration of the entire structure? If so, every effort should be made to identify the original color scheme and to paint the exterior these exact colors. The Matching Paint Colors section in this chapter describes procedures for this investigation. A word of warning: A few early builders used eccentric shades, and you may discover unattractive colors. In this situation you may be able to choose another color in the same family. When homeowners are doing a renovation, more leeway is possible in the color choices, but the colors should be close to ones considered appropriate for the style of the house.

THE RELATIONSHIP OF YOUR HOUSE TO OTHER HOMES ON THE STREET AND IN THE NEIGHBORHOOD

How will the colors relate to those selected by your neighbors, and how will they fit into the overall appearance of the street? Homeowners in urban areas particularly must address this question. Bright purple may be your favorite color, but painting a house this shade could jar a subdued neighborhood as well as disfigure the house's appearance. Determining a color scheme to harmonize with nearby houses is especially important when these are built in a similar style and are townhouses or row houses. If you live in a double house, be certain to consult with the homeowner next door and together develop a color combination for the entire double house. Such twins should be identical and not fight each other visually.

Caution: Other homes in the vicinity may be a hodgepodge of colors. In these circumstances, do not hesitate to be a pioneer and repaint your house with colors suitable to its style. Your house could become an example for others to emulate.

THE SIDING MATERIALS

In general, the walls (or main body) of an older house were painted one color, although in the late nineteenth century two-toned siding was popular. Clapboard and board and batten siding need regular repainting, and they undoubtedly underwent numerous color changes over the years. If shingle siding is stained, restain rather than paint it. Treasure the texture and the natural color of unpainted stone and brick. Paint brick or stone walls only when they have already been painted.

TRIM

The framing around windows and doors, corner boards, cornices, porches, and porticoes on older homes were frequently painted a different color from the body of the house to accent these features.

FINE TRIM AND DECORATIVE DETAILS

In some instances the narrow putty lines on the window muntins and small decorative details on older homes were painted a sharply contrasting shade. Color was used to call attention to the ornamentation.

WINDOW SASH

Originally, in some styles, the window sash were painted a color different from the trim or the siding. Often this sash color was darker than the trim, making the windows appear to recede into the walls of the house.

SHUTTERS AND BLINDS

Shutters and blinds were commonly dark tones such as evergreen greens, deep grays, or black, although variations occured in some styles.

OTHER PAINTING DECISIONS

Paint is temporary. No matter how well the surface is prepared or how soundly the paint is applied, eventually paint will chalk, check, crack, crumble, or flake. Once a color scheme is selected, the next decision is whether to paint the house yourself or hire a professional painter.

Rather than totally repainting a house every 4 to 6 years, another approach is to view painting as an ongoing process. Systematically touch up vulnerable parts. Some highly exposed sections of a house are more susceptible to paint problems. Check the house regularly to identify these areas. Window sills and exposed trim, for example, may require painting every two years. By keeping extra paint of the same color in reserve, you can then scrape, sand, and spot paint these areas. Whatever the approach, it is imperative that the preparation and the painting are done meticulously to add to the life of an older house.

DESIGN

The original exterior colors of an older home reinforced its architectural style and brought out its personality. Some initial colors were quiet and subdued, blending a home into the natural landscape; others were bold and forthright, making a house conspicuous. Many shades were cheerful; a few were somber. Prim colors adorned some older houses; numerous others had playful colors. All colors on older houses had one quality in common: They were never flashy. Some colors were lively, but rarely were they ostentatious or offensive to the eye.

As each style developed, certain colors were deemed more suitable for bringing out its characteristics than others. Within any one style, a narrow range of color choices may have emerged, or wide color variations might be appropriate. Color preferences also varied from locality to locality. Although there are few clear-cut rules, a variety of color schemes was often associated with irregular, asymmetrical older houses, and simpler color combinations were applied to more formal, symmetrical homes. But expect to find exceptions.

The initial finish colors on older houses also related to advances in paint making. Early paints were made by hand, usually combining white lead, linseed oil, and hand-ground coloring pigments. Water-base paints, such as whitewash, were sometimes used on masonry walls, fences, and outbuildings. Toward the end of the nineteenth century a revolution took place when manufacturers developed ready-mixed paints. Suddenly, homeowners could choose from a wide range of colors. At present certain paint companies carry early American colors resembling some original colors for a few styles. For an exact duplication of the initial colors, however, having the color mixed to order may be necessary.

COLOR GUIDELINES FOR OLDER HOUSES

Because of the differences among localities, the absence of precise color rules, and the varying individual preferences of the original owners, the color guidelines presented in the table on pages 185–187 are not set standards. They indicate a general framework for selecting colors in keeping with particular architectural styles at the time they were popular.

POSSIBLE PAINT COLORS FOR OLDER HOMES

Architectural Style	House Siding or Body	Trim	Shutters and Blinds	Sash
Seventeenth Century	Probably unpainted with exposed wood siding left to weather to soft, warm earth tones of browns or light grays	Same	Same	Same
Eighteenth Century— Georgian				

1700 to about 1750	Barn reds
	Whites (Virginia)
	Yellow ochres
	Dark evergreens
	Gray greens
	Bluish sage greens
	Warm grays
	Chocolate browns
	Ochres
	Taupes
	Tans
	Fawns
		Whites
		Creams
		Sometimes same color as body of the house
		
		Less common:
		  red browns
		  grays
		  yellows
			Deep greens
			Blacks	

Around 1750 to 1780	Creams Whites			Dark green putty lines, or entire sash in New England

Federal 1790 to 1830	Houses with wood siding, gentle pastel shades:
	  light yellows
	  creamy beiges
	  bluish grays
	  smoky blues
	  muted greens
	
	Off-whites
		Lighter tones than siding:
		  off-whites
		  creams
		  pale yellows
		  buffs
		  restrained blues
			Urban houses:
			  rich greens
			  dark reds
			  deep browns
			  blacks
			
			Creamy off-whites	

Greek Revival 1820 to 1860	Whites
	
	Rural New England soft shades:
	  pale yellows
	  light blue grays
	  buffs
	  muted green grays
	  smoky grays
		Whites
		
		For nonwhite houses:
		  gray blues
		  olive greens
		  buffs
		  evergreen greens
			Bottle greens
			Chrome greens
			Vivid greens
				Whites
				
				Putty lines:
				  black or
				  green black

Architectural Style	House Siding or Body	Trim	Shutters and Blinds	Sash
Gothic Revival 1820 to 1860	Light earthy colors: fawns warm grays gray tans stone grays stone browns smoky grays slate grays straw colors rose beiges chocolate browns	Same color as the body of the house but in a contrasting shade Light-colored home with darker trim Darker-colored home with lighter trim Creamy off-whites	Dark greens Deeper shade of body of the house Natural wood color, stained	
Italianate 1845 to 1880	Warm, neutral hues on early houses: earth browns muted stone grays yellow ochres peachy tans moss greens Later houses: yellows grayish greens terra-cotta reds dark browns blue grays	Early houses: creamy off-whites beiges same color as body of the house but in a darker or lighter shade Later houses: evergreen greens deep browns dark olive greens	Early houses: warm browns Later houses: deep forest greens reddish browns	Sometimes: blacks chocolate browns deep greens
Stick Style 1855 to 1900 Subdued At times a two-tone body	Natural weathered grays Neutral hues: soft browns light sage greens whites Maroons Terra-cotta reds Ochres	Dark grays Buffs Evergreen greens Dark browns Accent colors: blacks chrome yellows peachy tans	Dark forest greens	Sometimes: whites
Mansard 1860 to 1880 Deep, somber, and intense colors Contrasting colors	Maroons Rich earth tones: warm red browns stone grays lead grays blue grays dark terra-cotta reds chocolate browns umber browns olive greens evergreen greens sage greens Dark golden ochres Burnt oranges Parchments Yellowish beiges Soft tans	Color contrasts with the body of the house: evergreen greens light chocolates whites beiges creams yellows	Slate grays Green blacks Dark browns	Sometimes: velvety browns or grays
Romanesque 1875 to 1895	Natural masonry	Red browns Chocolate browns Dark stone grays		

Architectural Style	House Siding or Body	Trim	Shutters and Blinds	Sash

Queen Anne 1876 to 1900
 	
Mostly multicolored
 	
Harmonious tones, three to five on one house, to emphasize asymmetrical lines, varied textures, and decorative details
	Early houses:
	  warm brick reds
	  terra-cotta reds
	  buttercup yellows
	  deep sands
	  medium olives
	  fawns
	  deep greenish yellow
	    ochres
	  gray greens
	
	Later houses:
	  soft ash yellows
	  muted grays
	  olive greens
	  medium ochres
	  bluish bottle greens
	  tans
	  dark browns
	  sage greens
	  yellowish avocados
	  nutmegs
	  russets
	  sandish taupes
	
	Less common, with single colors or contrasting shades of the same color:
	  browns
	  grays
	  olives
		Wood houses:
		  maroons
		  medium chocolate
		    browns
		  slate grays
		  umber browns
		  evergreen greens
		  rich tans
		  chrome yellows
		  sage greens
		  sap greens
		  burnt siennas
		
		Stone or brick houses, earth colors:
		  burnt siennas
		  dark coppers
		  Indian reds
		  chocolate browns
		  sand colors
		  maroons
		  deep tans
		  rich ochres
		  dark burnt oranges
		  whites
		
		Less common, with houses having single body colors:
		  contrasting shades
		  of the same color
			Evergreen greens
			Dark reds
			Tans
			Dark blues
			
			Two tones
				Maroons
				Dark reds
				Olives
				Deep greens
				Alizarian crimsons
				Whites
				
				Putty lines:
				  sometimes vermilion

Shingle Style 1880 to 1900
 	
Muted, monochromatic earth tones
	Weathered or stained shingles:
	  deep grays
	  earth browns
	  silver grays
	  moss greens
		Natural wood oiled or stained with deep Venetian reds
		
		Less often, whites
				Similar to trim

Revivals of the Georgian and Federal Styles 1885 to 1940				
Georgian Revival	Whites Pale yellows Soft buffs Muted terra-cotta reds Pale olives Medium grays	Whites Creamy ivories	Dark bottle greens Deep olives At times, the same color as the body of the house	Whites (especially on brick or stone homes) Same color as trim Dark greens Sometimes black putty lines
Federal Revival		Brick houses: whites		

MATCHING PAINT COLORS

Let your house tell you about its original colors. When the homeowner desires the exact shade and color scheme of the initial paints, he or she should seek professional advice. Although the owner can expose samples of the original colors, it is sometimes difficult to know precisely what they were at the time of application. Paints, particularly the early ones, turn yellow, fade, or darken over the years, depending on the paint and its condition. A specialist in paint analysis may be of help by taking a number of samples from the house, analyzing the paint, and sending the owner a report, including the color noted by a color notation system and a description of its gloss and texture as well.

To save money, the homeowner, following directions from a professional, may take samples from the house and send them to the specialist to be investigated. The professional will then return to the owner a report designating color standards. The owner can write to the Munsell Color Company (2441 N. Calvert Street, Baltimore, MD 21218) for their color samples based on the specifications from the paint expert, enabling the owner to match the paint at a paint store.

As part of his or her work on the site, the color consultant usually counts paint layers on various parts of the house to understand the paint history of the house. This procedure the homeowner may be able to carry out alone. Use an X-acto knife with a curved blade to cut through all the paint layers to the base materials, making a crater about ½ inch across the top. Sand the sides of the exposed paint layers with 220-grit wet/dry finishing paper, applying a lubricating oil as you work to obtain a smooth surface now about 1 inch wide. Wipe the surface. Again, using the oil, polish the curve with 600-grit wet/dry paper. In excellent light with a good-quality hand magnifier, study the layers. Accumulated dirt or grease appearing as dark lines between layers indicates finish coats. Be alert for evidence of paint removal such as patches of old paint in crevices and corners where it could not be reached. This technique may also be useful to ascertain whether certain parts of the house are original. Compare the paint history of one section of a house with another section that you have determined was part of the structure when it was first built.

The owner can also try a simpler do-it-yourself procedure to match the original or later color layers. Choose a surface where it is unlikely there has been abrasion. Cut a bevel through the layers, and when you have determined which of the finish coat layers is to be duplicated, uncover a large area. Scrape dirt or skin off the old paint surface and try to match this color to a manufacturer's color chart or the Munsell Color System. Use a bright light and a 3-to-5 power magnifying glass. This technique is only as good as the eye of the individual involved; therefore, it is wise to ask several people to check the color. Have a paint dealer mix new paint according to the color sample. Also, the possible fading, yellowing, or darkening of the paint over time affects the results, but imprecise as it is, this method is worthwhile. To contribute to the knowledge of which paint colors were found on particular architectural styles, send a report of the findings to the local historical society and keep a record for future owners.

When paint buildup is excessive enough to demand removal of the paint, try to leave small patches of the old paint in locations where they will not be unsightly. They represent a record of paint history for researchers or subsequent owners.

PAINTING

Paint refreshes a house. An even more important reason for painting is to protect your home. Paint helps to keep out water which deteriorates the surfaces beneath and may stain wood. A wet surface is more likely to rot or corrode.

Painting a house is a duty countless homeowners undertake. Compared with other renovation work, the task is relatively simple. Homeowners can paint at their own pace, and they can realize a considerable savings because labor is the greatest cost of a professional paint job.

Among the reasons for calling on someone to help you are living in a tall house, feeling uneasy about working from a ladder, and having neither the time nor the stamina to do the work. Even though you have hired someone else to paint, a task you should carry out yourself beforehand is to hunt for problems in the house that will cause paint failure in a brief time. Take care of the roof, flashing, gutters and downspouts, or whatever requires work well before paint is put on the house.

Generally, paint on the outside of the house lasts from 4 to 6 years, although it does not remain clean, bright, or glossy for that long. The durability of paint depends on factors such as the condition of the house, the carefulness of the surface preparation, the skill of the painter, the quality of the paint, its protection from the sun and rain, and the climate. Window sills and exposed features may require repainting every 2 years.

TOUCHING UP PAINT

A conscientious maintenance program may nudge into the future the time when a house calls for a complete repainting. You may encounter paint failure from blistering, checking, excessive chalking, flaking, or crumbling in only one or a few sections of the house, possibly where it is exposed to strong sunlight or to condensation. Repaint only these areas of the house. Carefully prepare the surface by removing loose paint with a wire brush or scraper. To make a smooth, clean surface, sand over the edges of the spots where you have taken off the paint and remove all dust and grime. Prime bare wood, and repaint. If you do not have leftover paint of the same color stored away, take a chip of old paint to a paint dealer for matching. When touching up the surface, try to blend the new paint into the old. With just a little paint on the brush, move from the center of the newly painted area onto the old paint.

Paint that seems faded may be covered with dust or grime. In this case, hosing down the paint or washing it with water and a mild detergent will renew the paint job and avoid repainting.

PREPARING THE HOUSE

Because of the time and money that must be spent to paint, you would like the paint to last as long as possible. A house in first-rate shape offers the best chance of this happening. An inspection of the house comes first. Begin with the roof and flashing, the gutters and downspouts, and the walls. Chapters 4 and 8, Roofs and Walls, explain what to look for and how to take care of problems. Do any necessary repairs and replace missing or deteriorated parts.

Be alert for water stains and evidence of moisture, and try to find the cause. If moisture seems to be coming from inside, your home may require improvements such as better ventilation of the attic, exhaust fans in the bathroom or kitchen, or metal vents in the siding located between the studs. Cut back any trees or shrubs next to the house which may be hindering the surface from drying.

Look for deterioration of the surfaces you are about to paint. Check carefully horizontal ledges, such as window sills, railings, or ornamentation, which may hold moisture; also inspect porch columns, particularly near the bases. Fill cracks in the wood with linseed-oil putty or an appropriate sealant, and cut out badly degenerated wood and patch it with new wood. Before installing the new wood, soak it thoroughly with a wood preservative, especially on the ends. Prime the wood after the preservative has had time to dry.

Investigate all joints in the house before painting, including those between the wall and parts of the windows and doors, between the wall and corner trim, between the boards of the siding, between unlike materials such as wood and masonry, and at the place where the wall meets both the roof and the foundation. If you are hiring a painter, point out gaps in these joints and deteriorated caulking and ask the painter to caulk these areas. When sealing these openings yourself, remove the old caulk with a wire brush or a knife. Cleaning with a solvent may be necessary. Prime bare wood and porous surfaces and allow the primer to dry. Caulk. When painting the house, paint over the caulking.

At this time, replace loose or cracked putty or glazing compound and broken window glass. The sections Broken Glass Panes and Loose and Cracked Putty around the Window Glass in Chapter 11, Windows, describe how to do these jobs.

GETTING THE SURFACE READY

The time spent on getting a house ready can easily surpass the hours spent on the actual painting. No dirt, oil, mildew, corrosion, or loose, cracked, or badly chalking paint should remain on the surface. If these problems are hidden under a coat of paint, they will eventually reappear as peeling, cracking, crumbling, or flaking. A thorough preparation is worth the time and work involved because the paint will bind to the surface better and last much longer.

Removing Old Paint. One way, a tedious one, to remove loose paint from small areas is to use a wire brush, scraper, or sandpaper. To create a smooth surface, sand over the edges of the spots where the paint has been taken off and follow up with a primer. A surface riddled with deep cracks extending to the wood beneath may result from a paint buildup that has become excessive. When this is the case or when there are large areas of deteriorated paint, all the paint must be taken off. You may consider using attachments for a drill or rotary tools and sanders. Many of these, however, can gouge the surface, and for an even face you will have to smooth the surface afterward by a gentler means. Because of the hazard of lead poisoning these methods are dangerous for most houses built before 1950 where any lead paint lingers. Workers should wear a respirator and scrape and sand outdoors, if possible. Electric heat guns and chemical removers will more safely take off lead paint. No matter what method is used, a respirator is necessary. Get rid of scraped paint at once, and wash the clothes worn for removing paint. Use drop cloths and make certain no chips remain on the ground.

An electric heat gun and other heat tools soften paint and make scraping easier, although the process is still quite time consuming. Any paint that is left can be removed with a chemical remover. Used correctly and cautiously, heat tools are less likely than a torch to char wood and to start a fire. A torch is not recommended because of the danger of fire. Also, never take off paint by sandblasting. It can damage wood irreparably.

Another possibility for taking off large areas of paint is a chemical remover. These are available in various strengths. Check with a paint supply shop to find the one most suited to your needs, and test it on a small inconspicuous section of the house before proceeding. A semipaste product is best for vertical surfaces. Brush it on in one direction only. When the remover has covered the area for the length of time specified in the directions, test to find out if the paint is soft. If it is not, add another coat of stripper to the first application. Once the paint is soft, scrape off the sludge with a dull putty knife followed by steel wool. Some of the chemical removers contain wax or paraffin, which leaves a slight residue on the surface. Wash it well with a solvent, such as turpentine, before either priming or applying any other finish. The disadvantages of this method are its expense and the resulting toxic fumes, requiring its use in well-ventilated locations. Always wear gloves and protect your eyes when using a chemical remover.

A last resort for taking paint off various removable parts of the house like shutters, doors, windows, balustrades, or trim is to pay for a commercial stripping service. Warning: Harsh stripping processes can loosen joints, soften wood, raise the grain, lighten the wood's color, and destroy delicate molding. For these reasons many experts do not recommend this technique. When investigating a firm which strips wood, ask to see examples of the work in the different kinds of wood you are interested in. Be cautious when removing parts from the house so that you will not damage them.

Cleaning Old Paint. Mineral spirits or a detergent in water will clean off oil and grease. After you have washed the paint with a detergent, rinse the surface. Severely chalking paint will come off with a stiff-bristle brush. Also, paint that is chalking can be washed off with TSP (trisodium phosphate) and water. Rinse the surface well afterward. When the chalking is not too severe, an oil-base primer is all that is needed before repainting.

Sheltered areas of the house under the eaves, beneath the porch, and below a shield of trees may not require painting as often as other parts of the house. A washing with water and a detergent may refresh this paint. In any case, always wash these protected areas of the house before painting.

Treating Mildew. Damp, warm, shaded, and poorly ventilated locations are vulnerable to mildew, a mold which shows up as dark spots on the paint. To test for mildew, put a few drops of recently purchased household bleach on the stain. If the stain vanishes, mildew is its cause. Destroy the mildew before proceeding with the painting. Washing the stained area with ⅓ cup of TSP and ½ cup of house-

hold bleach in a gallon of warm water will kill the mold. Rinse well with fresh water and permit the paint to dry. Use a mildew-resistant paint for the affected parts of the house or add an antimildew formula to the paint you use.

Preparing Metal. Painting metal calls for special preparations. Wipe new metal with mineral spirits to take away the manufacturer's protective coating. On any corroded or rusted surface, use a wire brush or sandpaper and clean the surface down to bare metal. The next step is to apply a primer appropriate for the metal. If aluminum has an anodized or baked-enamel finish, sand it before priming to help the paint adhere.

Encountering Other Problems. The route to a good paint job includes removing rust found around nailheads with either steel wool or sandpaper. Prime the area around the nailhead with a rust-preventing primer. If the nailheads are recessed, press putty over them before priming and painting. Nail any boards that are loose.

Another problem to look for is a smooth or shiny surface on the existing paint. Sand this paint before repainting because new paint will not adhere to such a surface. To take care of knots or spots of resin on the surface of wood, sand or scrape these areas and cover them with a knot sealer, shellac, or aluminum paint before priming.

PRIMING

A primer helps the paint to form a strong bond with the surface whether the surface is an unpainted one or an area where the existing paint has been removed. A primer, however, is unnecessary if the painted surface to be coated is in good condition. A few drops of the finish coat in the primer will give it the same tone as the top coat. To ensure a thorough covering of the surface, apply the primer with a brush. Allow the primer to dry for a day or two before proceeding.

Be certain to obtain the correct primer for the type of surface to be coated. For example, masonry and metal each call for a particular primer. Covering an oil-base paint with latex paint requires an oil-base primer. Also, use a primer compatible with the finish coat. Check the manufacturer's directions or purchase the primer and paint from the same manufacturer.

PAINTING BRICK AND OTHER
MASONRY SURFACES

You will eliminate one maintenance chore—repainting—by never painting an unpainted masonry surface. Brick on an older house may have been painted because it was poor-quality, underfired brick and it demanded extra protection. Other reasons older brick buildings may have been painted or stuccoed are to seal the walls from moisture and to imitate stone. If possible, repaint these surfaces rather than attempt to strip the paint, a process which often badly damages the brick.

CHOOSING THE RIGHT PAINT

There are different paints for different parts of the house—the main body, trim, masonry, shingles, and porch floor and steps. Oil-base, or alkyd-base, and latex paints are the two types manufactured for the body of the house. Each has its advantages. In general, oil-base paints are better than latex paints for the older house because of their excellent penetrating ability and the harder surface they provide. Oil-base paints adhere better, too, especially when they are applied with a brush. Most oil-base paints have a glossier surface than latex brands and are easier to clean.

On the other hand, latex paints have better color retention. It is easier to clean up after painting because water will remove the paint. Latex paints dry quickly, and you can apply them to a slightly damp surface. They give a softer, flatter finish, if that characteristic is desired. They are more porous and, therefore, an appropriate choice for areas where moisture should penetrate.

When deciding upon paint, know what kind of paint is already on the house. If you do not, take a chip of the old paint to a paint store to obtain this information. Usually, the best results come from duplicating the kind of paint already on the house. Otherwise, problems can result. For instance, latex paint applied directly over an oil-base paint may separate the old paint from the surface.

The paint for trim such as windows, doors, cornices, and other ornamentation dries to a hard, glossy finish. The colors of trim paint are brighter than those manufactured for house paint. Trim paint is tougher, more durable, and easier to clean than house paint. Also, glossier paints will not chalk and stain the surfaces below them.

Some firms make the same paint for both masonry and shingles or shakes; others produce individual paints for these two uses. Latex paint is preferable for masonry or shingles and shakes because its high degree of porosity allows water which has worked its way behind these materials to evaporate. For masonry, a cement powder paint is also available.

Porch and deck paints are especially tough. They must stand up to the wear and abuse taken by these areas.

When purchasing paint, decide whether you need paint that is mildew resistant or that is meant to chalk slightly as a self-cleaning device. Chalking paints are undesirable for areas where the paint may run down and mar the surface beneath.

Stains are popular for exterior wood on the body of the house. They penetrate beneath the surface rather than coat the wood, revealing the grain. Stains range from the nearly transparent to the more opaque, which does not equal the hiding power found in paint. For the best results, use a stain on new wood. Paint should be completely removed from a painted surface before it is stained—often a difficult and tedious process.

BEING SAFE ON A LADDER

Your foremost concern when working on a ladder should be safety. Check the Safety Precautions section in Chapter 4, Roofs, for ways of decreasing hazards.

APPLYING THE PAINT

Paints and brushes influence how long the paint job will endure. Good quality is essential and always worth the extra expense. Because paint manufacturers frequently change their colors, it is wise to purchase more paint than the job requires to allow for future patching and minor repainting. Brushes provide an advantage on exterior wood because they urge the paint into the pores and cracks of the wood. For oil-base paint, purchase a natural-bristle brush; for latex paint, either polyester or nylon bristles. Consider a sprayer for large areas like fences and lattices, but not for a prime coat. Sprayers are ideal for stucco and masonry. When spraying, scrupulously cover with drop cloths the areas not to be coated.

For satisfactory results, outside painting must wait for choice weather—on days neither windy nor rainy when the temperature is between 40 and 90 degrees Fahrenheit. Only with latex paint can the surface to be painted remain slightly damp. While waiting for the ideal weather conditions, you can paint in the garage the storm windows, screens, and shutters removed from the house.

Always stir paint immediately before applying it. Dip the brush one-third the bristle length into the paint, and tap lightly against the side of the container to remove extra paint. As you work, brush from the unpainted to the freshly painted parts of the house. Begin applying paint at the top of the main body of the house, and proceed left to right as you move downward. If you are balancing on a ladder to reach the high areas, avoid positioning the ladder twice in the same spot by painting the trim as you go along. Otherwise, paint the trim after completing the body of the house. Never paint in full sunlight because the top of the paint film will dry out too quickly. Paint the areas the sun has already touched.

On new wood, give each surface a primer and two coats of the finish paint. Unless a drastic change in color is introduced, a painted surface in good condition calls for one coat of paint. You may decide to apply two coats to areas, such as a porch floor and steps or window sills, where extra protection is desired. Thin the first coat with a paint thinner. Check the paint to be certain it is dry, not sticky, before proceeding with another coat.

FAILING PAINT

As it ages, paint eventually chalks, checks, cracks, and flakes. Poor-quality paint, improper surface preparation, leaks in various parts of the house, condensation, incorrect paint application, or painting during unsatisfactory weather conditions bring about premature paint failure.

Checking. Shallow cracks on the paint film which finally pierce through to the surface beneath are described as checking. Among the causes of checking are low-quality paint, too much paint on the surface, and oil paint applied on a damp surface. When cracks have reached bare wood, take off all paint from these areas and then prime and paint.

Alligatoring. Alligatoring describes paint that is deeply cracked in an alligator-skin pattern. Applying another coat before the first is dry, putting an incompatible type of paint on existing paint, painting over a glossy surface, or using poor-quality paint are responsible for this condition. Before repainting, remove all paint having this problem.

Crumbling and Flaking. The problem of crumbling and flaking, in which pieces of paint drop from the surface, occurs because the surface was damp, oily, or insufficiently prepared before painting. Scrape and sand all crumbling and flaking paint and try to locate the source of the trouble before priming and painting.

Blistering. Blistering usually arises from moisture behind the paint. It can seep behind the paint from the outside through cracks in joints or from faulty flashing, gutters, downspouts, siding, or roofing. Moisture can work its way outward from the inside as well. Reasons why this could happen include poor ventilation or the lack of vapor barriers on insulated walls where there is high humidity such as in the kitchen or bathroom. Urea-formaldehyde foams injected as insulation into the wall system can cause

paint to blister. Finding the source of moisture is essential to correct this problem. Otherwise, new paint may blister again, sometimes within a few weeks of repainting.

Wrinkling. The novice painter in an out-and-out effort to coat the surface can put on too much paint. In this case, the paint may dry rapidly on the top and remain soft underneath. When the paint below the dry skin finally hardens, wrinkles occur. Other causes of wrinkling are not waiting for a first coat to dry before a second one is applied and painting in full sunlight. Sand light wrinkles on the surface, and remove the paint where the ridges are deeper.

Running and Sagging. When paint seems to slide down a wall, too heavy a coat may have been put on at one time. Also, paint applied over a shiny surface may cause running or sagging. Try sanding the surface or using paint remover to take off the paint.

SELECTING A PAINTER

If you decide to hire a painter to paint your house, select only a competent person or firm, preferably one experienced with older houses. Read Chapter 15, Calling in a Contractor, to learn about finding and choosing professional help, working out a contract, and arranging the payments. In addition to seeking suggestions from the local historical society, architects with experience in renovation work, and the other individuals and groups listed in Chapter 15, a possible way to locate a good painter is to ask for recommendations from the salesperson or owner of a hardware or paint supply store.

To save money and, possibly, to ensure that the work is done with the required thoroughness, the homeowner may be able to do part of the work, especially some of the time-consuming and expensive tasks. For example, the homeowner may caulk gaps in the joints, replace any deteriorated caulking, apply glazing compound around the window glass, clean surfaces, and scrape peeling and flaking paint before the painter arrives. In other instances, the owner may decide to scrape only small areas of cracking and peeling paint and to paint the lower portion of the structure and hire a painter to remove large sections of deteriorated paint and to paint the upper stories of the house.

Each painter bidding on the job should submit a contract spelling out every task. It should state where the new paint is to be applied, how much of the old paint is to be taken off, and how the job is to be done. Remember: A torch always presents a fire hazard, and for this reason you may choose to rule out this paint-removing method. The contract should also include the number of coats of paint, the type of paint (oil or latex), the brand and model of paint, and the paint colors, stating whether these will be ready-mixed or mixed by the painter. Make certain the painter plans to use a good-quality paint. When extensive preparation is necessary, a painter may not be able to give a firm price. In this case, ask for a not-to-exceed figure.

In evaluating estimates, do not allow the price to become the only selection criteria. A low bid may reflect poor-quality paint, inadequate preparation, and an intent to seek profits by extra charges later. A quality painting job may entail paying a higher price. Before making a choice, contact previous customers to learn whether they were satisfied with the quality of the work.

Painters may request an advance payment to purchase paint. Buy extra paint to have a supply for touching up in the future—especially important when the painter is mixing colors.

After selecting a painter, the owner has other responsibilities to ensure satisfactory results. Before allowing the painter to put on any paint, examine the surface preparation to be sure it is acceptable. Do not purchase a large amount of paint until you have agreed on the color. Test the color, whether ready-mixed or prepared by the painter, on a small area of the house, and wait for it to dry before making a decision. As the painting proceeds, make certain the correct number of coats are applied. Inspect the completed job carefully. Do not make a final payment until you are satisfied that all the work has been done and that it has been done well.

CHAPTER FOURTEEN

FOUNDATIONS AND BASEMENTS

Foundations are the strong, silent components of houses, extending from the earth or rock upon which buildings rest to the first-floor structures. They do not encompass large visible areas nor advertise themselves with flamboyant decorations. The functions of a foundation are major ones—to support the weight of the structure, to hold back the surrounding earth, and to protect the building from water, dampness, and insects. Improper foundation construction, uneven settling, insufficient elevation from the earth, poor perimeter drainage, deteriorating soft mortar, flaking stone, or crumbling brick are the chief threats to a foundation.

Before purchasing an older house, check to be certain the foundation is sound. Unbalanced settlement or extensive degeneration may require replacing portions of or all of the foundation, an expensive job which calls for professional help. Substantial foundation work should be executed before other improvements are carried out because in returning the house to a level position the walls and ceilings may crack. Once a foundation is stable, inspect it regularly and carry out any needed repairs immediately.

Walls and footings form the foundation. Footings are the foundation's base, and their function is to distribute the load to prevent uneven settling. In older houses footings may be either the same width as or wider than the foundation walls or they may be nonexistent. Many old houses have stone foundation walls which simply start off on earth below grade, sometimes but not always below the frost line (the lowest depth frost reaches) (Figure 14-1). Soil under the foundation should be undisturbed. For this reason good drainage around the foundation walls and footings extending below the frost line will help to achieve a stable foundation. To withstand the effects of moisture, foundation walls are stone, brick, cast concrete, or concrete block. Because of the builder's concern for the architectural appearance of the house, the material exposed to the eye above grade will at times differ from the material below. The thickness of the foundation wall may diminish to receive the first-floor framing.

DESIGN

Throughout the seventeenth century, houses built in New England generally rested close to the ground on low foundation walls of rough fieldstone invariably secured from the immediate vicinity. If the foundation was somewhat exposed, builders sometimes dressed the stones into regular shapes and laid them in even courses across the front of the house. In most instances, stonework on the back and sides of the house was laid in a more irregular manner. At times only a few flat stones supported the building, with the cellar excavated under just a small section of the house. At other times slightly higher foundation walls permitted a full basement for storage.

Stones were laid either without mortar or with clay in the joints. Mortar made with lime was rare because lime was costly and difficult to obtain. In localities where oysters were available, crushed oyster shells were frequently the source of lime in mortar. Seventeenth Century homes in Virginia usually had brick foundations with an oyster shell and sand mortar. The soft consistency of the oyster shells, however, made this type of mortar unreliable for foundations, as it tended to disintegrate easily. Because of the inadequacy of the mortar and the small size of the underpinnings, subsequent owners of Seventeenth Century houses usually undertook substantial rebuilding of the foundations.

In the early eighteenth century, quarried stone became increasingly popular for foundations. Depending on the locality, limestone, redstone, or stratified granite in crudely split blocks often was used. By the end of the eighteenth century regular blocks of dressed stone appeared frequently on the above-grade walls of foundations in New England homes.

Before 1750 brick, which is more porous and susceptible to disintegration from ground moisture, was rarely employed for foundations except in the South, but during the late Georgian period brick above-grade foundation walls were seen throughout the eastern seaboard. The bond pattern in the above-grade foundation wall usually duplicates the one on

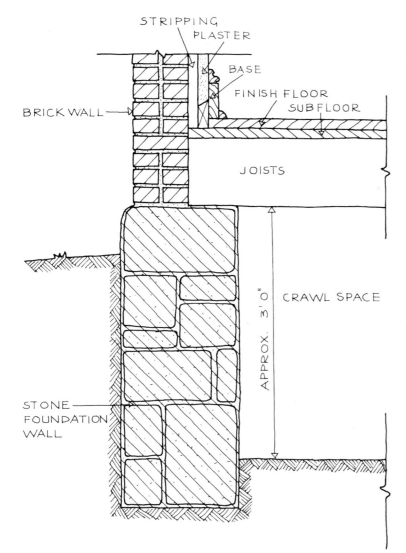

Figure 14-1. Parts of the foundation.

During the Federal period builders directed increasing attention to the exterior appearance of foundations. Craftsmanship improved, and builders often sought construction materials far from the site rather than use whatever stone was nearby. At times the foundations were built with large stones cut to resemble evenly spaced rectangular blocks, with a false joint incised into the exposed face of the stone. Granite became a favorite foundation material throughout the nineteenth century.

Stone and brick of various types continued to be the preferred construction materials for above-grade foundation walls during the nineteenth century. High foundations built of granite or brick or faced with marble were characteristic of Greek Revival houses, making them appear to be elevated on platforms similar to the ancient Greek temples. The only other nineteenth century architectural style to have a noticeably different type of foundation was the Shingle Style. Constructed of rough, natural stone often laid randomly, foundations of homes in this style may be close to the ground or extend partially or completely up the first-story walls.

With the advent of pressed brick at the end of the last century, above-grade foundation walls could be built with a material that was more durable and water-resistant than the earlier softer bricks. In most instances, lime mortar was used in nineteenth century foundations, although cement mortar was found on some foundations built toward the end of the century. Poured concrete or concrete block foundations, now and then concealed behind a stone or brick veneer, began to occur after 1890 and into the twentieth century along with the more traditional stone and brick foundations.

MAINTENANCE AND REPAIR

The owner of the older house does not have the assurance that the dwelling is supported by a modern foundation of cast concrete or concrete block that was well waterproofed on the outside at the time of construction and, perhaps, is guarded by a termite shield. The homeowner will be able to assume some repairs to the older foundation. For solving troubles such as severe bulges and cracks, active motion of the foundation, the need for waterproofing the exterior of the foundation, and extensive repairs or replacement of the foundation, the homeowner will probably decide to seek professional help.

CONSTRUCTION GUIDELINES

Knowing about safe construction practices for foundations may explain the cause of current trouble, will alert the owner to future difficulties, and will guide the homeowner incurring major work on the

the exterior walls, except when the walls are laid in the decorative Flemish bond. Then the foundation bricks are a simpler pattern. High foundation walls elevating the first-floor level became fashionable at this time, allowing light into the cellar and adding to the stateliness of these Georgian houses.

When the entire building is constructed of brick, a course of molded bricks, known as a water table or weathering, may act as a transition between the thicker foundation wall and the wall above. The slanted or rounded edges shed rain and snow away from the structure. The contour of the water table assumes numerous forms: simple convex slopes, concave shapes, or a combination of convex and concave profiles. Variations in water table designs occur among different localities, too.

foundation. The foundation should reach a minimum of 8 inches above the soil level, although greater height for the foundation is preferable, particularly where there are hard rains. At least 6 inches of the foundation, or more in wet climates, should be exposed between the siding and the ground (Figure 14-2).

A crawl space is the shallow area beneath a house without a basement, usually enclosed by foundation walls. Crawl spaces have their own minimum dimensions which provide access below first-floor structural members and make possible an inspection of the area, even if only by flashlight from an access door. Girders should be placed at least 24 inches above the ground, joists 36 inches above the soil in crawl spaces.

Any replacement wood should be treated with a preservative if it will touch the masonry or be within 8 inches of the ground. Wood already existing in this precarious location should be protected from moisture and treated with wood preservative to prolong its life.

CARE

Certain conditions are likely to cause problems within foundations, crawl spaces, or basements. Inspect these areas at least once a year.

- Find out if the gutters, downspouts, and water drainage systems are working properly and directing water away from the foundation. The best time to check is after a hard rain.

- Watch that any thick planting does not grow within 2 feet of the foundation—roots can cause movement and also retain moisture in the soil.

- Notice whether the soil and any walks and patios near the foundation always slope away from the house.

- Inspect the foundation materials on the outside and in the basement for cracks, bulges, or deterioration and the mortar for gaps or crumbling.

- Search the foundation or crawl space for signs of rot, moisture stains, or insect invasions. Be on the lookout for subterranean termites' shelter tubes, passageways ¼ to ½ inch wide between the soil and the termites' food supply in the wood.

- Examine the foundation or crawl space and the area around these for evidence of condensation or rising ground moisture.

- Investigate the joint between the sill and the foundation for any openings.

- Check outside spigots for leaking.

- Be alert for stains, rust, peeling paint, cracked floors, efflorescence (a powdery white substance on the surface), and other signs of moisture in the

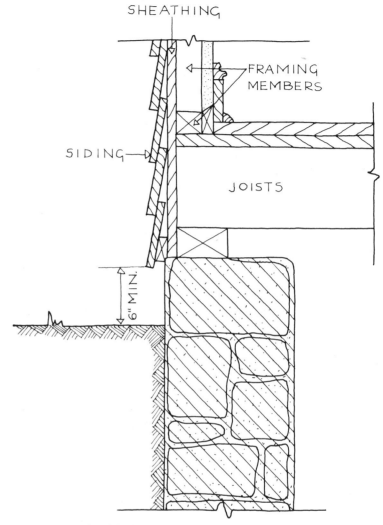

Figure 14-2. Height of the foundation.

basement. Also, in a finished basement, check the bottom of the walls for mold, mildew, and warping.

- Probe the wood framing members with an ice pick, screwdriver, or other sharp object. If the instrument penetrates the wood more than about ½ inch, break open a section of the wood to learn why it has deteriorated.

- Look for loosened floor tiles in a finished basement and efflorescence between the joints. Investigate beneath the loose tiles for evidence of dampness.

Settlement and Cracks. Foundations may settle or move. Shifting or shrinking soil is a frequent reason for this to happen. Perhaps the house was originally built on soil of insufficient bearing capacity.

Underground water (a stream, or pressure due to impervious soil such as clay) can cause big problems. Vibrations from traffic, tree roots near the foundation, flooding, lack of drainage away from the perimeter earth, the expansion and contraction of building materials, rotting timbers, insufficient footings, or a foundation built above the frost line may contribute to the movement of foundations. Signs of this activity may be an uneven eaveline, a sagging roof ridge, a crooked chimney, cracks in the exterior or interior walls or in the foundation, slanting floors, or binding or looseness of the windows or doors. One test for foundation settlement is to place a marble or ball on uncarpeted floors. If it rolls almost every time to the same side of several rooms, the foundation may be settling.

You must now determine if the foundation movement has halted. Attach two strips of metal overlapped in an X shape to the mortar with a nail at the top of each piece (Figure 14-3). Scribe, or mark, their starting position with a nail, or whatever will scratch metal. If the settlement is active, you will learn which way the wall is moving by observing the position of the scribe lines over a period of time. For an active crack and for any exceptionally large cracks, call in a structural engineer or a knowledgeable contractor for advice about the best way to proceed. Expensive underpinning of the foundation wall may be necessary.

Where you have determined that the foundation is stable, fill the cracks in a brick or stone foundation with mortar of the same strength as the original mortar. For a lime mortar foundation, use patching mortar containing lime and some cement. Also, maintain the mortar in the joints in good condition, repointing when necessary. For exposed walls, repair or replace any badly deteriorated stones or bricks with substitutes of the same size, color, and texture as the original material. (Walls that do not show need not match.) Work in small sections to prevent the collapse of the wall, and allow the mortar to harden before proceeding with additional replacing. Chapter 8, Walls, tells more about how to care for bricks and stones and how to repoint.

Sills. Sometimes a rotted sill, the horizontal timber that sits directly on the foundation, will produce sagging eaves or cracks in a house. If the sill is the source of the problem, replace the portion of the sill that has decayed. You may require the help of a carpenter to accomplish this task, and shoring and needling, or supporting the wall above where you are working with a beam, may be necessary. When checking the condition of the sill, be alert for decaying joists, beams, or studs that touch the sill, and replace any weakened portions of these members. One way to repair deteriorated joists or beams is to nail

or bolt a new piece of wood of at least the same size beside the deteriorated material. This new piece, or "scab," must be long enough to extend beyond the rotted areas so that it can be fastened into sound sections of the old wood.

Dampness. Dampness is a widespread problem in foundations, crawl spaces, and basements. The result is often rotting wood and invading insects and, thus, weakened materials. The first step in controlling dampness is to discover its source. Poor drainage is responsible for countless wet foundations. Gutters and downspouts that function well and water drainage systems, whether storm sewers, dry wells, or other satisfactory methods to carry water away from the house, may be the solution to a wet basement.

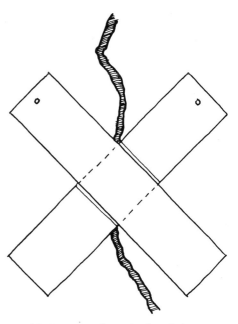

Figure 14-3. Testing to determine foundation movement.

Be sure that water is not entering through the window wells. A shield over the window well or a drain leading from the window well to a dry well at least 15 feet from the foundation are cures for this difficulty. The ground surrounding the foundation should slant away from the house for 6 feet or more. If it does not, you may be able to move earth to produce this slope. On a sloping lot, drains installed underground on the high side or a retaining wall built about 15 feet from the house on the uphill side of the lot may successfuly guide water past the house.

Seepage of water into the basement and condensation are common reasons for dampness. To test whether either of these is a problem, tape a small mirror or piece of aluminum foil to the foundation wall on the inside, sealing all the edges with tape. If after 24 hours the surface of the mirror or foil is moist, condensation is the trouble. If the surface is dry, but the back is damp, the moisture is seeping through the walls. Of course, it is not impossible for both conditions to be present at once. Continuous ventilation on dry days or a dehumidifier will often be the solution to condensation.

Seepage takes more effort to correct. This can be accomplished, perhaps, by sealing the walls of the basement with a waterproof coating after thoroughly cleaning the walls. Begin by making sure all cracks are filled—always an excellent preventive measure. One way to fill cracks is with mortar. Chip out loose material at the back of the crack until it becomes wider than the surface, a step not necessary when the crack is on the floor. Wet the crack and pack in mortar with a trowel. Keep the patch damp for about a week to allow it to cure.

When water gushes into the basement through a hole in the wall, make a plug out of a product such as a hydraulic or an epoxy compound, which hardens rapidly. An area where cracks frequently develop is where the walls meet the floor. These joints can be sealed with a patching cement. Chisel out more of the crack to enlarge it so that it is wider in the back than in the front, clean out the debris, and then insert the patching material with a trowel.

For more serious trouble other remedies become essential. One technique to reduce the amount of water in the basement is excavating a trench and installing drains to a sump pump *inside* the walls. Another solution may be digging soil away from the foundation on the exterior, installing drain tiles at the level of the footings, and applying a waterproof membrane to the exterior of the foundation wall. For this procedure, consider contacting a reputable firm specializing in waterproofing. Beware when a contractor suggests injecting a chemical into the ground under pressure to make the foundation watertight. This process frequently fails because the right soil conditions for its success are not present. In cases where water oozes through the basement floor, a sump pump may be the answer.

Another difficulty results from brick or stone walls that draw moisture from the ground. Poor drainage and soil that does not slope away from the foundation are sources of this trouble. If you have discovered that the drainage and the slope of the soil are not the source of the problem, call on an architect or engineer experienced with this "rising damp" problem. The specialist may recommend inserting a vapor barrier or a waterproof chemical into the walls to protect them and adjacent wood or other materials from deterioration.

Crawl Spaces. A leading problem with crawl spaces is excessive moisture rising from the ground or coming from condensation on materials near the crawl space under a heated building in cool weather or under an air-conditioned house in hot, humid weather. Any safeguards taken to keep crawl spaces dry will reduce the chance of insect invasions and of decay.

Vents installed around the perimeter of the foundation, preferably near the corners, will increase the movement of air within the crawl space. The area of all vent openings should total $\frac{1}{150}$ of the area under the house. Where vents are screened to keep out insects or rodents, the area must be one-third larger. In addition to vents, a ground cover of a strong vapor-resistant material will decrease the amount of moisture entering the crawl space. A ground cover becomes an effective remedy for moisture when the vents are closed in cold climates during the winter. Forty-five-pound or heavier roll roofing or 6-mil polyethylene sheets are good materials for this solid cover. Overlap the sheets about 2 inches and extend the soil cover to the foundation wall. Bricks or stones placed on the overlapping edges will hold down the sheets. When a crawl space has a ground cover, the vent area can be reduced to about $\frac{1}{1500}$ of the ground surface beneath the house. Unheated crawl spaces should be insulated. The vapor barrier should be above the insulation facing the heated room.

CHAPTER FIFTEEN

CALLING IN A CONTRACTOR

Perhaps your old metal roof leaks at the seams. Possibly you are planning an extensive renewal of an older house. How do you find honest and competent contractors? If you take the time to investigate prospective contractors whether you are looking for a general contractor or a subcontractor, you may never be the object of a fraud or the victim of shoddy or unfinished work. You may never pay twice—once for a botched job or a job never begun and again for the planned work. Be alert for dishonest contractors in the following situations:

- The deal seems too good to be true.
- The contractor demands a large percentage of the total cost before work begins.
- A fast talker threatens dreadful consequences if repairs are not done at once.
- You have difficulty obtaining an estimate or a contract in writing.
- Workers just happen to be in your neighborhood and offer a cheap price or even free work, possibly in exchange for your becoming a reference for anyone inquiring about the firm's work.

Following the process described in this chapter offers a good chance of a happy ending for you, your house, and your contractor.

DECIDING WHAT KIND OF HELP YOU REQUIRE

Before locating a contractor, scrupulously study Chapters 1, 3, and 16, Becoming Friends with Older Homes, Preparing for the Work, and Considering an Architect. These chapters explain how to understand your house and its problems, how to make decisions about the best way to proceed and about who is to do the work, and how to know what documents are necessary. After a realistic appraisal of your abilities, your stamina, and the time you can spend on the job, you may have concluded that professional help is necessary.

Do you require a general contractor? This expert is most helpful when the project includes several interrelated tasks or when speedy completion of the job is essential. A general contractor will perform the following services:

- Locates subcontractors, or specialists, for each task
- Finds and purchases all materials
- Plans the timing of the various jobs and coordinates the work of the subcontractors
- Supervises the work and ensures its satisfactory completion
- Resolves any disagreements between workers

As the work progresses, the owner pays the general contractor at prearranged times, and the general contractor is responsible for the cost of labor, materials, and other items, such as permits and insurance, written into the contract.

Turning the work over to a general contractor does not mean that the owner has nothing to do with the project. Whether or not an architect has been hired, the owner's advance planning is indispensible: There is no substitute for work well thought out ahead of time. The owner must understand what is involved from beginning to end. During the actual work the owner's supervision, daily if possible, is another way to ensure a satisfying outcome.

In addition, the owner may decide to locate extraordinary items such as an old paneled door, perhaps discovered in a wrecking-company yard, or a carved mantelpiece, tracked down in an antique shop. Allow plenty of time, and you will be ready when the contractor plans to install the item. An owner may vigorously hunt for matching materials, such as slate, brick, or tile, to replace a deteriorated section of a roof, wall, or hearth. Also, an energetic owner may take on much of the preparation including digging trenches, removing partitions, pulling up linoleum, scraping paint, or stripping wallpaper to keep costs to a minimum. Once the job has begun, working along with subcontractors on particular tasks is more difficult because the homeowner must meet the workers' schedules, which may not coincide with the owner's free time. This effort may be resented by the workers unless each has clearly defined tasks. The owner can, however, more easily accomplish finishing touches such as painting or sanding floors. Another possible path is hiring a general contractor for most of the work and finding by yourself subcontractors for specific jobs, possibly painting or roofing. Coordinate the work in a way not to conflict with the progress of the general contractor.

Some enterprising individuals act as the general contractor for work on their own houses. They must have time, patience, and perseverance. Experience helps, too — knowing what materials are appropriate and what problems are likely to occur in older homes. Such homeowners must be skillful in persuading others to perform well and on schedule, and they must be able to evaluate the work. One inducement encouraging an owner to take on the role of general contractor is the possible saving of 10 to 20 percent of the total cost of the project, but this amount will materialize only if the owner chooses the subcontractors wisely and shops around for the best prices on materials. Other rewards for the owner as general contractor include a greater understanding of the older structure and the pleasure of accomplishing a difficult task. In addition, the homeowner possesses a dedication to quality which may surpass the interest of any hired individual.

Serious drawbacks result from carrying out major work on a house without engaging a general contractor, particularly the forfeit of an expert's advice, which can be invaluable especially when no architect has been hired for the project. Also, the owner usually lives with disarray longer because he or she will not be able to schedule the work as efficiently as the contractor. In addition, obtaining a construction loan can be more difficult without a general contractor unless the owner can readily persuade the lender that the work will be completed competently.

Smaller jobs, work prolonged over several years, or a project where the owner intends to do much of the work can be carried out without a general contractor. In these cases the homeowner can hire the necessary subcontractors for each task, who will supply the labor, materials, and insurance and workers' benefits. Remember that for workers who are not subcontractors the homeowner is responsible for all insurance and benefits such as social security and workmen's compensation. Be sure, too, you have adequate insurance to cover a worker's accident or any damage to your home.

FINDING A CONTRACTOR

Ideal contractors are reliable, honest, and good businesspersons who pay workers and suppliers on time. They keep their word and live up to the written contract. They are competent, possessing the skills and experience with older houses to do a good job and to hire subcontractors and workers who take pride in their work. They are not elusive, but accessible to answer the owner's questions and to solve problems on the job. Also, they are individuals the homeowner works with comfortably. In addition, the owner of the older house should look for someone who appreciates the architectural features, materials, and workmanship of the structure and who has the ability to take care of these assets. A contractor should be open-minded to repairing existing materials, not someone who suggests massive, perhaps unnecessary, replacement. This individual should be knowledgeable about the permits required for the work and about the applicable building codes, which may give special consideration to saving original features of the house. A contractor who glances hastily at the work to be done, makes rapid assumptions, and resents taking the extra minutes to explain the inevitable puzzles of the older house is probably not someone you ought to permit to work on your home.

Where can this paragon of a general contractor or subcontractor be found? No computer service exists to match the homeowner with a suitable contractor, but advice may be as close as your friends, neighbors, and relatives. Ask them for names of contractors who have worked successfully on their homes. Contacting the owner of a house that is being renovated sensitively or that you admire for the unmistakable care that has gone into it may lead to excellent prospects. Real estate brokers, local bankers, building supply companies, lumberyards, and hardware and paint stores are other sources for names of good contractors. Seek suggestions from the owner of a store specializing in architectural parts or of an antique shop selling doors, windows, or mantelpieces from older houses. When an architect is on the job, he or she will usually know of competent contractors. If you have found an excellent carpenter, painter, or electrician, ask these individuals to recommend the professionals you are seeking. The local historical society and neighborhood development council are organizations that may be able to propose contractors. Stay away from the widely advertised home-improvement firms, for the results rarely will satisfy the knowledgeable owner of an older home.

If you have accumulated a long list of prospects, narrow it down to three to five names through preliminary investigation. The Selecting a Contractor section in this chapter gives ideas about checking on a contractor. Even if you have only a few names, make a brief investigation of each before obtaining bids to avoid wasting time meeting with an unsuitable contractor. While you are collecting names of contractors, apply for any necessary municipal or historic district commission approvals for the work planned. Then any changes can be made in the work plans before the contractors bid on the job.

OBTAINING BIDS

You and the architect, if one is involved, should meet with each prospective contractor individually at the site. Give each one the necessary copies of the work plans. These should be specific and should include the quality and quantity of all materials; brand names, model numbers, colors, and sizes; the nature of the work and the preparation desired; and a time schedule for completing the project. The documents should state that all work is to comply with applicable building codes and other local regulations. When contractors suggest changes or additions to the plans, ask them to submit these changes separately. Request bids in writing by a certain date, probably 3 or 4 weeks from the day the contractor has met with you.

Most often the bid will be in the form of a lump sum, or a total figure, for all of the work, which may be broken down into the cost of various tasks. The contractor working on an older home may encounter unforeseen deterioration — rotting wood behind the plaster walls, for instance. For this reason the contractor may submit a bid that states an hourly rate and the cost of materials plus an amount for overhead. If this is the case, after a discussion with the contractor when the proper assumptions are made about the work, the homeowner should set a total beyond which the contractor cannot bill the owner. This provides an incentive for the contractor to finish the work quickly. When a time-and-materials contract is submitted, encourage the contractor to state a lump sum for all possible items and set apart only a few tasks on a time-and-materials basis.

Once the bids are received, check them carefully against the work plan to be certain each bidder includes everything. Notice how long the bid is valid; some may extend for only 2 weeks. You can compare the cost of materials in the bid with prices offered by suppliers to be sure the prices quoted for materials are fair. When a bid seems too high or too low or when you have any questions, call the contractor for an explanation. Perhaps the high bid reflects extra effort to do a thorough job, or it may indicate the contractor does not want the work.

SELECTING A CONTRACTOR

Proceed carefully when selecting a contractor. Begin by finding out if the contractor is listed in the phone book and whether he or she has an office or merely an answering service. The here-today-gone-tomorrow operator usually does not establish an office, although a reputable contractor may have only an answering service. Ask additional questions such as how long the contractor has been in business. If the firm is new, learn about the contractor's previous experience and check with a former employer, if possible. Is the contractor licensed? A license is a sign of responsibility, and most respectable firms will have one. For plumbing, electrical, and mechanical work, the contractor should be licensed.

This next step is essential. Request a list of references. Ten is not too many names for a larger job. From this list, choose about three to investigate, including one or more recent jobs. Call these individuals and ask the following questions:

- What was the nature of the work? It is a good idea to learn whether the contractor has done jobs similar to the one you are proposing.
- Did problems occur? What were they? Who was at fault? How were they resolved?
- Was the work completed nearly on time?
- Was the work done in a neat and orderly manner with adequate cleanup afterward?
- Were there extra charges beyond the price in the written contract? Why?
- Was the contractor available when he or she was needed?
- Did the owner and the contractor work well together?
- Who supervised the work? Was the supervision thorough and efficient?
- Did the contractor return promptly to repair or complete work not done properly the first time?
- Were there problems with either suppliers or workers not being paid?

Finally, ask to visit the house to view the work. This inspection takes time, but it is the only way to obtain a direct impression of the quality of the work.

To help evaluate the contractors, call the Better Business Bureau or the local consumer protection agency to learn whether any complaints have been lodged against the contractors. What were they and how were they resolved? Also, you can acquire the names of the contractors' major suppliers and ask them whether they were paid on time.

When you have gathered this information and reviewed the bids, do not arbitrarily choose or dismiss the lowest or highest bidder. Try to determine from the information which one will do the best job. Hiring the contractor you have most confidence in may be the least expensive route in the long run.

WRITING A CONTRACT

Do not proceed without a written contract even for a small job. It will prevent misunderstanding, clarify responsiblities, specify the work to be done, and forestall dishonest dealings. Remember, too, that verbal contracts or oral changes to an existing written contract are not legally valid. The owner has a number of choices in preparing a contract. Sometimes the contractor presents the owner with a contract, a version which may be to the contractor's advantage. Check such a contract carefully and negotiate the desired changes, or have a lawyer review it for you before signing it. Often the architect for the project will prepare the contract. Another choice is to write your own contract or purchase a form from a nearby office of the American Institute of Architects. The most costly procedure initially is to hire a lawyer to prepare the contract for you. If the job is major, however, working with a knowledgeable lawyer will afford the homeowner excellent protection.

The contract should include plans and specifications. These may be attached to the contract, but a list of the documents and the number of pages for each must be noted in the contract. These should state all the specific data such as the type, color, size, manufacturer, and quality of materials. The contract may note that the customer has final approval of some items, possibly in which the contractor will be matching existing materials.

A payment schedule should appear in the contract. Specify how much money, if any, is to be paid at the time the contract is signed or when the work begins. The actual amount, which may be as much as 25 percent, depends on whether costly special items or supplies must be ordered ahead of time. List the points in the work when additional sums are to be paid. No matter how intimidating the contractor may become, never pay the sums until the agreed-upon amount of work has been completed. When the job is finished, the owner should hold back 10 percent (although this percentage may be less on a larger job) until he or she has had time to inspect the work thoroughly, compare the actual work to the plans and specifications in the contract, and live

with the results for a brief time, no more than 30 days, to be certain everything functions properly. The amount withheld acts as an incentive for the contractor to return to correct any problems. When you are assured that the work is completed in accord with the contract, make the final payment promptly.

Also appearing in the contract should be the cost of the work, a statement that the job will conform to all pertinent local codes, and the length of time for which the labor and materials are guaranteed—at least 1 year. Require proof of insurance, particularly adequate workmen's compensation and liability insurance, and a release of liens furnished by the contractor either before or at the time of final payment. This document frees the owner from any financial responsibility if the contractor does not pay subcontractors, workers, or suppliers.

The contract should state the approximate dates when work is to begin and end, possibly with a schedule added for various phases of the job. It should mention the written procedure established for making any future changes in the work, should list the steps to be taken to terminate the contract, and should include the requirements for cleanup.

Two copies of the contract are necessary—one for the contractor and one for the owner. The contractor and all owners of the property should sign the document, but only after the owners have read and understood it.

WORKING WITH A CONTRACTOR

It is up to you to look out for your own interests and to make certain the contractor follows the plans, specifications, and other details of the written contract. If you have questions about what is being done or discover shoddy workmanship or damage to your house, speak to the contractor at once rather than let the work go on. In extreme circumstances when you are convinced the contractor cannot do the job competently, terminate the contract, which can be a complex procedure, and hire someone else to complete the work.

Once you have found a qualified contractor, someone who takes an interest in the quirks of an older home, relax. The effort consumed along the way to discovering this individual or firm will pay off in a house well tended.

CHAPTER SIXTEEN

CONSIDERING AN ARCHITECT

Bringing out the best in an older house is what renovation is all about. Many times this mission can be fulfilled by entrusting some or all of the evaluation, design, and work supervision to a competent architect.

Just as with other professions, misconceptions and myths build up around architects. One of these fallacies is that good design costs more money. Architects' fees are, of course, an extra expense, but the services paid for will make the most of the available funds. In renovating older houses, a good architect will uncover the authentic features and architectural details, create replacements to sensitively match the originals, and design new additions sympathetic to the older fabric and parts of the house. Another myth is that architects isolate themselves in ivory towers dreaming up fanciful new structures. Some do, but others are experts in the idiosyncrasies of older homes. Their training and experience can save you much unnecessary time, effort, and expense.

Before deciding whether to hire an architect, consider why you are undertaking the project and what you hope to accomplish. Sometimes an architect is clearly necessary, and you should be familiar with these situations. Architects provide a wide range of services and can act as consultants on a short-term basis for a modest fee or oversee all aspects of the job. Knowing about these possibilities, a client's obligations, and the various fee, payment, and contract arrangements will enable you to make a more informed decision.

WHEN IS AN ARCHITECT HELPFUL?

Renovating an older house can be a complex job with a number of puzzling or serious problems. In some cases, these challenges can best be clarified and solved by securing the skills of a registered architect.

Careful consideration should be given to hiring an architect for the following reasons.

MAJOR RENOVATION OR RESTORATION WORK

Unless a homeowner has substantial experience, it is advisable to hire an architect for major renovation or restoration work. An architect can provide invaluable assistance when there are serious structural problems, such as a shifting foundation, or if an older house is in poor physical condition outside and inside. Homeowners intent on accurately capturing the house's original character or on having an authentic restoration definitely need an architect. Large projects often proceed in phases, and an architect can identify the correct order for undertaking improvements to avoid costly mistakes.

Spending money to save money seems paradoxical, but the dollars spent on an architect's fee could produce significant savings in construction costs. Older houses, for example, often have structural problems or obsolete utility systems hidden from view. Renovations applied on top of them are chancy and would only call for removal. Moreover, architects can suggest methods for construction and replacement that save on labor costs. With a limited budget, making the best use of the money available for any renovation work is essential, and an architect can help determine where to make the most appropriate investments and not waste money.

HOMEOWNERS LACKING SKILLS OR INTEREST IN RENOVATION WORK

Before proceeding, homeowners need to be honest with themselves in evaluating how much renovation work they could or should do alone. Think about the considerations listed in the section Deciding Who Is to Do the Work in Chapter 3, Preparing for the Work, and answer these questions:

- Can you visualize different design possibilities for the house?
- Do you have the skills to assess thoroughly the physical condition of the house, to determine

what parts should be salvaged, and to develop plans?

- Are you familiar with the building codes, zoning ordinances, and permit procedures?
- Are you interested in undertaking all aspects of the job or only certain parts?

Homeowners with no experience, skills, or personal interest in renovation work or with a tight time schedule for the job should consider seeking an architect's assistance. In these situations, putting a house in the hands of a contractor, no matter how qualified, could lead to irreversible damage to the historic honesty of the house.

REPLACING IMPORTANT FEATURES

Older houses can be troublesome: Roofs will wear out, wooden siding can rot, and porches may sag. When total replacement is necessary, an architect probably should be consulted.

Replacement is a delicate procedure because it may affect the structure of the house or other features and because duplicating the original components as closely as possible is important. Architects can be helpful not only in designing suitable replacements but in selecting appropriate materials and making certain the older parts of the house are adequately protected from any damage during new construction.

REMOVING UNSIGHTLY EARLIER ALTERATIONS

Previous owners may have violated the integrity of an older house by making shoddy alterations, unsightly modern "improvements," or improperly executed repairs. If prior physical changes have disfigured the house's historic character, they may require removing. An architect can suggest proper procedures for eliminating ugly alterations without damaging the fabric of the house and can recommend appropriate replacements.

CONSTRUCTING ADDITIONS

Because older houses were built to suit the needs of earlier generations, your home may not meet today's living requirements or fit with your personal life style. Maybe the house is too small and you would like to add new rooms. When considering major additions, an architect should be consulted. Carelessly designed additions will fight visually with an older house. An architect can select the most suitable location for an addition, preferably in an inconspicuous area, and design the new construction to blend with the proportions, architectural details, and materials of the original house.

CHANGING USE

Persons purchasing a nonresidential building intending to transform it into a home should hire an architect to oversee the conversion. Older buildings, such as carriage houses, barns, or former firehouses, often can become attractive residences. Architects can identify the features which give these buildings charm, design renovations to complement the original structure, create functional layouts to answer the client's needs, and prepare plans for the utility and heating systems. Unless you have had experience, it is risky to attempt a conversion without an architect or to proceed with only a contractor who may not value the building's special features.

DEVISING A RENOVATION PLAN

Restorations, large-scale renovations, and even small improvements should be based on a carefully thought-out organization plan defining the work and its order and methods. An architect can help develop a work plan to avoid needless mistakes and also provide preliminary cost estimates. Major restorations may require a more comprehensive and detailed master plan where an architect's contribution is essential.

EVALUATING AN OLDER HOME

Architects familiar with older houses can help determine when the home was built, confirm its architectural style, and identify key features worth retaining. Sometimes they can answer these questions simply by observing the physical evidence of the house, or they may undertake more extensive research.

FINDING AN ARCHITECT

After deciding to hire an architect, the next step is to search for several architects knowledgeable about renovation work. Although many architects have this expertise, be prepared to invest what might amount to considerable time to find just the right one for your home. In the long run, it is well worth the effort.

Investigate a number of potential sources:

- Contact friends who had an architect for similar renovation work and ask for a frank evaluation of the architect's competency, the quality of the work, and their satisfaction with the architectural services. Was the schedule followed? Was the budget met?
- Look around the neighborhood for examples of residential or even commercial renovations with

fine-quality design and workmanship. Ask the owner for the name of the architect.

- Get in touch with the local chapter of the American Institute of Architects. Some chapters have special historic resources committees whose members are knowledgeable about older buildings.

- Seek out the local historical society or preservation group. These organizations, however, may hesitate to give names unless they have supervised successful projects and can actually testify to the architect's competence. Request names of members who have had architectural assistance with renovations or who could give suggestions. Certain local historical societies have architects on their staffs who might help establish the construction date and style of your house, identify historically accurate exterior colors, do smaller renovations, or recommend qualified local contractors and craftworkers. Some may be willing to assist on larger renovations by working on their off-duty hours.

- Request assistance from a municipal historical or landmarks commission, especially if the house is in a historic district.

- Check with a nearby university having an architectural school offering courses on preservation. Speak with the faculty giving these courses as well as with the dean of the architectural school.

- Find out if the house is in a designated public renewal area. If so, discover whether there is an assistance center providing architectural advice for homeowners in the renewal district. Clients often must be within a certain income range, and the center may charge a nominal service fee.

- Inquire for information from state and national organizations. State historic preservation officers generally keep lists of architects who are responsible for restoration projects under the state's supervision. The American Institute of Architects' state preservation coordinators may have suggestions. The National Trust for Historic Preservation in Washington, D.C., also has regional and field offices and maintains consultant files. The National Park Service and other federal agencies concerned with historic preservation might be additional sources. With some of these organizations, legal or policy considerations may prevent them from providing specific names of architects.

Try to make personal inquiries to organizations either through a visit or by telephone. Explain the project and the services you need. Find out if they will recommend an architect in your vicinity or tell you about similar renovation or restoration projects. Patience and persistence are necessary because it may take several calls or visits to secure this information.

SELECTING AN ARCHITECT

Once this search yields the names of several qualified architects, the next step is to select the one who answers your requirements within your budget, a sometimes difficult assessment. As with any profession, the individuals practicing architecture have a wide spectrum of talent and integrity. Choosing the right one is important because a client and architect must develop good rapport and mutual trust for a successful project.

SKILLS AND QUALITIES TO LOOK FOR

Those architects most likely to provide satisfactory services have the following abilities and characteristics.

Technical Expertise. Knowledge about the structural aspects of older houses and former building practices is essential, although engineering evaluations may be subcontracted. Never assume an architect possesses technical know-how about earlier construction techniques. Another limitation to watch for is an architect with a large firm who specializes in one service offered, for example, in writing specifications, and who has little experience with an overall project. Look instead for an architect who is more of a generalist, familiar with all aspects of old construction.

Design Competence. For a successful renovation an architect often has to visualize the aesthetic possibilities inherent in an older house—an essential ability for an addition or a major replacement. An architect can have adequate technical expertise, but only mediocre design skills. Carefully examine examples of an architect's renovation work for evidence of creative competence.

Respect for the Historical Integrity of Older Houses. An architect for renovations should not only be familiar with different architectural styles, but respect the historical qualities of the house. Respect comes from understanding, and an architect must be willing to be a detective: to identify the original features, investigate the structure, discover any newer additions, and evaluate their merit. Without this respect a well-intentioned architect could harm an older home by devising alterations permanently disfiguring its historic characteristics or even damaging its structural fabric.

Empathy. A good architect allows an older house to be itself. The historical evidence guides the design. In some instances, designing with empathy means an architect has to subordinate his or her personal preferences. Prima donnas who want to transform an older house into a perfect replica of its style or to leave their own indelible mark on a house are not architects you want to hire. A certain humility is needed because renovations are often unassuming or even inconspicuous. An architect should also be sympathetic to the client's objectives. If the project is modest, do not select someone intent on a grandiose scheme.

Patience. Identifying original parts, devising appropriate replacements, and coping with unexpected discoveries hidden beneath the surface can be time consuming and frustrating. An architect needs patience—and so does the homeowner!

Forthrightness. To develop a good working relationship, an architect and client must be open and direct and communicate easily with one another. Seek an architect who is willing to listen to your suggestions and to respond in a candid manner. You must also have faith in the architect's integrity.

Compatibility. Compatibility between a homeowner and an architect is an essential but elusive quality. It is either there or not, and only you will know. Because renovations entail countless decisions, some disagreements will undoubtedly occur. When a client and an architect are basically in accord, however, they can look forward to a successful mutual undertaking with a minimum of friction. Try to choose an architect you feel comfortable with, and one who does not intimidate you. As a warning, a few architects, like some artists, have extremely sensitive natures and are difficult to deal with. Although the work may be satisfactory, do not expect a smooth relationship if you pick a temperamental individual. Ask an architect's former clients whether they felt their relationship was compatible, and trust your own intuition.

SELECTION PROCEDURES

Before contacting any architects, develop a clear description of the work required. Even though your work plan may change after discussions with an architect and more research, start out with a specific and realistic outline of your objectives and budget.

Contact the architects found through your search and explain the project. Find out about the services they offer and the ones they think you will need. Ask for their résumés, describing their professional training and experience, and for a list of former clients. Inquire whether they are registered in your state or associated with a registered architect. Arrange to see some of the architect's renovation work to evaluate the quality of its design and workmanship.

After this initial screening, narrow the list to two or three names. A personal interview will help you assess an architect's attitude toward your project and whether you are compatible. Find out if your job will fit into the office's schedule. Share any existing floor plans and elevations of the house and explain your budget. Many architects do not charge for an initial on-site interview at your home, but a few expect a consultation fee, which is a small investment if it assists your evaluation.

Once each architect understands your project and decides what services you need, ask for a written proposal. Proposals provide a firm basis for comparing services and fees. For small jobs a simple letter of agreement outlining the services, time schedule, fees, and payment arrangements may be sufficient. Larger projects often require more detailed proposals and may include dividing the work into phases with separate fees. In extensive renovations you may consider hiring an architect on a step-by-step basis, approving later phases only if you are satisfied with the preliminary work.

Proposals should state who will be the architect in charge of the job and the other persons providing assistance. This seems obvious, but if you are considering a larger firm, you do not want to assume you are hiring a certain architect only to discover later that your job has been delegated to someone else.

Read the proposals carefully. Be certain they are specific and include all the services requested. If the fees differ markedly, check to see if each architect is offering similar services. Otherwise, valid comparisons are impossible. Several proposals may yield a range of fees. In making your selection, do not use fees as the only yardstick. Take into account architectural skills, technical expertise, experience, and personal qualities as well as the ability to perform on a schedule and within your budget. Contact their references. If any were dissatisfied, give the architect an opportunity to offer an explanation of the problem.

Once your selection is made, two copies of the letter of agreement or the proposal should be signed by both the architect and the client, each keeping one. Remember, no architecural work should begin until these documents are signed. The Contracts, Fees, and Payments section of this chapter describes the more formal contracts required for extensive renovations.

ARCHITECTURAL SERVICES

The architectural services depend on the requirements of your project, on your requests, and on your budget. They range from a few hours of consultation on an hourly or daily basis to overseeing the entire job from preliminary design to construction observation.

A brief consultation with an architect often is a sensible way to proceed. Renovation concerns which might be addressed on a consultation basis include:

- Determining the age and architectural style of the house
- Identifying features worthy of preserving
- Replacing a major component, such as a roof, porch, or dormer, where structural problems may be encountered
- Removing improper former alterations
- Establishing a renovation plan
- Recommending local sources for replacement features, materials, or ornamentation and competent contractors or craftworkers
- Interpreting building codes and securing the necessary permits

Although the full scope of architectural services may not be needed for your project, you should be aware of what services are available. There are five general phases: schematic design, design development, construction documents, bidding and negotiating with contractors, and observation of construction including administration of the construction contract.

SCHEMATIC DESIGN

Schematic design involves historical research, examining the house's physical condition, establishing goals for the project, and preparing alternative designs, thus setting the framework for the subsequent work.

At the outset, an architect thoroughly investigates the structure to identify any major problems in the construction, foundation, and overall physical condition. If necessary, a specialized structural engineer may be hired as a consultant. Knowing the hidden structural difficulties from the beginning will prevent them from haunting you later, ensure against doing a cosmetic renovation, and help in determining the work plan and schedule. A preliminary analysis of the utility and drainage systems will point out problems or the need for updating. Architects can also offer suggestions for improved insulation and other energy-saving measures.

For larger renovations an architect must become familiar with all the house's components. What features are original? Which ones have been altered, removed, or added later? What is the condition of the architectural details? Any old photographs or other data pertaining to the house's history should be studied.

The client and architect will next have to identify exactly what work to accomplish. A simple listing may be adequate. For larger projects or full-scale restorations, an architect may prepare a more detailed report. The original project may change if the architect discovers structural deficiencies or makes other recommendations. From the outset, express your ideas fully to avoid later dissatisfaction.

Architects usually include preliminary sketches and some drawings in this preliminary planning phase. If you do not have the house's floor plans and elevations, an architect may have to prepare measured drawings. For small jobs these drawings require a minimum amount of time. Extensive projects need floor plans and elevations showing exact measurements. These are an accurate record of existing conditions and will be useful for any future work. Houses of major historical significance may have drawings on file with the Historic American Buildings Survey. If you suspect your house has particular historic merit, check with the Historic American Buildings Survey, for copies of these drawings are available. When securing measured drawings proves too expensive, consider hiring an architectural student to do this job.

Architects may do preliminary sketches of proposed renovations illustrating different design concepts. An exterior elevation gives a clear idea of any outside changes. Do not expect detailed drawings at this stage because it is a time for exploring general design ideas. An architect also can prepare a preliminary cost estimate of the proposed work. This is only a rough calculation, but it will show whether the work is within your budget or whether certain work must be postponed or eliminated.

For elaborate restorations or large-scale renovations a historic structure report may be needed and is required if federal funds are involved for a house listed on the National Register of Historic Places. Sometimes a carefully delineated master or comprehensive plan is called for. Feasibility studies address technical, physical, aesthetic, and economic questions and can be useful when adapting an older building to a new use.

DESIGN DEVELOPMENT

In the design development phase architects refine their initial designs, prepare final design drawings, develop preliminary working drawings and specifications, and readjust the cost estimates to reflect changes in the project.

Before developing final designs, architects must make certain the renovation conforms to local codes. The utility systems must be thoroughly checked and plans devised for any improvements. When a project involves a change in the building's existing

use or a major addition, architects will review the local zoning ordinance, help with the application for any variances, and assist with securing permits or filing other documents needed for government approvals. The initial approval steps usually occur in this phase, followed by the submission of more detailed documentation in the next phase. If the house is in a historic district, you and your architect should look into the requirements and find out which, if any, exterior changes are prohibited.

Depending on the renovation's magnitude, the design drawings may include elevations, floor plans, sections, architectural details, and site plans, when there are substantial additions. Perspective drawings showing the house in three dimensions are not always necessary, but they can help a client to better envision the renovations and encourage banks to lend money for these improvements. Architects may prepare preliminary working drawings and an outline of specifications, especially when the project involves major work. The cost estimates are recalculated on the basis of the final architectural design; the structural, mechanical, and utility changes; and the outline specifications.

Before giving your approval to proceed to the next phase, carefully review with your architect all of this stage's work to be certain you agree with the recommendations. If you cannot visualize the changes or question some ideas, bring these concerns to your architect's attention. Once the job progresses, it becomes increasingly difficult to make changes without incurring unnecessary time and expense.

CONSTRUCTION DOCUMENTS

The construction documents, or a full set of final working drawings and specifications, constitute the basis for bidding the job and dictate all the construction requirements. To ensure competent work, these documents must be meticulously accurate and not slipshod.

Remember, too, that the construction documents together with the written contract form the legally binding agreement between the homeowner and the builder. These documents provide safeguards for all concerned: the assurance to you and your architect that the work will be carried out as specified and to the builder that unreasonable changes will not be demanded. If subsequent changes arise, the consent of all three participants is required along with an appropriate readjustment of project costs. Realistically, however, be prepared for some change orders because surprises occur in renovation work. Be certain the work and additional costs are clearly spelled out. To keep costs in line, try to avoid picayune changes.

Working drawings set forth the project's exact dimensions for the builder. The specifications are a written description of the materials, workmanship, construction methods, and techniques to be employed by the builder and are more detailed for an older home than for most new houses. Among the items architects should include in renovation specifications are:

- A complete description of any new materials and the recommended building methods. These specifications are important because the new work should match the old as closely as possible rather than seem glaringly new. For example, if a deteriorated porch needs replacing, there should be a precise description of the design, material, size, and placement of columns and balusters; any ornamentation; the material of the steps, flooring, footings, or foundations; the lattice underneath the porch; the shape, pitch, and materials of the roof; the flashing materials; the type and location of gutters and downspouts; and the paint colors, including the suggested manufacturer.

- A clear instruction for builders and craftworkers to take every precaution to protect all original components of the home during construction. Work must proceed with the utmost care to avoid breakage or irreversible damage.

- A requirement not to remove any parts or pieces of the house from the property without your permission. The homeowner, in conjunction with the architect, has the responsibility for deciding which components to salvage and which to throw away. As a general rule, retain any original parts, such as old shutters, that you are not putting back. In some cases, keeping a sample of an early material or item may be sufficient as a record for future owners. When architectural features must be removed temporarily, clearly identify each piece, tag with a brief description of where the piece came from, and store it in a safe, dry place until it is put back.

- A statement emphasizing the importance of quality workmanship. Competent work is necessary all the way down to replacing the smallest feature.

After completing the construction documents, an architect will prepare a final cost estimate for the job. Thoroughly review the working drawings, specifications, and final cost estimate with your architect before giving your approval for the job to proceed.

BIDDING AND NEGOTIATING WITH CONTRACTORS

Unless the job is small or you have sufficient experience to serve as general contractor or to do all the work, hiring a general contractor becomes the next step. The architect can suggest qualified contractors as well as craftworkers and subcontractors, recommend various contracts appropriate for renovations, organize the bidding, negotiate with the potential contractors, and assist the homeowner with making a choice. Whether to negotiate a price with one contractor or to have competitive bidding depends on the size of the job, the confidence you and your architect have in one contractor, and the involvement of public funding. For a fuller explanation of selection procedures for contractors, see Chapter 15, Calling in a Contractor.

CONSTRUCTION OBSERVATION AND CONTRACT ADMINISTRATION

During construction an architect acts on behalf of the homeowner to make certain the working drawings and specifications are accurately followed by the contractor, subcontractors, and craftworkers. An experienced contractor conducts the daily job supervision, but an architect should make frequent visits to the project to observe whether the work is properly executed, the materials and techniques are correct, and the time schedule is being met. In addition, an architect may examine samples and check any tasks requiring especially skillful workmanship. The contractor should keep detailed records for the architect and, if necessary, the client to review. When disputes arise, the architect may also serve as a liaison between the homeowner and the contractor to help resolve the problems.

The architect is responsible for interpreting the requirements of the contract documents and evaluating the contractor's performance. If an architect determines a portion of the work does not conform to the contract, he or she may reject this part of the work and require the contractor to redo it at the contractor's expense because of the contractual obligations.

Renovations often involve unknowns, such as hidden structural flaws, which become visible during construction. A good contractor will immediately inform the architect of these before proceeding. Minor changes not involving cost adjustments may be approved by the architect. Major changes could require redoing portions of the working drawings and specifications, change orders (or amendments to the contractor's contract), and a renegotiated price. These change orders are prepared by the architect for the homeowner's approval.

Upon periodic billing by the contractor, the architect inspects the work and, when satisfied that it meets the contract's requirements, gives approval of payment for work completed to date. When the architect issues a certificate of payment, the client is obligated to pay the contractor. This sequence is repeated until the project is completed.

For more extensive restorations or for clients who can afford the extra expense, consider asking an architect to prepare a set of "as-built" drawings illustrating the finished project. These drawings involve an additional fee, but they will be an invaluable record for future owners and for a local historical society. Architects can also supply clients with a renovation maintenance plan offering suggestions for ongoing upkeep to avoid major repairs. In some cases, it is useful to have an architect's final report of the project for your records.

HELPING YOUR ARCHITECT

A good working relationship between a client and an architect does not just happen: It is two way. Both have responsibilities to fulfill to help make the project successful. By assisting an architect, an owner receives rewards beyond the satisfaction of helping create a quality renovation job—learning more about an older house and, in the process, cultivating an enjoyable partnership.

There are a number of ways a homeowner can aid an architect.

PREPARE A WORK PLAN

At the outset, prepare a precise plan and budget for the renovation work you want done. This plan probably will be revised to incorporate the architect's suggestions, but your ideas will give direction to the project.

UNDERTAKE RESEARCH

You can save an architect time and effort by gathering whatever information you can about the house. Search for old photographs. Trace the property deed. Contact the local historical society.

BE RESPECTFUL AND CONSIDERATE

Architects must answer to the needs of other clients as well as to your project. Respect his or her schedule and be considerate about your requests. Avoid insisting upon frequent or extensive changes in the work, which in the later phases only add extra charges. Do not pester an architect with calls about trivial items or interfere with the contractor, subcontractors, and craftworkers. Instead, keep a list of your questions and concerns and review these periodically with the architect. If you have valid complaints, let your architect know about them, but also do not hesitate to give praise for work you like.

BE PROMPT

Being prompt is both a courtesy and a necessity to meet the work's timetable. When an architect seeks your advice and approvals, avoid delays in responding. Punctuality is also vital in paying your bills both to the architect and to the contractor.

SHOW YOUR INTEREST IN THE PROJECT

Caring is contagious. Homeowners who genuinely care about their older house and want a truly competent job are likely to inspire an architect to share their feelings. Your work will become more than just another job for the office; it will become one which receives extra attention and effort.

BE AWARE OF AN ARCHITECT'S JOB

Clients who try to understand what an architect does are likely not to make unreasonable demands. Be aware that an architect is guided by certain restrictions such as structural necessities, historical accuracy, codes, and the budget. If problems arise, be careful not to blame your architect without first learning about the problems' sources, as many may be beyond the architect's control.

To fulfill your obligations as the client takes commitment, foresight, and effort. Do not disappear and turn everything over to the architect or, conversely, constantly bombard an architect with unneeded or unrealistic demands. Learn to trust your architect's professional expertise and judgment, and enjoy doing your share.

CONTRACTS, FEES, AND PAYMENTS

No matter how small the project or how simple the arrangements with an architect, the exact architectural services, the fee, and the payment schedule should be clearly spelled out in writing and signed to avoid unnecessary disagreements. As the work progresses, amendments can be made to delete or add other services if needed.

For small and simple jobs a letter of agreement may suffice. This letter, particularly appropriate for consulting work, may be written by either the architect or the homeowner, and copies should be signed by both parties before work begins. It should include the scope of work, the fee, the payment arrangement, and the time schedule. The fee is based on the architect's estimate of the services required, the time involved, and his or her own skills, experience, and knowledge.

Consulting services may be charged in several ways: hourly, daily, and as a fixed fee or lump sum. Another arrangement safeguards the client by combining an hourly or daily rate with a not-to-exceed maximum fee, setting a limit and calling for the owner's consent before an architect goes beyond this ceiling figure. Architects are also entitled to reimbursement for additional expenses associated with the work: travel, copying and reproduction charges, long-distance phone calls, and permit fees or other governmental approvals requiring payments. If a structural engineer or other consultants are to be hired, find out their fees beforehand. Learn whether these are included in the architect's fee or billed directly to the client.

Major renovations and full restorations require a more formal contract. Most architects employ the standard American Institute of Architects form, usually with amendments or deletions to reflect the project's requirements. Be certain to include a provision stating you will be given quality reproductions of all drawings, plans, reports, photographs, or other pertinent documents for your files because the originals belong to the architect. Before signing a contract, discuss its provisions with the architect and, for your own protection, review the contract with a lawyer.

There are various fee arrangements:

PERCENTAGE OF THE CONSTRUCTION COSTS

An architect's fee based on a fixed percentage of the total construction cost is used primarily for new construction. The percentage as specified by the American Institute of Architects varies from 10 to 15 percent. Several problems are encountered in using this calculation for renovation work. Because of contingencies, setting a firm construction price is often difficult until certain work is done on older houses. Restoration projects as well as some renovation jobs, moreover, usually need skilled craftworkers with higher labor costs than the craftworkers who are required in new construction. The homeowner in these cases would pay a proportionately higher fee to the architect. Sometimes there is little actual construction in renovations, but considerable time is spent on other work such as research, identification of the work, or preparation of cost estimates. An architect deserves a fair compensation for these services. Many times, too, renovation projects do not need full architectural services, and a percentage arrangement is not appropriate.

NEGOTIATED FIXED FEE PLUS EXPENSES

If specific architectural services can be clearly defined, a negotiated fixed fee plus expenses may be suitable. The architect is paid a set fee, which may be negotiated, and additional compensation for expenses.

REIMBURSABLE FEE

Because renovation and restoration projects involve many surprises, a reimbursable fee is often the most fair and appropriate payment method for both parties. A homeowner pays an architect for the actual amount of work done on the job. In this arrangement, an architect bills on an hourly rate with the time of other employees, such as draftspersons and secretaries, billed at their pay rates. These direct costs are then multiplied by a factor to compensate for overhead and profit. For a more definite fee, ask an architect to include a not-to-exceed limit. During the work if the fees approach this ceiling too quickly, renegotiate the price. Perhaps some work can be reduced or some services omitted.

Contracts as well as letters of agreement should include billing procedures. Architects customarily bill monthly, but billing may be on a periodic basis or at the completion of each work phase. As an act of good faith, a small retaining fee is appreciated by many architects especially on larger renovations or on projects involving substantial front-end expenses. Some may ask for this before beginning their work.

When you have discovered a knowledgeable, competent architect who respects and enjoys older houses, your home will have a friend. And so will you.

CHAPTER SEVENTEEN

ENERGY AND THE OLDER HOUSE

A popular misconception exists that older homes are inherently less energy efficient than new houses. It is a misconception because although older houses are often less energy efficient than newer ones, they do not have to be—they can in fact become as efficient or even more efficient. "Energy efficient" refers primarily to total heating and cooling costs. Obviously, the use of electricity or gas for cooking, clothes drying, or lighting will be similar in older and newer homes.

To understand the superior energy potential of the older house, taking a look at its original heating and cooling system is necessary. Surprisingly, in the 1700s and 1800s the science of thermal comfort was well developed, even if the technology was not.

Imagine a Victorian sitting room on a frigid January evening. The master and mistress of the house are ensconced in high-backed wing chairs, facing the glow of a coal fire from a grate in the fireplace. They wear heavy Victorian robes and sit with their feet up on needlepoint-covered stools. A thick rug conceals the floor, and one or two smaller rugs lie on top of it at strategic points of wear. Wall hangings make the room somewhat dark, but a kerosene or oil lamp on the table between the two Victorians casts a cheery yellow light for sewing, crafts, and reading. Floor-length draperies enclose the windows, muting the howling wind outdoors. There is no central heat.

It is 10 degrees outside. If the temperature in the sitting room were to be measured, it would be between 50 and 60 degrees. The occupants are comfortable, however, for a number of reasons. Those high-backed wing chairs keep drafts off their faces and necks and, to some extent, reflect the radiant energy of the fire upon them. They, of course, absorb the radiant heat from the fire directly upon their faces and hands.

The wall hangings and floor-to-ceiling draperies prevent heat from their bodies and the room air from radiating or conducting to cold wall or window surfaces. Rugs keep their slippered feet from chills as they later retire, taking coals from the fire in a bedwarming pan to remove the chill from the sheets. They will draw the thick draperies of their bedroom tightly closed before retiring in their heavy nightwear under quilts and comforters. A fire in the bedroom fireplace will warm them as they dress in the morning while the kitchen stove heats their morning water needs, their coffee, and the kitchen.

Scarcely a picture of privation, is it? And no central heat, remember. Is it only 100 years, or 75 years, or even 50 years since middle-class Americans lived this way? Where did the ideas come from that:

- Central heating is best?
- You have to heat all rooms of a house to 70 degrees?
- Fireplaces and woodstoves are for atmosphere?
- Draperies should be light and translucent?
- Clothes should be worn only in single or double layers?

The vertical multistory Victorian house was, in effect, a natural zoned-heat system and worked then to good efficiency. One or more fireplaces or heating woodstoves and the big kitchen range kept the first floor warm while heat from the first story rose naturally up the stairs and through the ceilings to keep the second-floor sleeping areas well above freezing.

In the summer the double-hung windows were lowered from the top and raised from the bottom to allow the cooler air in at the bottom and to exhaust warmer air at the top. This technique works only with those full-length Victorian screen sashes, not with newfangled triple-track aluminum ones. Perhaps a ceiling fan kept air in constant motion around the room. A cool pitcher of iced lemonade sat on a wicker table on the screened porch. Sleeping porches on the second floor let the occupants escape tossing and turning on the hottest nights.

Before believing you are being asked to turn back your clock to those visions of yesteryear, be assured this is not the intent. This description is merely designed to demonstrate the thesis that energy *inefficiency* is a modern disease. Nothing in an older house is inherently inefficient or wasteful.

CENTRAL HEATING

Few, if any, houses today lack a central heating system. Most will have oil- or gas-fired air, water, or steam heating plants ranging in age from 60 years to brand new. Surprisingly, the efficiency of many older furnaces and boilers is only a few percentage points below their modern equivalents.

In most cases a central heating system was installed years after the house was built. Exposed pipes are often the clue to this. Whether original or not, an older house will likely have either ducted warm-air heat, with air rising by gravity or forced by a fan; steam heat in a one- or two-pipe distribution system; or hot-water heat. Usually an older home will have a fireplace on each floor, frequently located on interior, rather than exterior, walls.

Older warm-air furnace systems used the principle that hot air rises and cold air falls to distribute heat. A network of relatively large sheet-metal pipes (7 to 10 inches in diameter) rose from the furnace through the interior walls. Larger cold-air return ducts at the exterior walls directed air back to the furnace to be warmed. Modern forced air systems reverse this by forcing the warm air out the cold perimeter and returning it in the center of the house. This promotes very even heating throughout the room, but it is not very efficient. Far better, from an energy-conserving standpoint, is the older practice of warm interior portions and cooler exterior walls.

One-pipe steam distribution systems send steam throughout the house and return condensed water by way of the same pipe, pitched on a loop which descends slightly downward as it travels around the basement. Two-pipe steam systems often look the same, except that a second pipe runs from each radiator back to the steam loop. Hot-water systems use a loop through which hot water passes. They are *always* two-pipe systems.

Identifying which type of system you have is fairly simple. If radiators have only one pipe entering them from the floor, the system is steam heated. If two pipes enter radiators, look for a 1- or 2-inch metal gadget on one end of the radiator, usually near the upper end. This is a steam-air vent, and it indicates a steam system. If there is none, or only a very small plug, it is a hot-water system.

In the basement you may find a wide variety of central-heat generating units. Some hot-water heating systems also produce hot water for the plumbing system. These range from poor to fair efficiency and, perhaps more importantly, from poor to excellent consistency of supply. Because modern gas and electric water heaters are of much better efficiency, replacement is often a sound option.

Depending on how long you expect to occupy the house, its orientation to the sun, the absence of large trees shading the house, and on state, local, and federal tax incentives as well as local fuel costs, solar hot-water heating may make some sense. Careful calculation is important. Also, find out whether the solar collectors can be placed on a rearward face of the roof to avoid detracting from the appearance of the front roof.

The most important measures to increase the energy efficiency of an older house are those which improve its resistance to heat loss. Storm windows and weatherstripping are covered in Chapters 10 and 11, Doors and Doorways and Windows. Weatherstripping is extremely important and relatively inexpensive to achieve. Although storm windows can be quite expensive, their effectiveness is not related to price because cheap plastic film works as well or better than the most expensive triple-track aluminum.

INSULATION

Roof and wall insulation are two ways to make an older house more energy efficient (Figure 17-1). It is usually possible for the homeowner to add roof insulation without professional assistance. Start by checking to see if any insulation can be found above the last-inhabited floor of the house, in the attic, or in the crawl space. If so, determine two things: how much insulation exists and whether it has a vapor barrier beneath it. With a ruler, measure the depth of the insulation layer or layers, and then pick up a corner of insulation and see if it is attached to an aluminum foil or tarred kraft paper layer.

When insulation does not exist or is inadequate based upon the map and table shown in Figure 17-2, plan on installing insulation as soon as possible. R-numbers indicate the resistance of insulation to heat flow. The higher the number, the better the material retards heat flow.

If insulation without a vapor barrier is discovered, it is advisable to remove the present insulation, if possible, put in a vapor barrier, replace the old insulation, and add to it.

The owners of a house with no roof insulation at all will have the easiest time. Nine-inch-thick batts of fiberglass insulation with vapor barrier attached can be laid between the joists of the ceiling or stapled to the rafters of the roof. Do not press down or compress the insulation. The vapor barrier must be next to the heated side of the house.

Depending on the presence of a vapor barrier in the old insulation, additional insulation (mineral wool) may be raked over the old insulation or added in rolls or batts. Such rolls or batts should not have a vapor barrier or should have holes slashed in the vapor barrier every few inches. Old insulation without a vapor barrier can be placed on top of a plastic sheet or put on top of a new first layer of insulation with an integral vapor barrier.

Roof insulation is an essential energy conservation step: It may save as much as 25 percent of your current fuel bill. It is the first and most important action you can and should take.

Next, consider wall insulation. Here, unless interior plaster is removed in the renovation process or exterior wall surfaces are being totally replaced, the homeowner is not advised to attempt insulating the walls as a do-it-yourself project.

One thorny question which must be faced concerning wall insulation is that of vapor barriers. Their purpose is to prevent water vapor from traveling from room air through the wall surface and into the insulation where it may condense into water, reducing the effectiveness of the insulation and, worse, causing rot and mildew (Figure 17-3). This danger is probably overrated. Unless the heating system includes a humidifier, or a portable humidifier is used, there will normally not be enough water vapor in the air during the heating season to cause a problem, except in kitchen and bathroom areas. In these areas, and others if desired, vinyl wall coverings or vapor barrier paints now available can be used to avert any potential problem.

Warning: If aluminum or vinyl siding is used, you can almost expect condensation problems in wall cavities with or without insulation unless a vapor barrier is installed. Thus advice not to use such sidings from a historic preservation point of view is also well advised from a technical standpoint.

Contractors should be called in to estimate on wall insulation. Unfortunately, the homeowner thus enters a jungle in which dwell some of the nastiest (as well as the nicest) varieties of the *genus renovaterri*. Third-party recommendations are very useful here, as is a check with the local Better Business Bureau to see if there have been any complaints about the contractors from whom you have requested estimates. Chapter 15, Calling in a Contractor, gives more information about finding and working with a contractor.

The insulation material a contractor chooses is important. Primary materials are mineral wool and treated cellulose. The safety of mineral wool is well established, and federal standards for fire-resistant treatment of cellulose remove most questions about this material. Concerns about formaldehyde vapors have caused the use of urea-formaldehyde foam, with its superb insulating capabilities, to be banned.

Ideally, all walls of a house should be insulated. But if this is not financially feasible, insulation of the north and west walls can be done at one time, and the south and east walls, later. Heat is not intelligent; it will not rush to uninsulated walls to escape

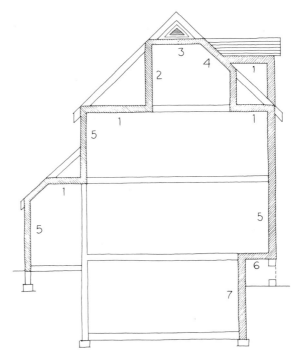

Figure 17-1. Where to insulate an older home. Key to numbers shown in sketch: (1) ceilings below an unheated area; (2) "knee" walls of a finished attic-level room; (3) floor of a crawl attic; (4) the sloping portion of the roof in a finished attic (leave an air space between insulation and roof); (5) exterior walls; (6) floors above cold crawl spaces, floors above a porch or an unheated garage; (7) walls of a heated basement.

any more than it did before other walls were insulated. Wall insulation will pay quite substantial dividends in the older house because the ratio of wall area to roof area is quite high in comparison to modern houses. A savings of 20 to 30 percent is not uncommon. Expensive it may well be; effective it surely will be.

REDUCTION OF DEMAND

Without any investment whatsoever, the owner of an older house can take a step to lower heating bills by 5 to 25 percent. Night setback of thermostats by 5 or better yet 10 degrees will accomplish a 6 to 12 percent savings. If the house is empty during the day, the same setback will achieve similar savings in addition.

Inexpensive automatic setback replacement thermostats can be easily installed by the homeowner to make certain that setback occurs every day. If your normal high setting is 65 to 68 degrees, a 10-degree setback at night will be quite reasonable. An extra quilt or an electric blanket can provide the additional heat required.

	Ceiling 38, wall 19, floor 22		Ceiling 30, wall 19, floor 19
Ceiling 33, wall 19, floor 22		Ceiling 26, wall 19, floor 13
Ceiling 19, wall 11, floor 11		Ceiling 26, wall 13, floor 11

| | R-number | | | | | |
Insulation type	11	13	19	22	30	38
BATTS/BLANKETS						
Fiberglass	3½″	4″	6″	7″	9½″	12″
Rock wool	3″	4″	5½″	6″	8½″	11″
LOOSE-FILL						
Fiberglass	5″	5½″	8½″	10″	13½″	17″
Rock wool	4″	4½″	6½″	8″	10½″	13″
Cellulose	3″	3½″	5½″	6″	8½″	11″
Vermiculite	5″	6″	9″	10″	14″	18″
RIGID BOARD						
Polystyrene (extruded)	3″	3½″	5″	5½″	7½″	9½″
Polystyrene (bead board)	3″	3½″	5½″	6″	8½″	10½″
Urethane	2″	2″	3″	3½″	5″	6″
Fiberglass	3″	3½″	5″	5½″	7½″	9½″

Figure 17-2. Recommended R-numbers for insulation in the ceilings,
walls, and floors facing unheated areas.

If you are still setting the thermostat at a high of 70 to 75 degrees, try to move this back gradually to 68 degrees. Especially after a lifetime, changing a mental and physical conception of warm versus cold is hard, but there is ample reason to do it, both financial and moral. There is also sufficient evidence to suggest that colds and respiratory infections are decreased when temperatures are maintained at a slightly lower level.

A second reduction in demand can be achieved by lowering the temperature setting of the hot-water heater to 120 degrees. The only catch here is to be certain that an electric dishwasher will operate properly. Most will. Despite advertising claims, so-called sanitizer cycles using 145-degree water are no more effective in germ killing than those using 120-degree water. To kill germs, use boiling water at 212 degrees! In addition, flow reducers installed in faucets and shower heads can decrease water flow without reducing water pressure, thus effectively diminishing hot-water energy usage.

IMPROVING CENTRAL HEATING SYSTEM EFFICIENCY

The final step in improving energy efficiency in an older house is to improve the efficiency of the central heating system. Owners of hot-water or steam systems should have their systems drained at least once a year and refilled using a corrosion inhibitor. The buildup of deposits and corrosion in steam and hot-water systems can decrease efficiency by as much as 25 percent. All oil-fired burners should be tuned up once a year by a qualified repairperson. Gas burners should be cleaned at least once every 2 years.

A multitude of new products, such as heat recovery devices and flue dampers, have been designed to improve furnace efficiency. Heat recovery devices can help if and only if you have an underheated area within 10 feet of the furnace which requires heat. Flue dampers, while perfectly safe when properly installed, and now standard on many new furnaces,

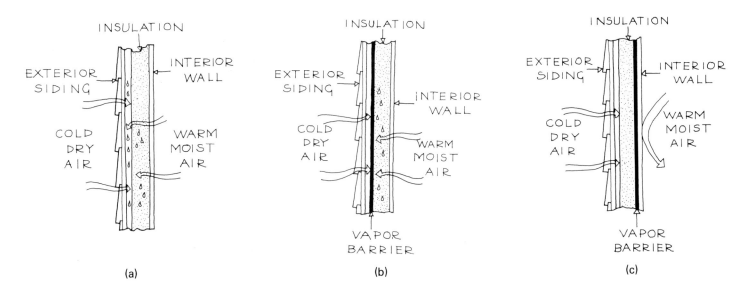

Figure 17-3. (a) Wall with no vapor barrier; (b) wall with vapor barrier incorrectly positioned; (c) wall with vapor barrier correctly positioned.

are somewhat risky investments because the amount of savings they will generate depends heavily upon the specific circumstances in the house. Average savings will probably be about 10 percent, and the average payback period will range from 2½ to 4 years. Other measures such as insulation and weatherstripping have much shorter financial recovery periods and should be accomplished first.

The insulation of steam and hot-water pipes, including domestic hot-water supply lines, as well as the insulation of warm-air ducts is an easy-to-accomplish, inexpensive way to improve efficiency. Hardware stores, lumber yards, and do-it-yourself stores offer the supplies and advice to get the job done.

Finally, if you have cut back the demand for heat, reduced heat losses through walls and roof, and made the house as tight as possible by weatherstripping, you may have arrived at a point where downsizing the furnace makes sense, particularly if the furnace is due for replacement. Because less heat is needed from the furnace to heat a house effectively, you can benefit from a smaller furnace cycling on and off less rapidly. From an efficiency standpoint the properly sized furnace will run full time to keep the house at the maximum desired temperature on the coldest day.

Another possibility for oil burners is the flame retention head, an invention which reduces the amount of fuel burned for a given output of heat. It can be inexpensively retrofitted to many oil burners. Ask an oil burner serviceperson for advice. Also, consider obtaining your oil burner service from an independent contractor, not from your fuel dealer. A fuel dealer's job is to sell oil, not save it.

Avoid gimmicks and gadgets, fuel additives, "magic catalysts," and anyone promising to cut your fuel costs by any means other than the outlined three methods:

- Reducing heat losses
- Reducing heat demand
- Improving furnace efficiency

THE SAGA OF OLDER HOMES

Older homes fade
Time ravishes
Humans abuse
Understanding illuminates
Love renews.

ADDITIONAL READING AND REFERENCE

DESIGN

Bicknell, A. J. *Victorian Village Builder*. Watkins Glen, N.Y.: Published for the Athenaeum of Nineteenth Century America by The American Life Foundation and Study Institute, 1976.

———— and W. T. Comstock. *Victorian Architecture—Two Pattern Books*. Watkins Glen, N.Y.: American Life Foundation and Study Institute, 1975, originally published as Bicknell, A. J., *Detail, Cottage and Constructive Architecture*, 1873, and Comstock, William T., *Modern Architectural Designs and Details*, 1881.

Downing, Andrew Jackson. *The Architecture of Country Houses*. New York: Dover Publications, Inc., 1969; New York: D. Appleton & Company, Inc., 1850.

Early American Society Books. *Colonial Architecture in Massachusetts, Colonial Architecture in New England, Early Homes of Massachusetts, Early Homes of New England, Early Homes of New York and the Mid-Atlantic States, Early Homes of Rhode Island, Early Homes in the Southern States, Survey of Early American Design*, from material originally published as *The White Pine Series of Architectural Monographs*, edited by Russell F. Whitehead and Frank Chouteau Brown. New York: Arno Press, 1977.

Foley, Mary Mix. *The American House*. New York: Harper & Row, 1980.

Gillon, Edmund, V., Jr., and Clay Lancaster. *Victorian Houses: A Treasury of Lesser-Known Examples*. New York: Dover Publications, Inc., 1973.

Gowans, Alan. *Images of American Living*. New York: Harper & Row, 1976.

Grow, Lawrence. *Old House Plans*. New York: Universe Books, 1978.

Hamlin, Talbot. *Greek Revival Architecture in America*. New York: Dover Publications, Inc., 1964; Fair Lawn, N.J.: Oxford University Press, 1944.

Harris, Cyril M., ed. *Historic Architecture Sourcebook*. New York: McGraw-Hill Book Company, 1977.

Morrison, Hugh. *Early American Architecture*. New York: Oxford University Press, 1952.

Pierson, William H., Jr. *American Buildings and Their Architects: The Colonial and Neo-Classical Styles*. Garden City, N.Y.: Anchor Books, Doubleday & Company, Inc., 1976.

Poppeliers, John, S. Allen Chambers, and Nancy B. Schwartz. *What Style Is It?* Washington, D.C.: The Preservation Press of the National Trust for Historic Preservation, 1977.

Scully, Vincent J., Jr. *The Shingle Style*. New Haven, Conn.: Yale University Press, 1955.

Waldhorn, Judith. *A Gift to the Street*, photographs by Carol Olwell. San Francisco: Antelope Island Press, 1977.

Whiffen, Marcus. *American Architecture Since 1780: A Guide to the Styles*. Cambridge, Mass.: The MIT Press, 1969.

Williams, Henry Lionel, and Ottalie K. Williams. *A Guide to Old American Houses 1700–1900*. Cranbury, N.J.: A. S. Barnes & Co., Inc., 1962.

———— and ————. *Old American Houses 1700–1850—How to Restore, Remodel and Reproduce Them*. New York: Bonanza Books, Crown Publishers, Inc., 1967.

MAINTENANCE AND REPAIR

Batcheler, Penelope H. "Paint Color Research and Restoration," Technical Leaflet 15. Nashville, Tenn.: American Association for State and Local History, 1968.

Becker, Norman. *The Complete Book of Home Inspection*. New York: McGraw-Hill Book Company, 1980.

Better Homes and Gardens Books. *Complete Guide to Home Repair, Maintenance & Improvement*, edited by Larry Clayton and Noel Seney. Des Moines: Meredith Publishing Company, 1980.

Bruns, R. M., and the staff of Home-Tech Systems. *How to Buy and Fix Up an Older House*. Bethesda, Md.: Home-Tech Publications, 1978.

Bullock, Orin M. *The Restoration Manual*. Norwalk, Conn.: Silvermine Publishers, 1966.

City of Oakland Planning Department. *Rehab Right*. Oakland, Calif.: City of Oakland Planning Department, 1978.

Dietz, Albert G. H. *Dwelling House Construction*, 4th ed. Cambridge, Mass.: The MIT Press, 1974; Princeton, N.J.: D. Van Nostrand Company, Inc., 1946, 1954.

Grow, Lawrence. *The Old House Catalog*. New York: Universe Books, published yearly.

Mack, Robert C. "The Cleaning and Waterproof Coating of Masonry Buildings," *Preservation Brief No. 1*. Washington, D.C.: Technical Preservation Services Division, Office of Archaeology and Historic Preservation, Heritage Conservation and Recreation Service, U.S. Department of the Interior, November 1975.

————. "Repointing Mortar Joints in Historic Brick Buildings," *Preservation Brief No. 2*. Washington, D.C.: Technical Preservation Services Division, Office of Archaeology and Historic Preservation, National Park Service, U.S. Department of the Interior, April 1976.

Myers, John H. "Aluminum and Vinyl Sidings on Historic Buildings," *Preservation Brief No. 8*. Washington, D.C.:

Technical Preservation Services Division, Heritage Conservation and Recreation Service, U.S. Department of the Interior, August 1979.

———. "The Repair of Historic Wooden Windows," *Preservation Brief No. 9.* Washington, D.C.: Technical Preservation Services Division, Heritage Conservation and Recreation Service, U.S. Department of the Interior.

The Old-House Journal. Edited by Clem Labine. New York: The Old-House Journal Corporation, published monthly.

Reader's Digest. *Complete Do-It-Yourself Manual.* Pleasantville, N.Y.: The Reader's Digest Association, Inc., 1977.

Smith, Baird M. "Conserving Energy in Historic Buildings." *Preservation Brief No. 3.* Washington, D.C.: Technical Preservation Services Division, Office of Archaeology and Historic Preservation, Heritage Conservation and Recreation Service, U.S. Department of the Interior, April 1978.

Stanforth, Deirdre, and Martha Stamm. *Buying and Renovating a House in the City: A Practical Guide.* New York: Alfred A. Knopf, Inc., 1972.

Stephen, George. *Remodeling Old Houses Without Destroying Their Character.* New York: Alfred A. Knopf, Inc., 1974.

Sweetser, Sarah M. "Roofing for Historic Buildings," *Preservation Brief No. 4.* Washington, D.C.: Technical Preservation Services Division, Office of Archaeology and Historic Preservation, Heritage Conservation and Recreation Service, U.S. Department of the Interior, February 1978.

U.S. Department of Agriculture Forest Service. *Principles for Protecting Wood Buildings from Decay,* USDA Forest Service Research Paper FPL 190. Madison, Wis.: U.S. Department of Agriculture, 1973.

Vila, Bob, with Jane Davison. *This Old House.* Boston: Little, Brown and Company, 1980.

ILLUSTRATION CREDITS

FIGURE 2-1. After a photograph of the Parson Capen House in *Early Homes of Massachusetts*, New York: Arno Press, Inc., and The Early American Society, Inc., 1977.

FIGURE 2-2. After a photograph in *The American Fireplace* by Henry Kauffman, New York: Galahad Books, 1972, by permission of the Virginia State Library, Richmond.

FIGURE 2-5. After a photograph by Nicholas Dean in *Portland* by Greater Portland Landmarks, Inc., Portland, Maine, 1972.

FIGURE 2-6. Based on a photograph in *Building With Nantucket in Mind* by J. Christopher Lang, Nantucket, Mass.: Nantucket Historic District Commission, 1978.

FIGURE 2-8. After a photograph by Allen Stross in the Historic American Buildings Survey, Library of Congress.

FIGURE 2-10. After a drawing in *Victorian Village Builder* by A. J. Bicknell, Norristown, Pa.: American Life Foundation, 1976.

FIGURE 2-11. After a photograph in *Evolution of Masonry Construction in American Architectural Styles* by Maximilian L. Ferro, Downers Grove, Ill.: Service Master Industries, Inc., 1976.

FIGURE 2-12. After a photograph in *Victorian Houses: A Treasury of Lesser-Known Examples* by Edmund V. Gillon, Jr., and Clay Lancaster, New York: Dover Publications, Inc., 1973.

FIGURE 2-13. After a photograph by Gerda Peterich in the Historic American Buildings Survey, Library of Congress.

FIGURE 4-1. Based on a drawing in *Colonial Architecture in Massachusetts*, New York: Arno Press, Inc., and The Early American Society, Inc., 1977.

FIGURE 4-6. After a drawing in *Victorian Village Builder* by A. J. Bicknell, Norristown, Pa.: American Life Foundation, 1976.

FIGURE 4-13. After a drawing in *Slate Roofs* by the Vermont Structural Slate Co., Inc., Fair Haven, Vt., 1926.

FIGURE 4-16. Based on a drawing in *Architectural Graphic Standards* by George Ramsey and Harold Reeve Sleeper, New York: John Wiley and Sons, Inc., 4th ed., 1941.

FIGURE 4-17. After a drawing in *Architectural Graphic Standards* by George Ramsey and Harold Reeve Sleeper.

FIGURE 4-18. After a drawing in *Wood-Frame House Construction* by L. O. Anderson, Washington, D.C.: U.S. Government Printing Office, 1975.

FIGURE 5-1. After a photograph in *Early Homes of Massachusetts*, New York: Arno Press, Inc., and The Early American Society, Inc., 1977.

FIGURE 5-2. Based on a drawing in *A Guide to Old American Houses 1700–1900* by Henry Lionel Williams and Ottalie K. Williams, © 1962 by Henry Lionel and Ottalie K. Williams, published by A. S. Barnes & Company, Inc. All rights reserved.

FIGURE 5-3. After a drawing by Phillip White after Forman in *Early American Architecture* by Hugh Morrison, New York: Oxford University Press, 1952.

FIGURE 5-7. After a drawing in *Greek Revival Details* by Carl Schmidt, Scottsville, N.Y., 1968.

FIGURE 5-8. After a drawing in *The Model Architect*, Volume II, by Samuel Sloan, Philadelphia: E. S. Sloan & Co., 1852.

FIGURE 5-9. After a drawing in *The Architecture of Country Houses* by Andrew Jackson Downing, New York: Dover Publications, Inc., 1969.

FIGURE 5-10. After a drawing in *Old House Plans* by Lawrence Grow, New York: Universe Books, 1978.

FIGURE 5-11. After a drawing in *Victorian Village Builder* by A. J. Bicknell, Norristown, Pa.: American Life Foundation, 1976.

FIGURE 5-12. After a photograph of the Harold Allen House in the Historic American Buildings Survey, Library of Congress.

FIGURE 6-1. Based on a photograph by Wayne Andrews in *Early American Architecture* by Hugh Morrison, New York: Oxford University Press, 1952.

FIGURE 6-3. Based on a photograph in *Colonial Architecture in New England*, New York: Arno Press, Inc., and The Early American Society, Inc., 1977.

FIGURE 6-4. Based on a photograph in *Victorian Houses: A Treasury of Lesser-Known Examples* by Edmund V. Gillon, Jr., and Clay Lancaster, New York: Dover Publications, Inc., 1973.

FIGURE 6-6. Based on a photograph in *How to Love and Care for Your Old Building in New Bedford* by Maximilian L. Ferro, New Bedford, Mass.: Office of Neighborhood Historic Preservation, 1977.

FIGURE 6-7. Based on a photograph in *Victorian Houses: A Treasury of Lesser-Known Examples* by Edmund V. Gillon, Jr., and Clay Lancaster, New York: Dover Publications, Inc., 1973.

FIGURE 6-9. Based on a photograph in *A Gift to the Street* by Carol Olwell (photographs) and Judith Lynch Waldhorn (commentary), St. George, Utah: Antelope Island Press, 1977.

FIGURE 6-10. Based on a photograph in *A Gift to the Street* by Carol Olwell.

FIGURE 6-11. Based on a photograph in *The Shingle Style* by Vincent J. Scully, Jr., New Haven, Conn.: Yale University Press, 1955.

FIGURE 6-13. Based on a photograph in *How to Love and Care for Your Old Building in New Bedford* by Maximilian L. Ferro, New Bedford, Mass.: Office of Neighborhood Historic Preservation, 1977.

FIGURE 6-14. Based on a photograph in *Victorian Houses: A Treasury of Lesser-Known Examples* by Edmund V. Gillon, Jr., and Clay Lancaster, New York: Dover Publications, Inc., 1973.

FIGURE 6-15. After a drawing in *Dwelling House Construction* by Albert G. H. Dietz, Cambridge, Mass.: The MIT Press, 4th ed., 1974, by permission of the MIT Press.

FIGURE 7-2. After a photograph in *Survey of Early American Design*, New York: Arno Press, Inc., and The Early American Society, Inc., 1977.

FIGURE 7-4. After a photograph in *Early Homes of New York and The Mid-Atlantic States*, New York: Arno Press, Inc., and The Early American Society, Inc., 1977.

FIGURE 7-5.   After a photograph in *Victorian Houses: A Treasury of Lesser-Known Examples* by Edmund V. Gillon, Jr., and Clay Lancaster, New York: Dover Publications, Inc., 1973.

FIGURE 7-6.   Based on a drawing in *The Building of Galena* by Carl H. Johnson, Jr., Galena, Ill.: 1977, and a photograph in *How to Love and Care for Your Old Building in New Bedford* by Maximilian L. Ferro, New Bedford, Mass.: Office of Neighborhood Historic Preservation, 1977.

FIGURE 7-7.   After a photograph in *How to Love and Care for Your Old Building in New Bedford* by Maximilian L. Ferro.

FIGURE 7-8.   After a photograph in *Victorian Houses: A Treasury of Lesser-Known Examples* by Edmund V. Gillon, Jr., and Clay Lancaster, New York: Dover Publications, Inc., 1973.

FIGURE 7-10.   After a photograph in *Evolution of Masonry Construction in American Architectural Styles* by Maximilian L. Ferro, Downers Grove, Ill.: Service Master Industries, Inc., 1976.

FIGURE 7-11.   After a photograph in *How to Love and Care for Your Old Building in New Bedford* by Maximilian L. Ferro, New Bedford, Mass.: Office of Neighborhood Historic Preservation, 1977.

FIGURE 7-12.   After a photograph in *How to Love and Care for Your Old Building in New Bedford* by Maximilian L. Ferro.

FIGURE 7-13.   Based on a drawing in *Old House Plans* by Lawrence Grow, New York: Universe Books, 1978.

FIGURE 7-15.   After a photograph in *How to Love and Care for Your Old Building in New Bedford* by Maximilian L. Ferro, New Bedford, Mass.: Office of Neighborhood Historic Preservation, 1977.

FIGURE 7-17.   Based on a drawing in *Slate Roofs* by the Vermont Structural Slate Co., Inc., Fair Haven, Vt., 1926.

FIGURE 8-10.   Based on a drawing in "Property Owner's Guide to the Maintenance and Repair of Stone Buildings," by Cornelia Brooke Gilder, Albany, N.Y.: Preservation League of New York, Inc., 1977.

FIGURE 8-11.   Based on a drawing in *Architectural Graphic Standards* by George Ramsey and Harold Reeve Sleeper, New York: John Wiley and Sons, Inc., 4th ed., 1941.

FIGURE 8-13.   After a drawing in "Wood Siding," Home and Garden Bulletin No. 203, Washington, D.C.: U.S. Government Printing Office, 1975.

FIGURE 9-1.   After a drawing by H. C. Forman in *Early American Architecture* by Hugh Morrison, New York: Oxford University Press, 1952.

FIGURE 9-2.   Based on a photograph in *Early Homes of Massachusetts*, New York: Arno Press, Inc., and The Early American Society, Inc., 1977.

FIGURE 9-3.   After a drawing in *Historic Architecture Sourcebook* by Cyril M. Harris, New York: McGraw-Hill Book Company, 1977.

FIGURE 9-4.   After a drawing in *Historic Architecture Sourcebook* by Cyril M. Harris.

FIGURE 9-5.   Based on a photograph in *Colonial Architecture in New England*, New York: Arno Press, Inc., and The Early American Society, Inc., 1977.

FIGURE 9-6.   After a drawing in *Early Domestic Architecture of Connecticut* by J. Frederick Kelly, New York: Dover Publications, Inc., 1969.

FIGURE 9-7.   Based on a photograph by Frances Benjamin Johnston in the Historic American Buildings Survey, Library of Congress.

FIGURE 9-8.   Based on a photograph in *Images of American Living* by Alan Gowans, New York: Harper & Row, Inc., 1976.

FIGURE 9-9.   Based on a photograph in *Greek Revival Architecture in America* by Talbot Hamlin, New York: Dover Publications, Inc., 1944.

FIGURE 9-10.   Based on a photograph in *Victorian Houses: A Treasury of Lesser-Known Examples* by Edmund V. Gillon, Jr., and Clay Lancaster, New York: Dover Publications, Inc., 1973.

FIGURE 9-11.   Based on a photograph in *Victorian Houses: A Treasury of Lesser-Known Examples* by Edmund V. Gillon, Jr., and Clay Lancaster, New York: Dover Publications, Inc., 1973.

FIGURE 9-14.   After a drawing in *Victorian Architecture—Two Pattern Books*, Watkins Glen, N.Y.: American Life Foundation and Study Institute, 1975.

FIGURE 9-15.   Based on a photograph in *Victorian Houses: A Treasury of Lesser-Known Examples* by Edmund V. Gillon, Jr., and Clay Lancaster, New York: Dover Publications, Inc., 1973.

FIGURE 9-17.   Based on a drawing in *Old House Plans* by Lawrence Grow, New York: Universe Books, 1978.

FIGURE 9-18.   Based on a photograph in *Victorian Houses: A Treasury of Lesser-Known Examples* by Edmund V. Gillon, Jr., and Clay Lancaster, New York: Dover Publications, Inc., 1973.

FIGURE 9-21.   After a drawing in *Victorian Architecture—Two Pattern Books*, Watkins Glen, N.Y.: American Life Foundation and Study Institute, 1975.

FIGURE 9-23.   Based on a photograph in *The Shingle Style* by Vincent J. Scully, Jr., New Haven, Conn.: Yale University Press, 1955.

FIGURE 9-28.   Based on a drawing in "Simple Home Repairs . . . Outside," Washington, D.C.: U.S. Government Printing Office, January, 1978.

FIGURE 10-3.   Based on a drawing in *Early Homes of Rhode Island*, New York: Arno Press, Inc., and The Early American Society, Inc., 1977.

FIGURE 10-4.   Based on a drawing in *Colonial Architecture in Massachusetts*, New York: Arno Press, Inc., and The Early American Society, Inc., 1977.

FIGURE 10-6.   Based on a photograph by Jack E. Boucher in the Historic American Buildings Survey, Library of Congress.

FIGURE 10-10.   Based on a drawing in *Cottage Residences* by Andrew Jackson Downing, New York: Wiley and Putnam, 1842.

FIGURE 10-12.   After a drawing in *Victorian Village Builder* by A. J. Bicknell, Norristown, Pa.: American Life Foundation, 1976.

FIGURE 10-13.   Based on drawings in *Late Victorian Architectural Details*, Norristown, Pa.: American Life Foundation, 1978.

FIGURE 10-14.   After a drawing in *Victorian Architecture—Two Pattern Books*, Watkins Glen, N.Y.: American Life Foundation and Study Institute, 1975.

FIGURE 10-16.   Based on photographs in *A Gift to the Street* by Carol Olwell (photographs) and Judith Lynch Waldhorn (commentary), St. George, Utah: Antelope Island Press, 1977.

FIGURE 10-17.   Based on a photograph in *The Shingle Style* by Vincent J. Scully, Jr., New Haven, Conn.: Yale University Press, 1955.

Queen Anne Window.   After a photograph in *A Gift to the Street* by Carol Olwell (photographs) and Judith Lynch Waldhorn (commentary), St. George, Utah: Antelope Island Press, 1977.

FIGURE 11-1.   Based on drawings in *Colonial Architecture in Massachusetts* and *Colonial Architecture in New England*, New York: Arno Press, Inc., and The Early American Society, Inc., 1977.

FIGURE 11-2.   After drawings in *The Restoration Manual* by Orin M. Bullock, Jr., Norwalk, Conn.: Silvermine Publishers, Inc., 1966.

FIGURE 11-6.   Based on photographs in *Survey of Early American Design*, New York: Arno Press, Inc., and The Early American Society, Inc., 1977, and in *Images of American Living* by Alan Gowans, New York: Harper and Row, Inc., 1976.

FIGURE 11-7. After a drawing in *Early Homes of Massachusetts*, New York: Arno Press, Inc., and The Early American Society, Inc., 1977.

FIGURE 11-8. After a drawing in *Domestic Architecture of the American Colonies and of the Early Republic* by Fiske Kimball, New York: Dover Publications, Inc., 1966.

FIGURE 11-9. Based on a drawing in *Greek Revival Details* by Carl Schmidt, Scottsville, N.Y., 1968.

FIGURE 11-10. Based on a drawing in *Greek Revival Details* by Carl Schmidt.

FIGURE 11-12. Based on a drawing in *Greek Revival Details* by Carl Schmidt.

FIGURE 11-13. Based on a photograph in *Greek Revival Details* by Carl Schmidt.

FIGURE 11-14. Based on a window in *Victorian Houses: A Treasury of Lesser-Known Examples* by Edmund V. Gillon, Jr., and Clay Lancaster, New York: Dover Publications, Inc., 1973.

FIGURE 11-15. Based on a photograph in *How to Love and Care for Your Old Building in New Bedford* by Maximilian L. Ferro, New Bedford, Mass.: Office of Neighborhood Historic Preservation, 1977.

FIGURE 11-18. Based on a drawing in *The Architecture of Country Houses* by Andrew Jackson Downing, New York: Dover Publications, Inc., 1969.

FIGURE 11-19. Based on a drawing in *Historic Architecture Sourcebook* by Cyril M. Harris, New York: McGraw-Hill Book Company, 1977.

FIGURE 11-20. Based on a drawing in *Historic Architecture Sourcebook* by Cyril M. Harris.

FIGURE 11-21. Based on a drawing in *The Architecture of Country Houses* by Andrew Jackson Downing, New York: Dover Publications, Inc., 1969.

FIGURE 11-25. Based on a photograph in *How to Love and Care for Your Old Building in New Bedford* by Maximilian L. Ferro, New Bedford, Mass.: Office of Neighborhood Historic Preservation, 1977.

FIGURE 11-26. Based on a photograph in *Victorian Houses: A Treasury of Lesser-Known Examples* by Edmund V. Gillon, Jr., and Clay Lancaster, New York: Dover Publications, Inc., 1973.

FIGURE 11-27. Based on a photograph in *How to Love and Care for Your Old Building in New Bedford* by Maximilian L. Ferro, New Bedford, Mass.: Office of Neighborhood Historic Preservation, 1977.

FIGURE 11-29. After a drawing in *Victorian Architecture—Two Pattern Books*, Watkins Glen, N.Y.: American Life Foundation and Study Institute, 1975.

FIGURE 11-30. After a drawing in *Victorian Village Builder* by A. J. Bicknell, Norristown, Pa.: American Life Foundation, 1976.

FIGURE 11-31. After a drawing in *Victorian Village Builder* by A. J. Bicknell.

FIGURE 11-32. After drawings in *Victorian Village Builder* by A. J. Bicknell.

FIGURE 11-33. Based on photographs in *Evolution of Masonry Construction in American Architectural Styles* by Maximilian L. Ferro, Downers Grove, Ill.: Service Master Industries, Inc., 1976, and in *Old House Plans* by Lawrence Grow, New York: Universe Books, 1978.

FIGURE 11-34. After a drawing in *Late Victorian Architectural Details*, Norristown, Pa.: American Life Foundation, 1978.

FIGURE 11-35. After photographs in *A Gift to the Street* by Carol Olwell (photographs) and Judith Lynch Waldhorn (commentary), St. George, Utah: Antelope Island Press, 1977.

FIGURE 11-36. Based on a drawing in *Old House Plans* by Lawrence Grow, New York: Universe Books, 1978.

FIGURE 11-37. After drawings in *Late Victorian Architectural Details*, Norristown, Pa.: American Life Foundation, 1978.

FIGURE 11-38. Based on photographs in *The Shingle Style* by Vincent J. Scully, Jr., New Haven, Conn.: Yale University Press, 1955.

FIGURE 11-39. Based on a drawing in *Old House Plans* by Lawrence Grow, New York: Universe Books, 1978.

FIGURE 11-43. After a drawing in *Late Victorian Architectural Details*, Norristown, Pa.: American Life Foundation, 1978.

FIGURE 12-1. Based on a drawing in *Old American Houses 1700–1850* by Henry Lionel Williams and Ottalie K. Williams, New York: Bonanza Books, Crown Publishers, Inc., 1967.

FIGURE 12-5. Inspired by *Old Philadelphia Houses on Society Hill*, copyright © 1966 by Elizabeth B. McCall, permission by Architectural Book Publishing Co., Inc., New York.

FIGURE 12-6. Inspired by *Old Philadelphia Houses on Society Hill*, copyright © 1966 by Elizabeth B. McCall, permission by Architectural Book Publishing Co., Inc., New York.

FIGURE 12-10. Based on drawings in *Greek Revival Details* by Carl Schmidt, Scottsville, N.Y., 1968.

FIGURE 17-1. Based on an illustration in *The Complete Book of Home Inspection* by Norman Becker, New York: McGraw-Hill Book Company, 1980.

FIGURE 17-2. After illustrations in *The Complete Book of Home Inspection* by Norman Becker.

FIGURE 17-3. Based on illustrations in *The Complete Book of Home Inspection* by Norman Becker.

INDEX

Page numbers in **boldface type** indicate definitions.

About the Authors and the Illustrator

SHIRLEY HANSON is a planning consultant and a writer. Her participation in historic preservation began in 1966 in Chestnut Hill, Philadelphia. Her activities encompass overseeing building restoration and renovation projects, carrying out architectural surveys, initiating educational slide lectures and walking tours, publicizing preservation projects, and conducting fund-raising efforts. She has been a long-term contributor to the *Chestnut Hill Local* newspaper. Shirley Hanson received a Bachelor of Arts from Smith College and a Master of City Planning from the University of Pennsylvania.

NANCY HUBBY is a planning consultant with 15 years of experience in environmental planning and historic preservation projects. She has directed, developed, and promoted conservation plans for numerous preservation organizations and municipalities, and has been the Director of Planning for two Philadelphia architectural firms. Her historic preservation work includes supervising the renovation and restoration of several buildings, conducting architectural surveys, and coordinating fund-raising campaigns. She was the photographer for this book. Nancy Hubby received a Bachelor of Arts degree from Wellesley College, a Bachelor of Fine Arts from Yale University, and a Master of City Planning from the University of Pennsylvania.

BETTY ANDERSON came to architectural illustration via studies in landscape design at Radcliffe Institute and Temple University and work in the restoration of older gardens in a landscape architect's office in Cambridge, Massachusetts. A graduate of Wellesley College with a Master of Arts in History from Columbia University, she lives in Philadelphia with her husband and three sons.